Beyoncé

Published in 2025 by Welbeck
An Imprint of HEADLINE PUBLISHING GROUP LIMITED

1

Cataloguing in Publication Data is available from the British Library

ISBN 9781035423743

Printed in China

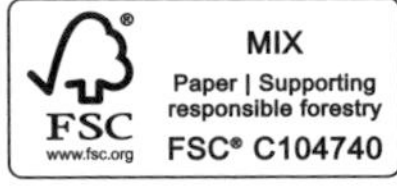

Headline's policy is to use papers that are natural, renewable and recyclable
products and made from wood grown in well-managed forests and other controlled
sources. The logging and manufacturing processes are expected to conform to the
environmental regulations of the country of origin.

HEADLINE PUBLISHING GROUP LIMITED
An Hachette UK Company
Carmelite House
50 Victoria Embankment
London EC4Y 0DZ

The authorized representative in the EEA is Hachette Ireland,
8 Castlecourt Centre, Dublin 15, D15 XTP3, Ireland (email: info@hbgi.ie)

www.headline.co.uk
www.hachette.co.uk

Beyoncé

The story of a fashion legend

Lauren Cochrane

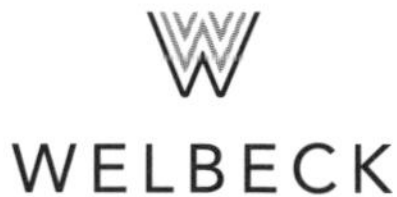

WELBECK

CHAPTER 3

Completely unique: Beyoncé's looks
160

CHAPTER 4

Breaking our soul: Renaissance World Tour style
202

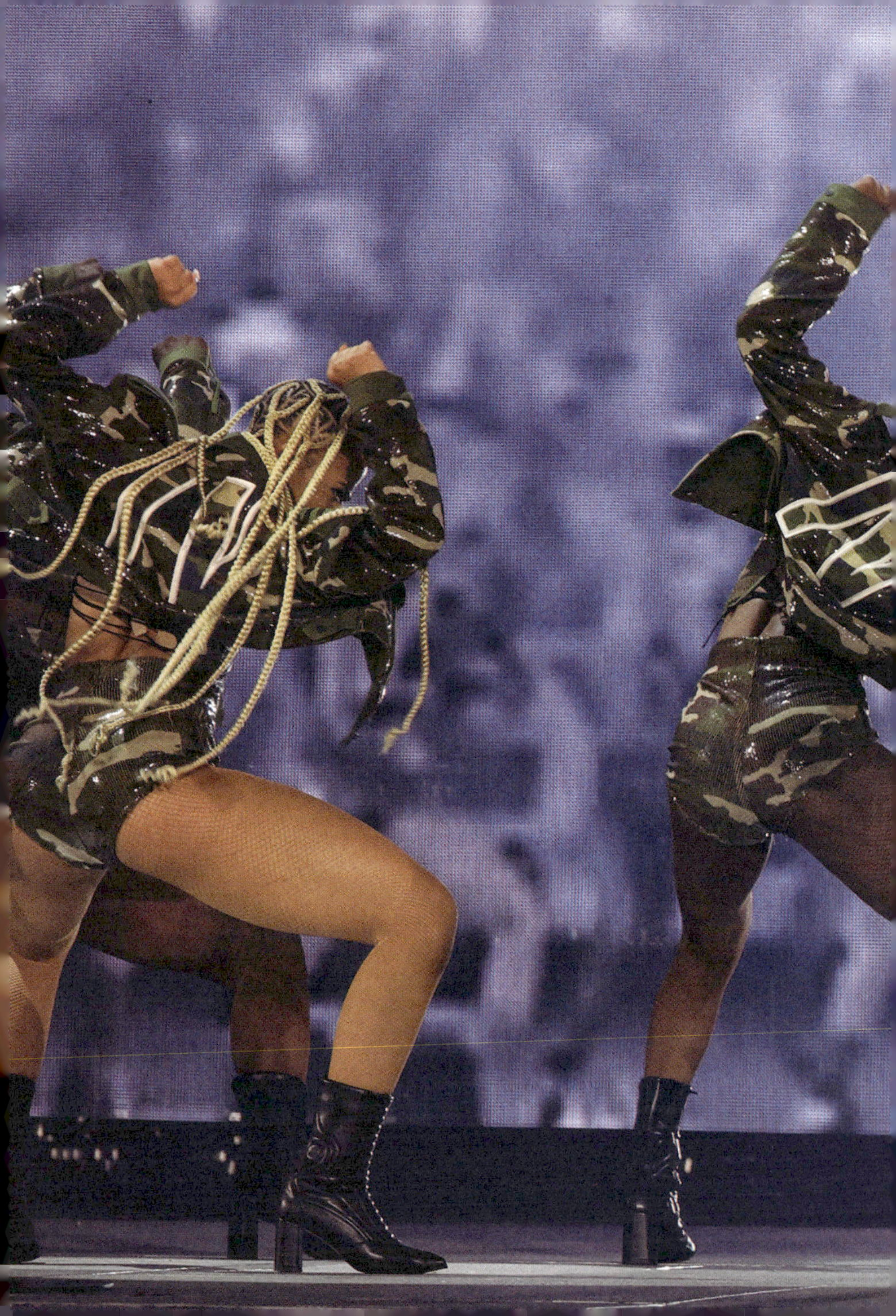

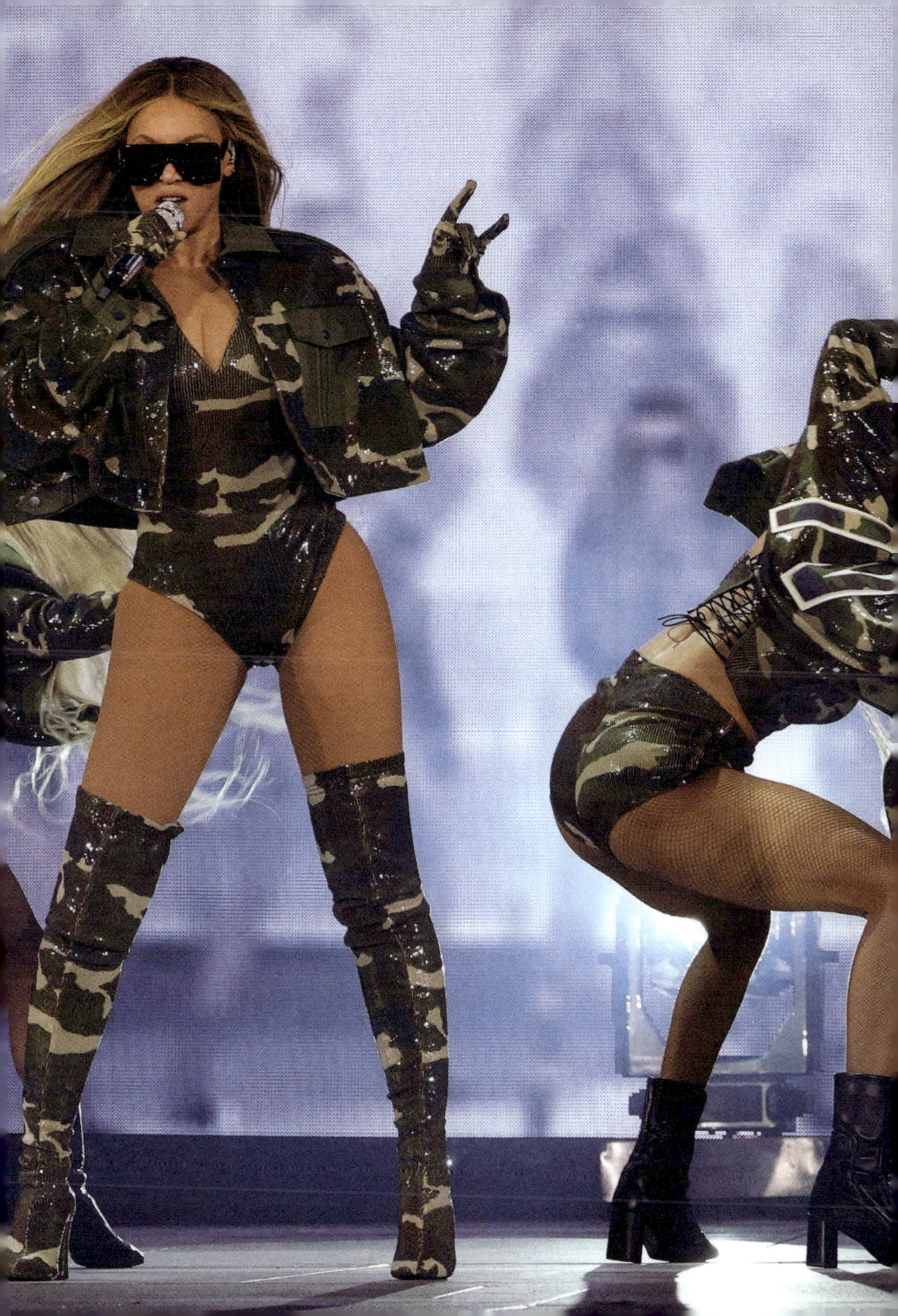

Introduction

In 2003, Beyoncé Giselle Knowles was fresh off the back of a triumphant first solo single 'Crazy in Love' and on the cover of *The Face* magazine. In the accompanying article, she discussed everything from dancing to fashion and a certain rapper called Jay-Z. Even then, she was known for her work ethic. Asked about it, she explained exactly why she worked as hard as she did. "Because I want to be remembered," she said, "and I want to be respected. And I want to be an icon."

Twenty-odd years later, she has completed those last two ambitions with aplomb and while the first is, thankfully, not relevant yet, there's little doubt it will be achieved. Over a career that has – to date – featured eight solo albums, six tours, thirty-two Grammys and several fashion labels, she is less a singer and more a phenomenon. Or, to quote the understatement of Wikipedia, "she is regarded as an influential cultural figure of the 21st century".

PREVIOUS Ready to go: Beyoncé and her army of dancers assemble for the Renaissance tour.

OPPOSITE Silver and sparkle: a distinctly Beyoncé take on high shine for stagewear in 2023.

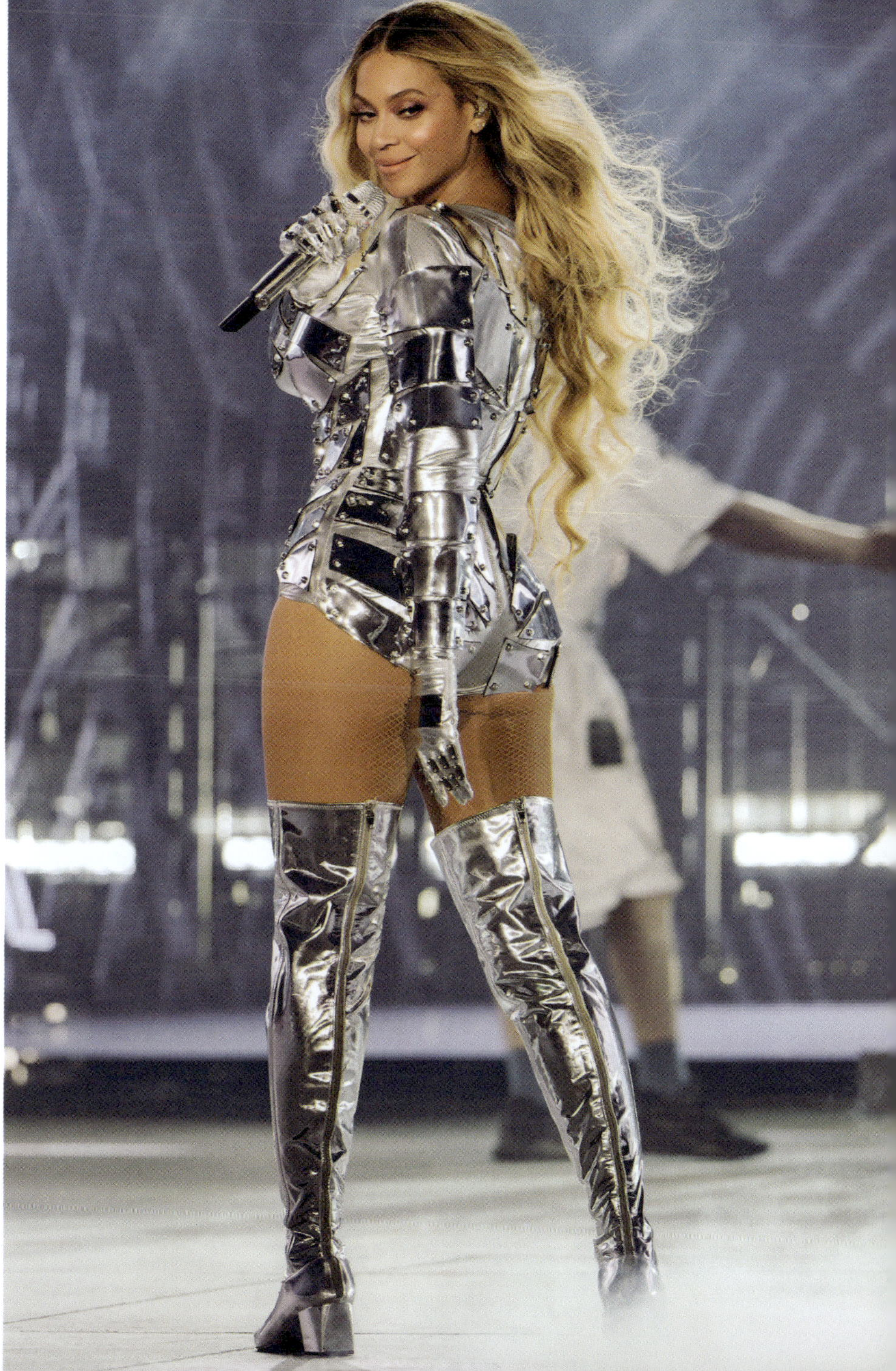

Of course, the majority of this regard comes from the sheer weight of talent that Beyoncé has – as a singer, a dancer, a curator and businesswoman, she is the full package. But she also knows the power of clothes, whether that's to look great on the red carpet, to wow on stage or as a way to signal different ideas without saying anything at all. This ability started early – as it might for someone who was first in the spotlight at the age of eight – and it came from who she surrounded herself with. Growing up with sister Solange and father Mathew in Houston, Texas, formative experiences came chiefly from her mother, Tina Knowles, who went on to design Destiny's Child's costumes, and her Uncle Johnny. Tina's best friend Johnny (who died of complications due to AIDS when Beyoncé was 17) made her prom dress, as anyone who has listened to the lyrics of 'Heated' knows, but he also did much more besides. When Beyoncé dedicated her seventh album *Renaissance* to him in 2023, her mother picked up the story on Instagram. "He helped me raise [Beyoncé and Solange]," she wrote, "and influenced their style and uniqueness!"

Beyoncé's style and uniqueness has developed further over the years. She's moved from a fresh-faced starlet in all manner of cut-out designs created by Tina to a red-carpet pro who might wear an Old Hollywood strapless gown as much as a latex dress with puffed sleeves. For each album cycle since she went solo, fans have been treated to new looks – whether the stripped-back, cyber-sexy look of 'Single Ladies', the holiday vibes of 'Drunk in Love' or the at-the-club look of *Renaissance*.

The way Beyoncé has used clothing to try on different characters – and not just alter ego Sasha Fierce – was learnt early on. Talking to CNN about fashion in 2011, she said, "What's exciting about being a woman is there is this variety of beautiful clothes that can bring out whatever you feel inside."

Fashion is, as *Harper's Bazaar* wrote in 2021, also part of how she has changed our world. "Beyoncé has become much more than a pop icon," said writer Kaitlyn Greenidge. "She's a cultural force who has transformed the way we understand the power of art to change how we see ourselves and each other."

The spirit of this idea is there through her outfits and also what she produces, whether that's Ivy Park, her clothing line, or Cécred, a haircare range launched in 2024. Then there's fan culture. The Beyhive are a particularly well-dressed army of fans. Through her gigs, Beyoncé has been a pioneer when it comes to providing a space where all looks are welcome and cowboy hats are encouraged.

Arguably, the focus on fashion for Beyoncé has increased over the years, certainly from that 2003 interview. Jess Cartner-Morley, writing in the *Guardian*, pinpoints the moment she ramped up her use of clothing to the 'Formation' video in 2016, arguing that until that point "being fashionable was not really what Beyoncé was about." That changed with a video that featured labels including Gucci, Zimmermann and Alessandra Rich. "As of this weekend, Beyoncé runs the world again. And this time, she is using fashion as armour and ammunition."

"[Fashion is] a tool for finding your own identity.

It transcends style and it's a time capsule of all of our greatest milestones."

BEYONCÉ

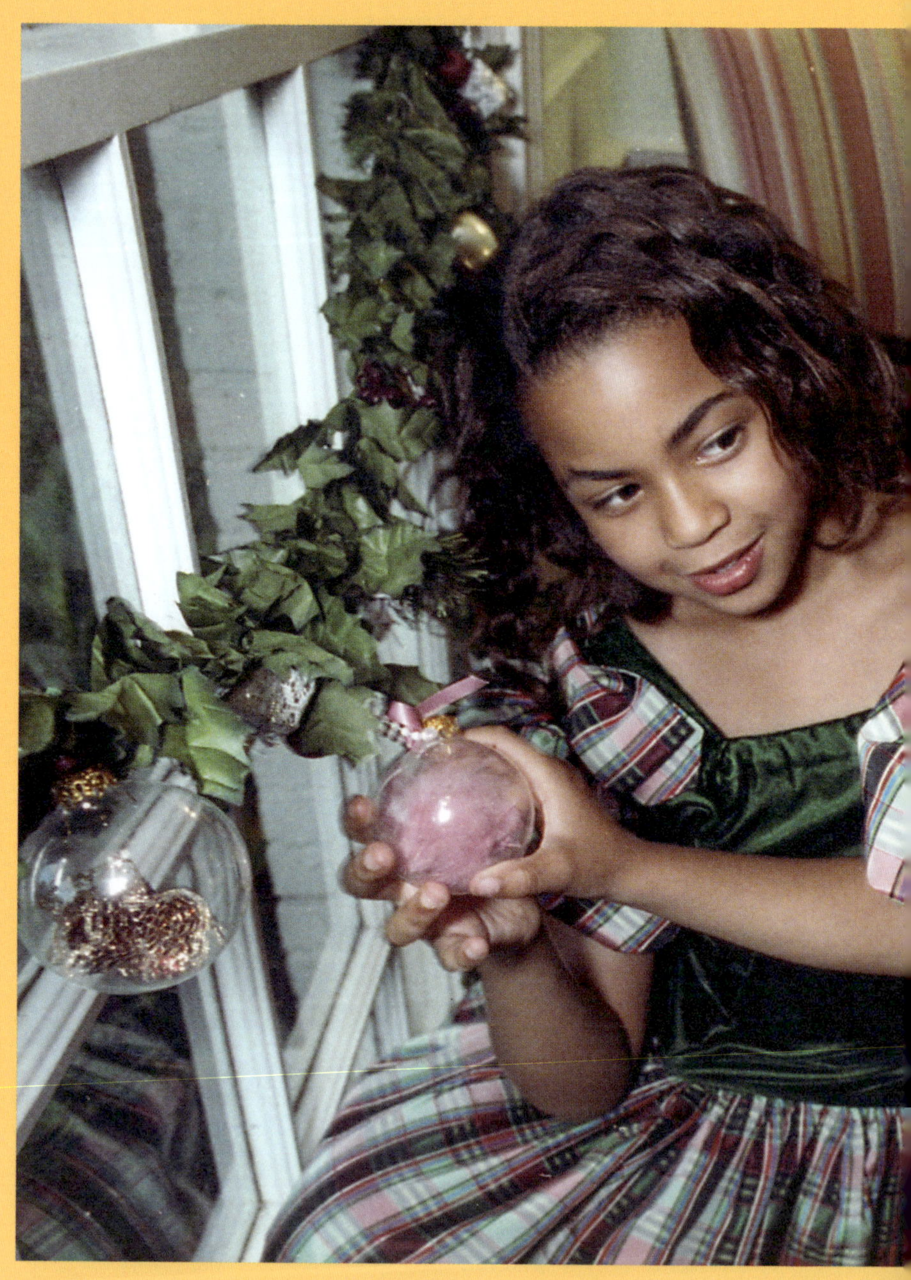

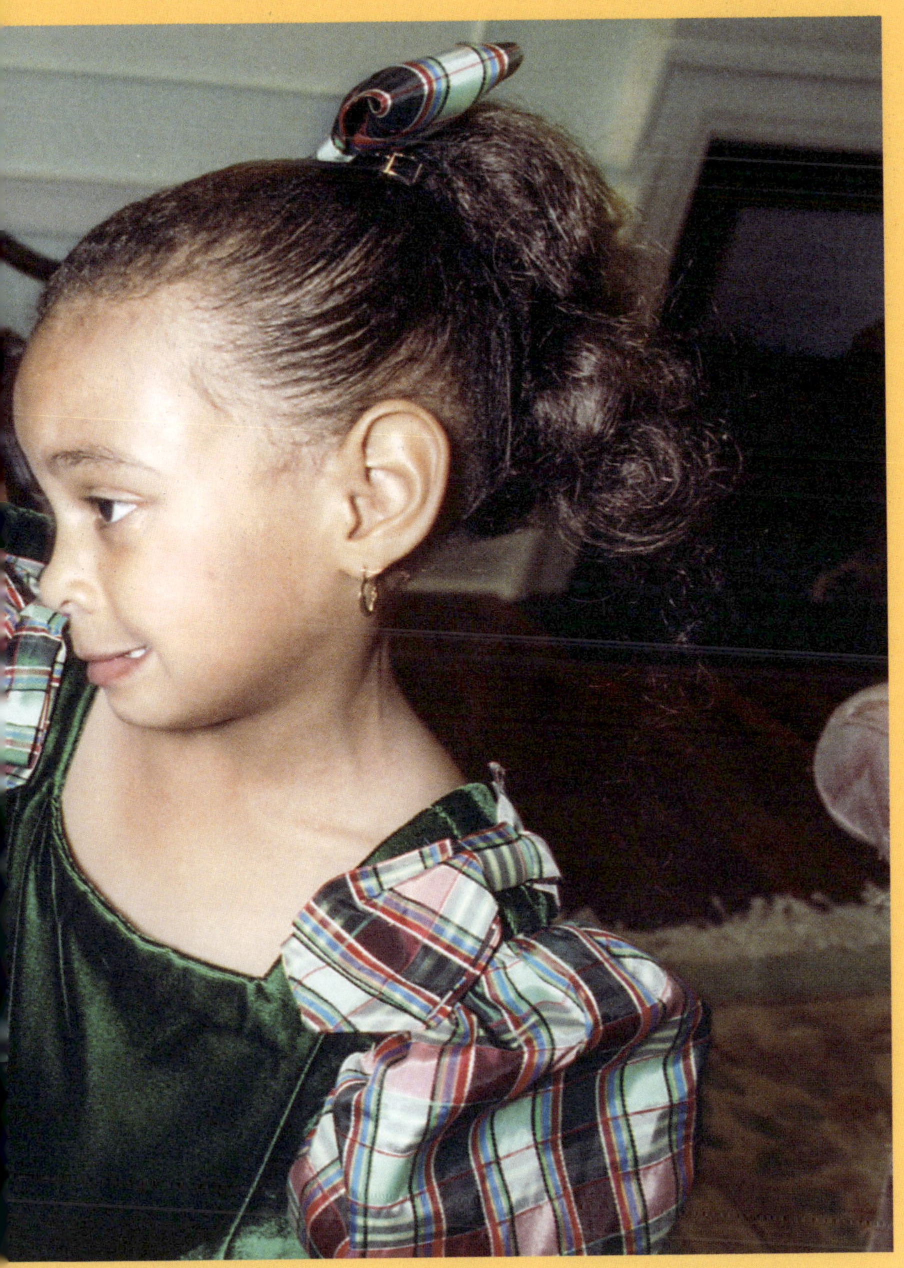

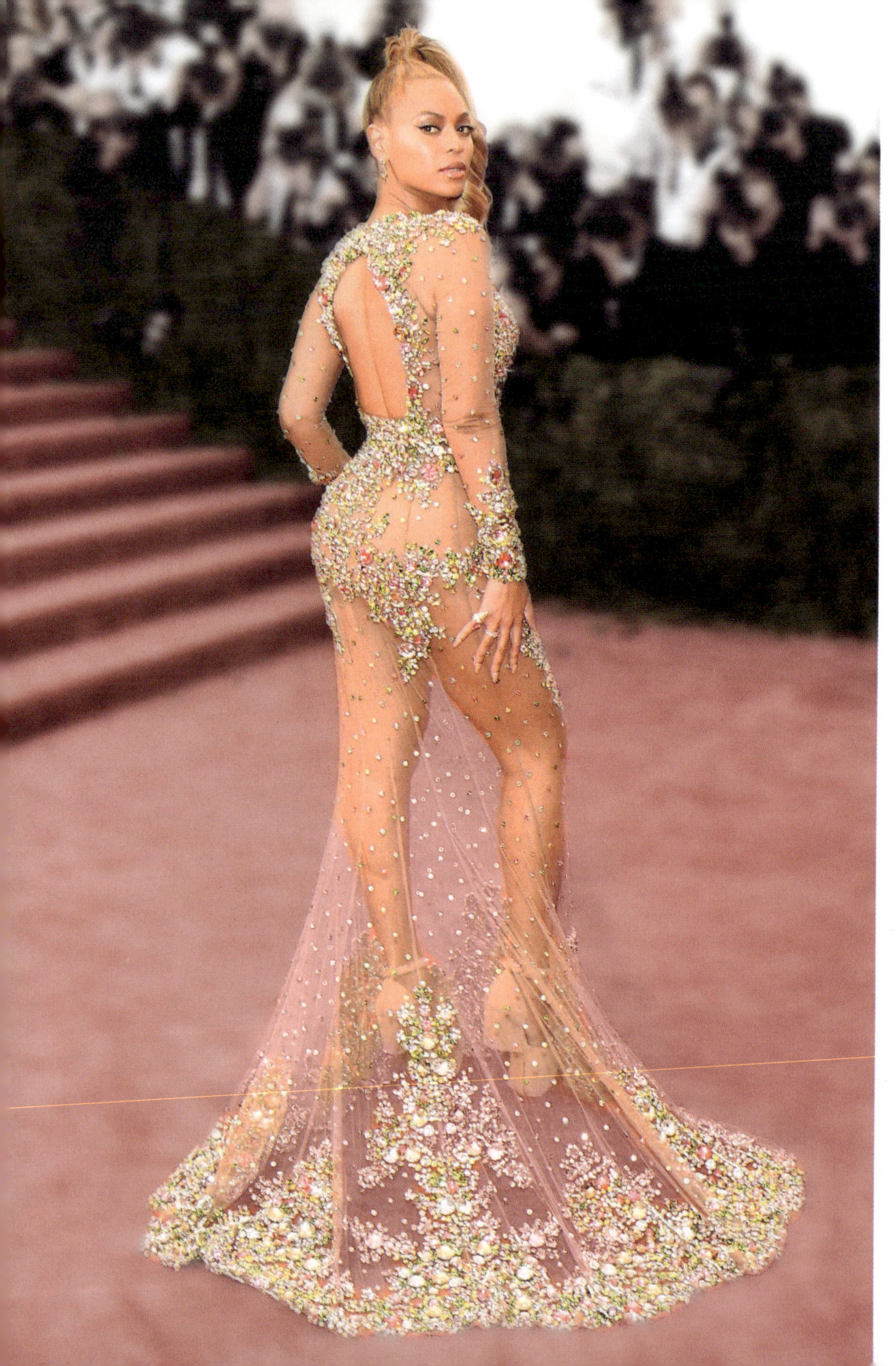

2016 was a big year for Beyoncé. As well as releasing the
'Formation' video, she launched Ivy Park and won the Fashion
Icon Award at the prestigious CFDA Fashion Awards. Chair
Diane von Furstenberg paid tribute to the star's ability to
channel her personality into her style: "Talent, heart, strength
and courage. That is what true style is about and all of that is
what Beyoncé is the best example of," said the designer.

In her CFDA acceptance speech, Beyoncé paid tribute to her
mother and her Uncle Johnny as well as earlier generations
in her family who worked with clothes. Typically, her take
on fashion was emotive, thoughtful and purposeful – tied to
memories of Tina making clothes for crucial events in her
life, including her wedding day. "This to me is the true power
and potential of fashion," she said. "It's a tool for finding your
own identity. It transcends style and it's a time capsule of all
of our greatest milestones."

More than 30 years after she first found herself in the spotlight,
Beyoncé's fashion prowess is established and the story of how
she got there is told in this book. It's one to take in, marvel at
and – perhaps – think about someone no longer here. Writing
about Uncle Johnny in 2023, Tina explained how proud he
would have been of where Beyoncé had got to today. "He is
smiling from Heaven at Bey right now! Saying you did that Ms
Thing!!" wrote Tina. She certainly did – and then some.

PREVIOUS Christmas with the Knowleses: Beyoncé and sister
Solange get festive decorating the tree in 1990, aged eight
and four respectively. Stardom beckoned for both.

OPPOSITE A 2015 wow at the Met Gala in Givenchy: the ponytail
worn with such an exquisite creation provides the perfect contrast.

On the wall:

CHAPTER 1

The Destiny's Child years

The perfect match – or not

By the time Destiny's Child were signed to Columbia Records in 1997, Beyoncé – and her then-bandmates LaTavia Roberson, Kelly Rowland and LeToya Luckett – were well-versed in girl-group dressing. They first started working on their style in 1990 as part of a previous incarnation, the excellently named Girls Tyme (fans will recognize the name from the sample at the start of the track 'Flawless'). In an image of the time, a pre-teen Beyoncé and her bandmates are seen wearing very nineties floral waistcoats, with different coloured T-shirts.

Fast forward to the 1997 incarnation and this matching-but-not-matching theme had developed. The four women in the group would often be wearing variations on a theme – black and white, as per a publicity photograph from 1997, or transparent, with Beyoncé in a lace cardigan to attend the Soul Train Music Awards in 1998, accompanied by Kelly Rowland in mesh and everyone's midriff proudly on display. It could also be subtler – band members in black with slightly different cut tops, or some in skirts and others in trousers, bringing a "spot the difference" to photo ops.

The start of things to come: Beyoncé and bandmates bring a new – and very nineties – take on monochrome.

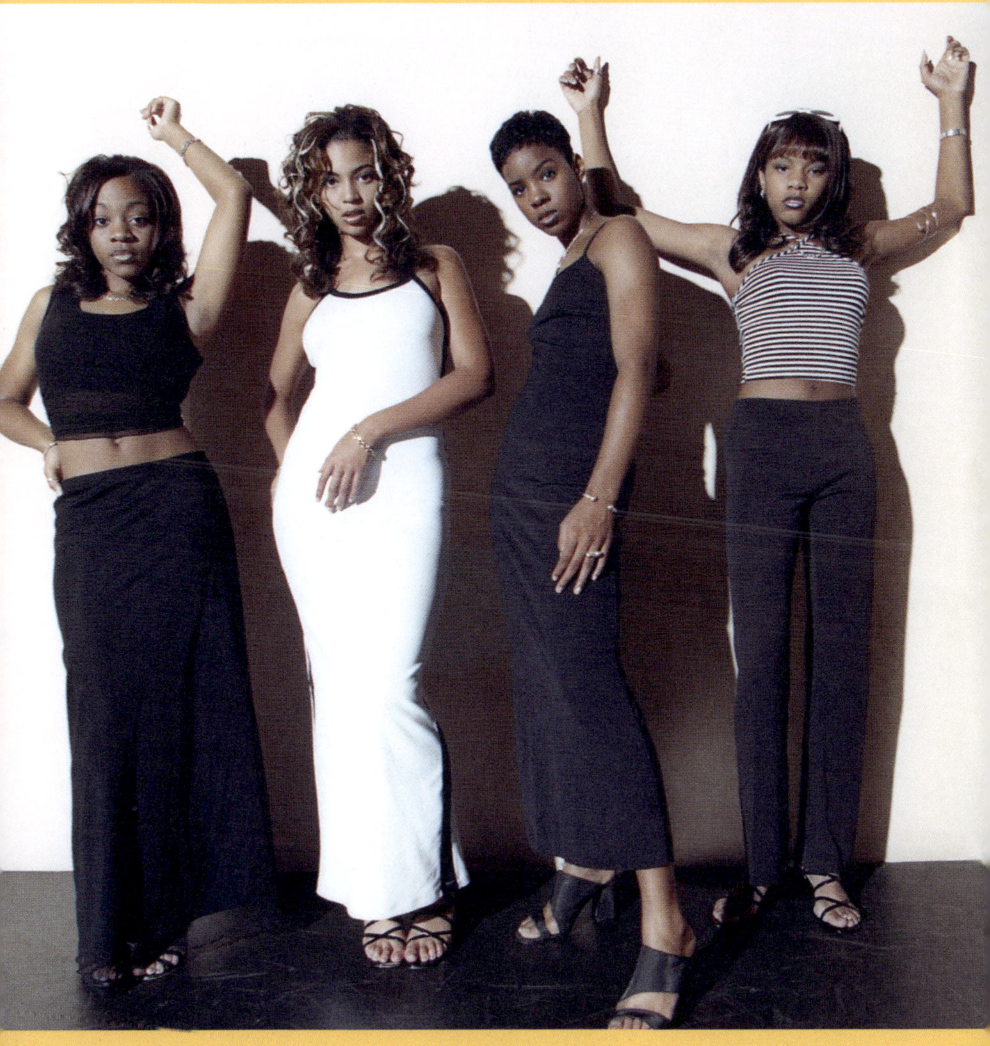

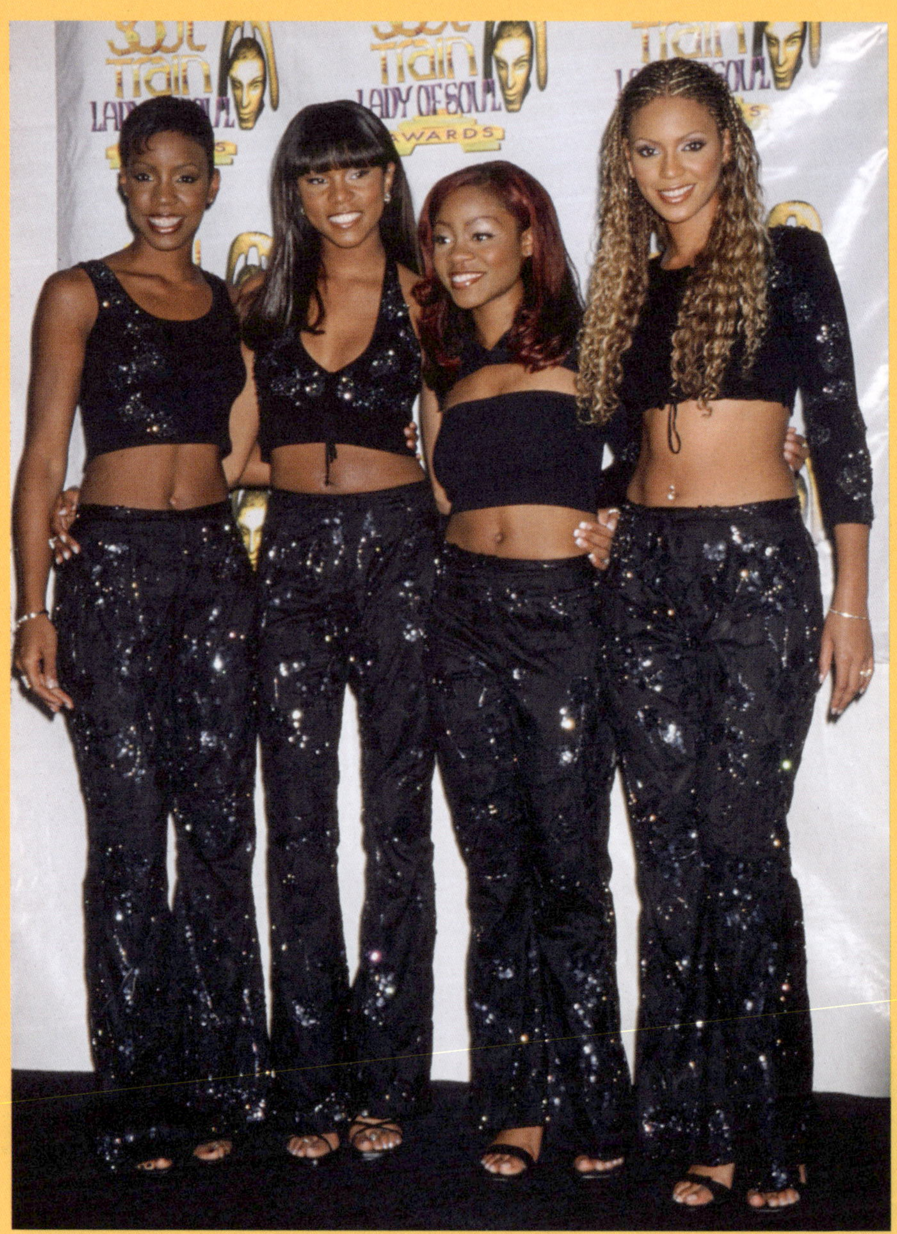
SOUL TRAIN
LADY OF SOUL
AWARDS

Of course, all of this was to introduce the Destiny's Child take on girl-group style of the time. Drawing on a history of bands like The Supremes and The Ronettes wearing matching immaculate frocks in the sixties, 1997 was a golden era for R&B groups – and their style. If TLC and SWV tended to stick to a streetwear-inspired look (think oversized, often with Timberlands), En Vogue were glamorous and grown-up. Destiny's Child, by contrast, went for something of a mixture, but a winning formula. "Their 'vibe' is an all-new hybrid of En Vogue glamour, TLC attitude, the futuristic soundscape of Missy Elliott with the soul and spiritual intensity of Motown," wrote Sylvia Patterson for *The Face* magazine in 2001. Not a bad recipe, you'd have to say.

OPPOSITE Black sparkles with a difference: the contrasting tops worn by each member of Destiny's Child subtly switched up the formula for girl-group glamour.

OVERLEAF Smile for the camera: a Destiny's Child early line-up brings their groomed but relaxed look to the rod carpet.

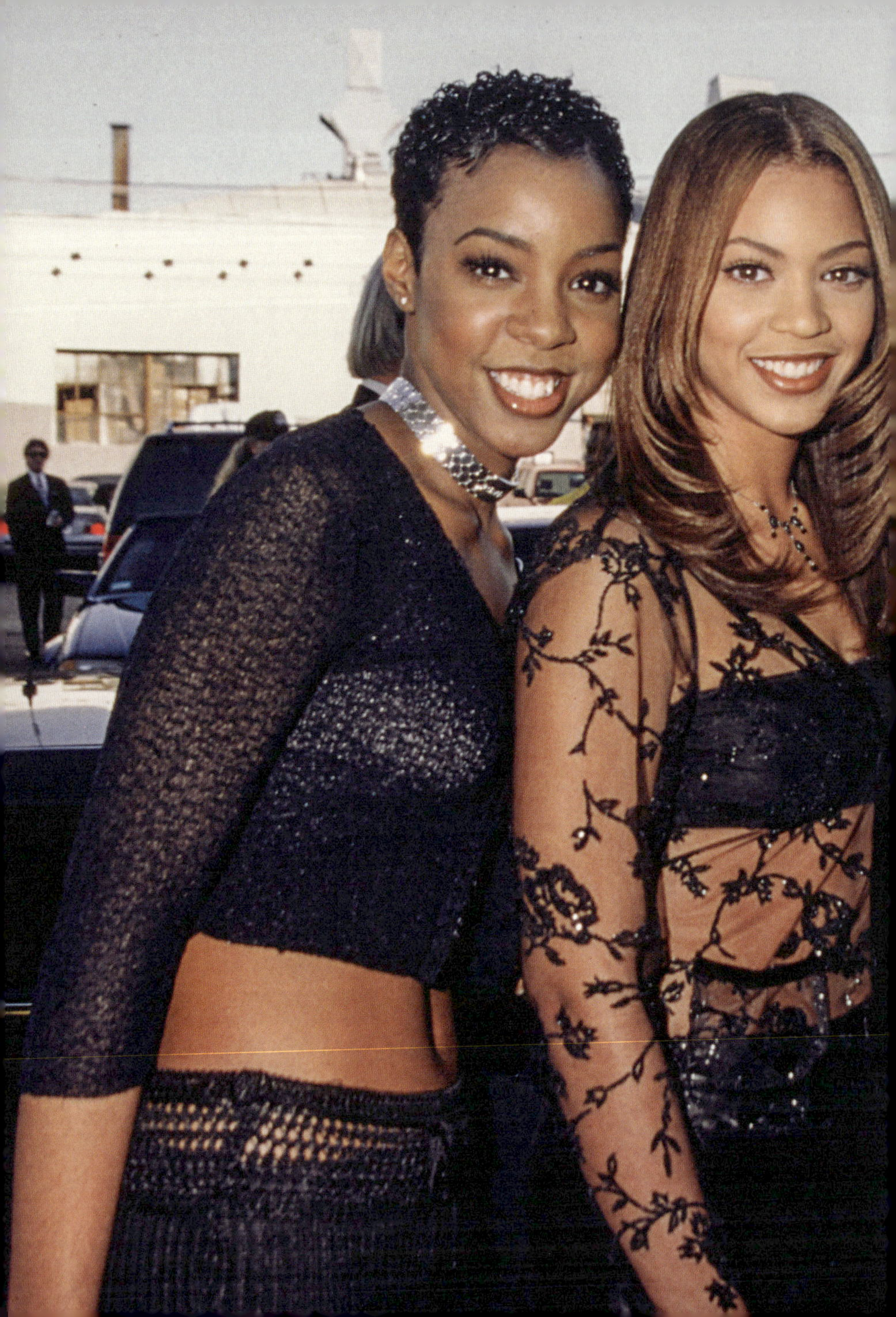

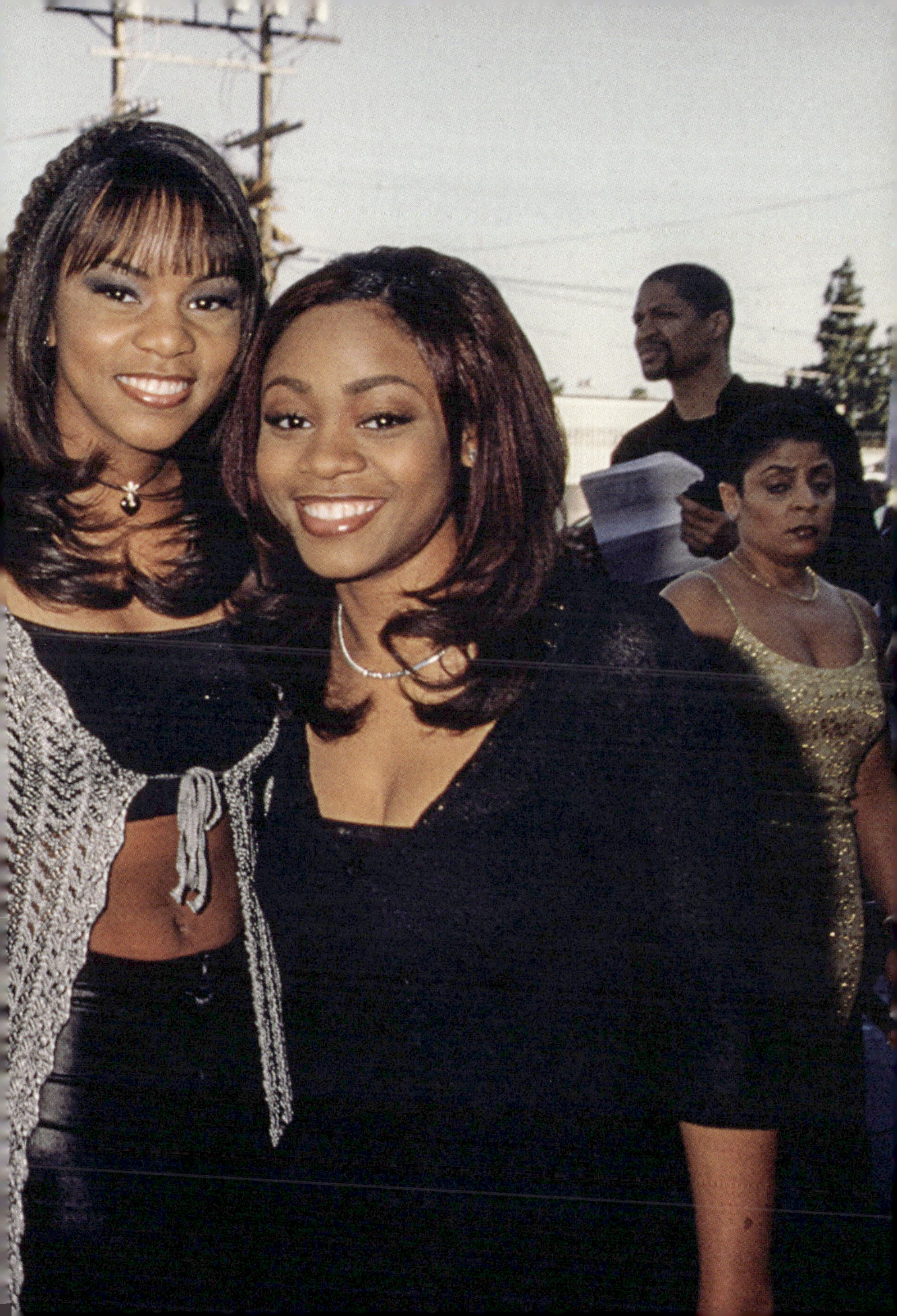

Stuck in the middle

The Destiny's Child era was distinctive for various reasons – hit after hit after hit, multiple line-ups and, of course, copious amounts of midriff. As young women in the public eye in the late nineties and early noughties, the exposure of this body part was a given.

The group was far from alone. Early pictures of The Spice Girls show them all with sporting acres of midriff, while stars like Aaliyah and All Saints regularly wore a sports bra combined with low-slung oversized workwear trousers. However, in recent times, Beyoncé and her bandmates have particularly become icons of the look, largely for the Y2K of it all – AKA their ability to combine flashing midriff with other buzzy trends. See an image of them performing in 1997 in matching velour tracksuits or another from 1999 of them attending the MOBO Awards in shades of sweet pastels that might now be known as mermaidcore.

OPPOSITE Soft, but also sexy: Destiny's Child give a co-sign to velour, a nineties favourite – with midriff proudly on display.

OVERLEAF A pastel dream: sweet shades of pink and blue make up the colour scheme for awards ceremony outfits in 1999.

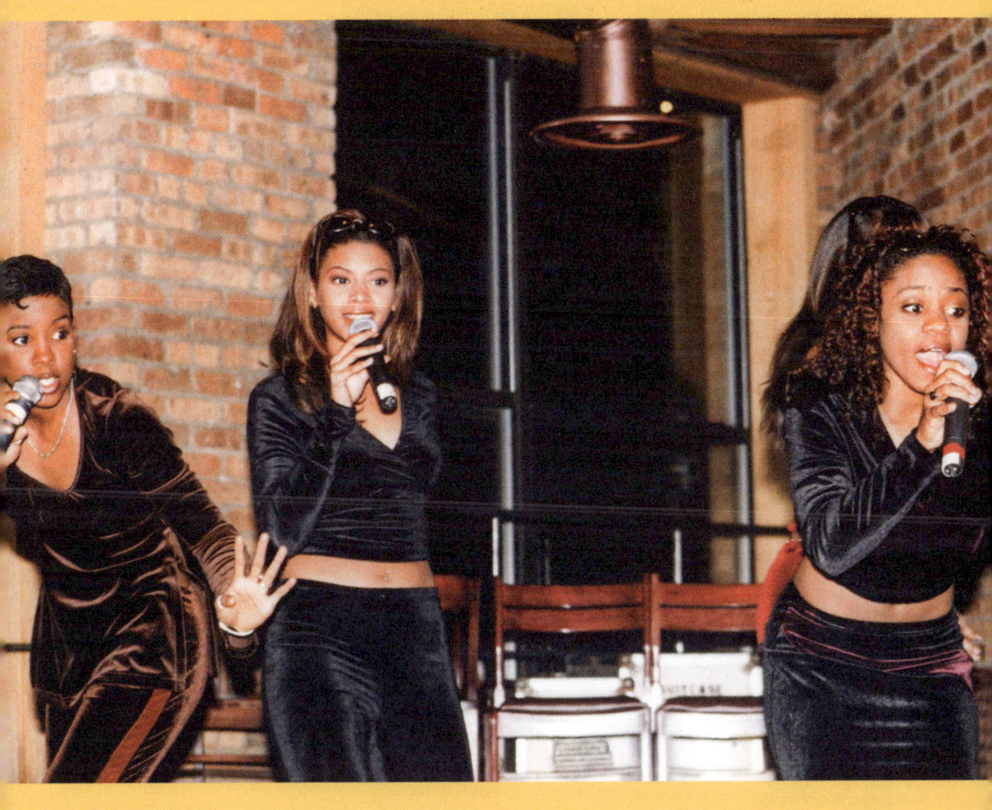

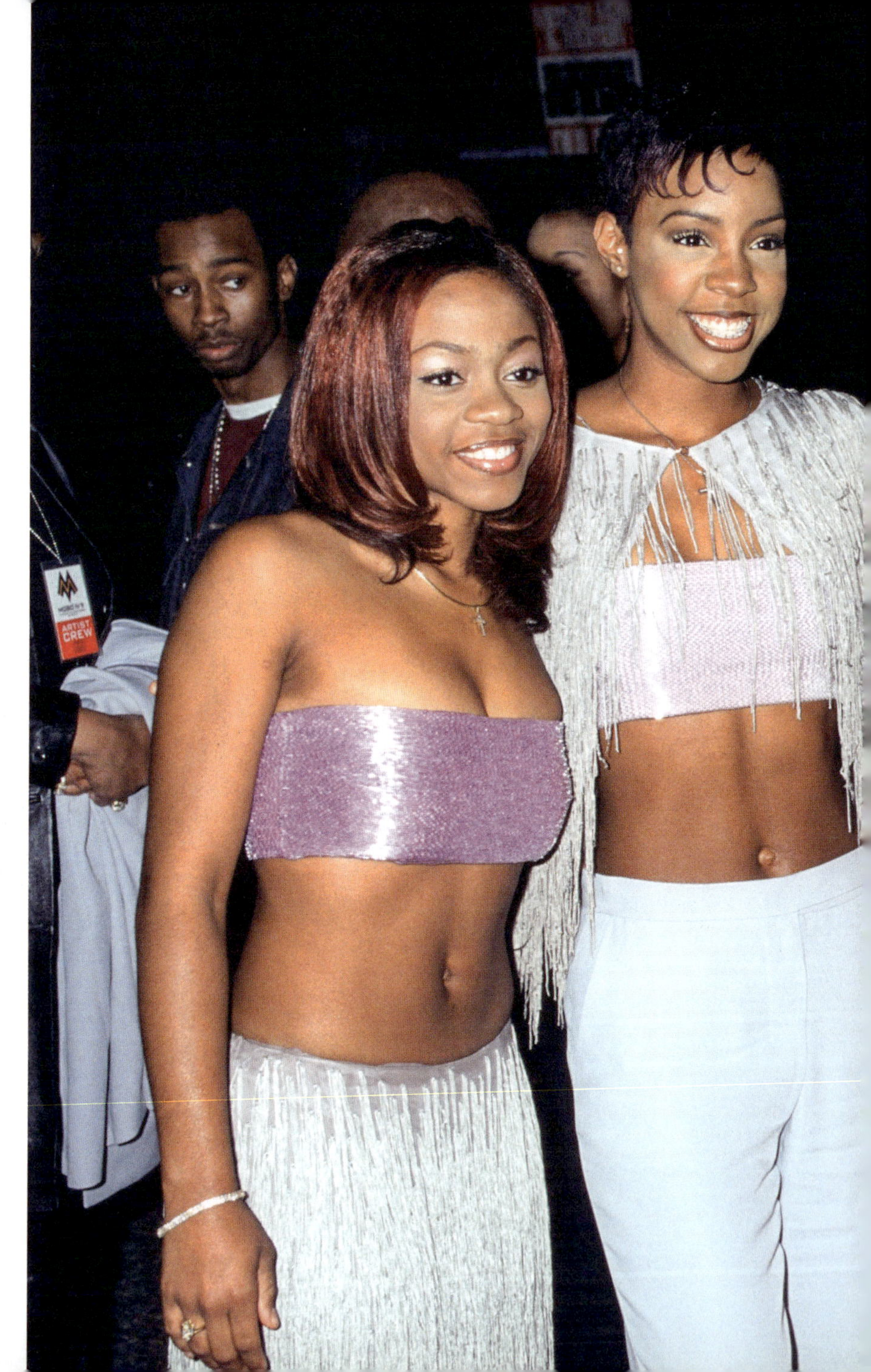
MOBO TV'S
ARTIST
CREW

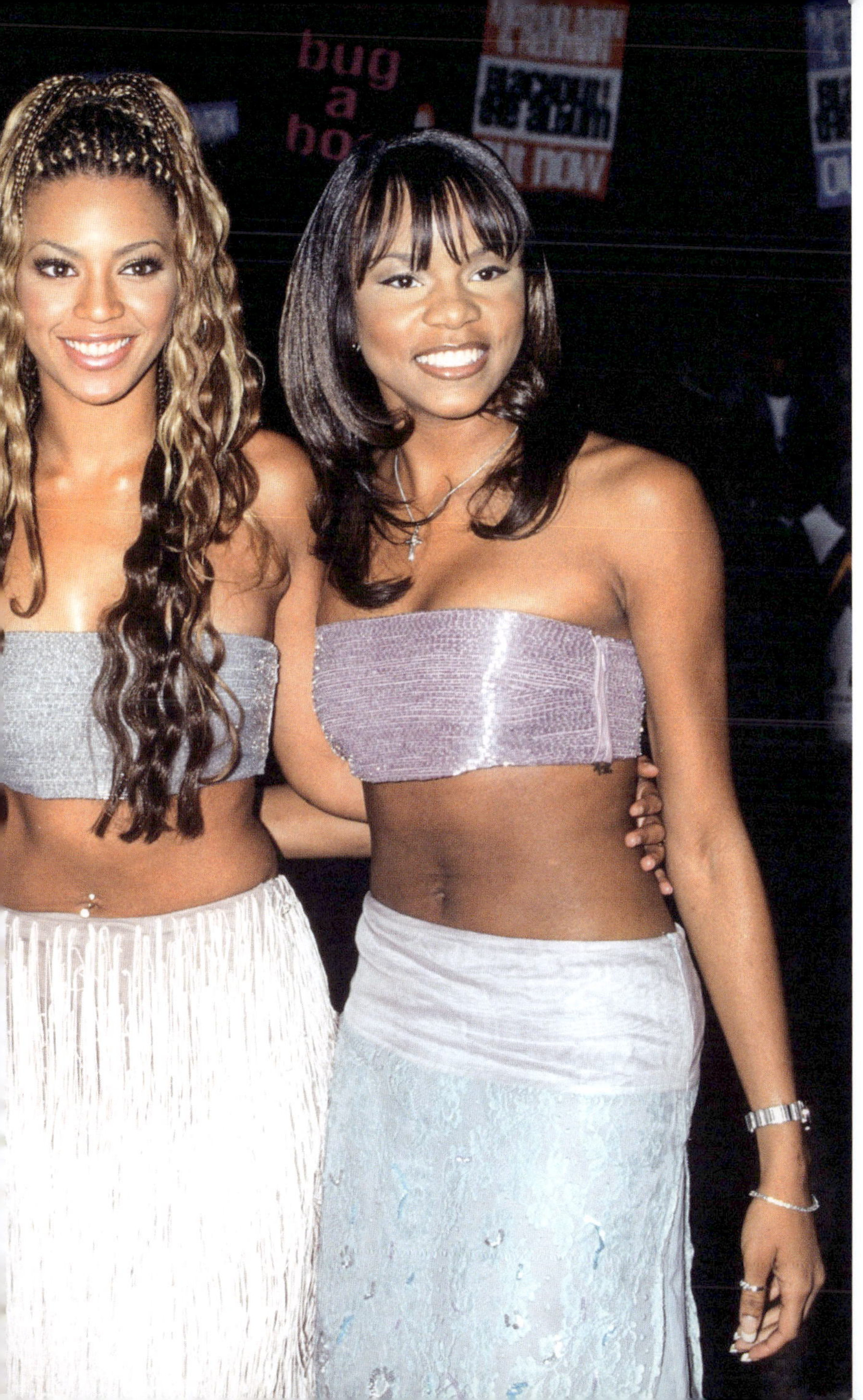

bug
a
boo

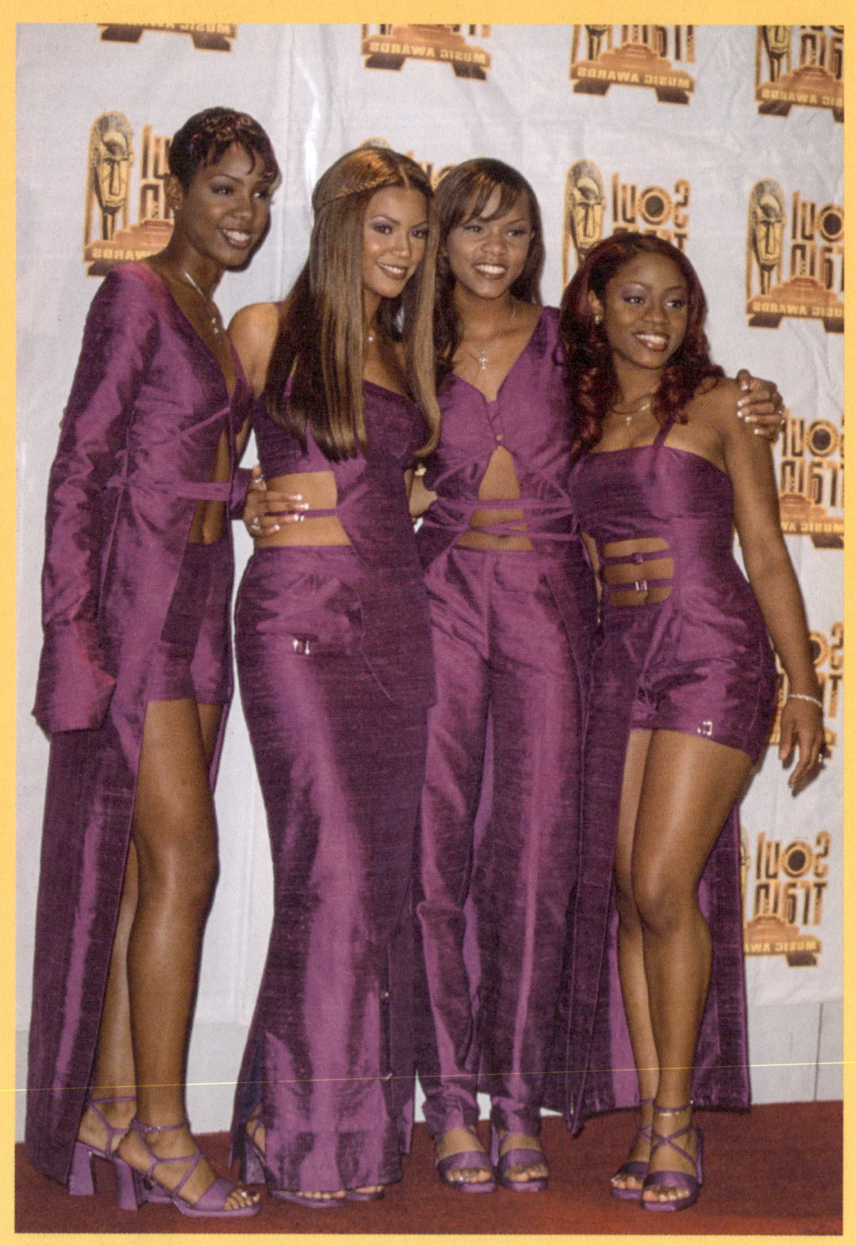

These weren't just outfits destined for a future as nostalgic images shared on social media. Some became part of the classic imagery of the group too, as with a performance at the VH1/Vogue Fashion Awards in 2000. Dressed in white with rhinestones, the new line-up of Beyoncé, Kelly Rowland and Michelle Williams performed 'Independent Women Part I' – the soundtrack to the hit movie *Charlie's Angels* – and took another step on the road to becoming icons of girl-group style.

Beyoncé has kept midriff part of her trademark look too, whether with cropped pieces to perform at Coachella or cut-out dresses on the red carpet. Far from something just for one era, the look is now a signature.

OPPOSITE Purple reign: a soon-to-disband Destiny's Child line-up bring matching-but-not-matching style to the BET Soul Train Awards.

OVERLEAF And then there were three: the final line-up of Beyoncé, Kelly Rowland and Michelle Williams take the Destiny's Child signature look to another level in white and rhinestones.

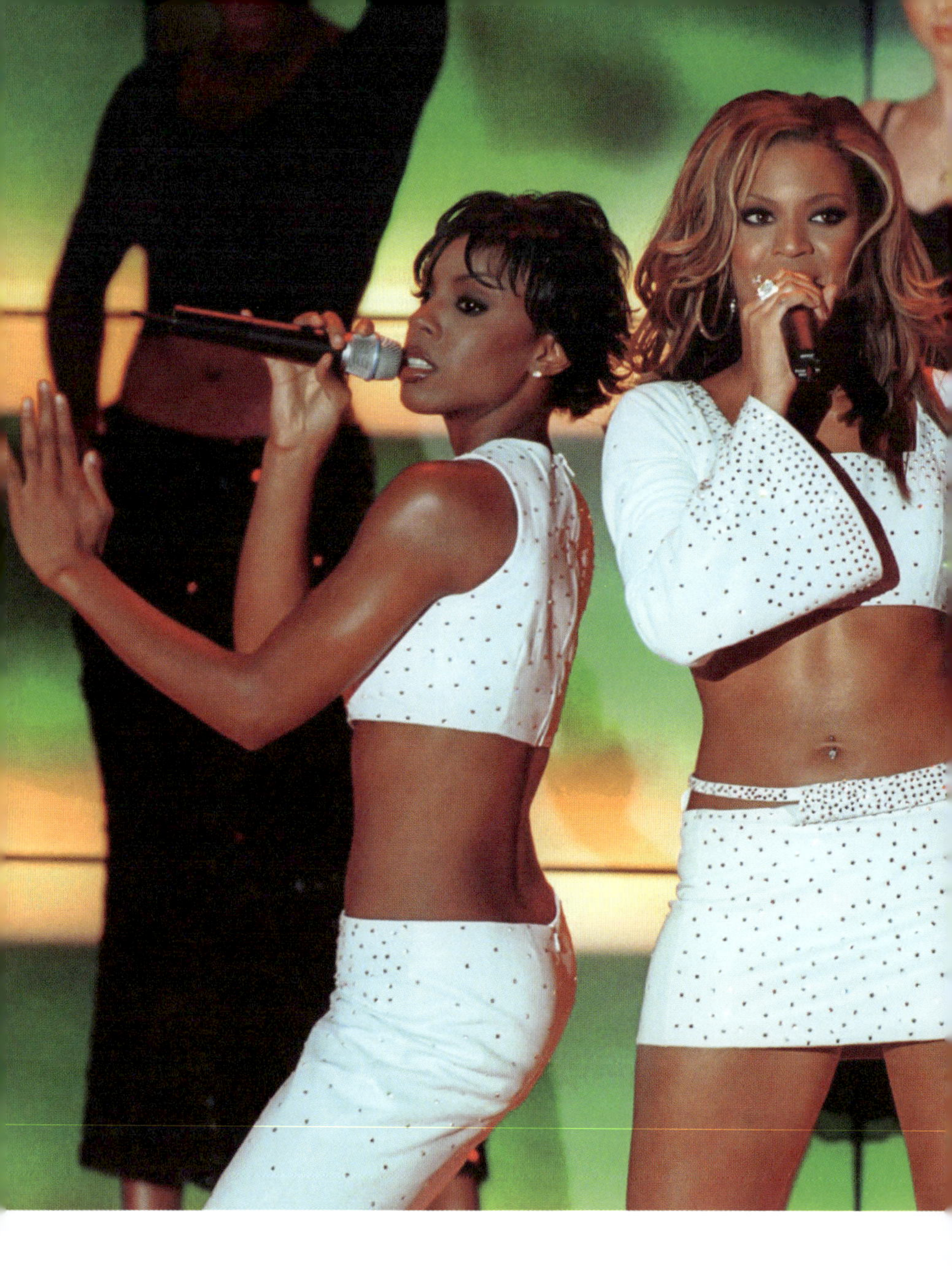

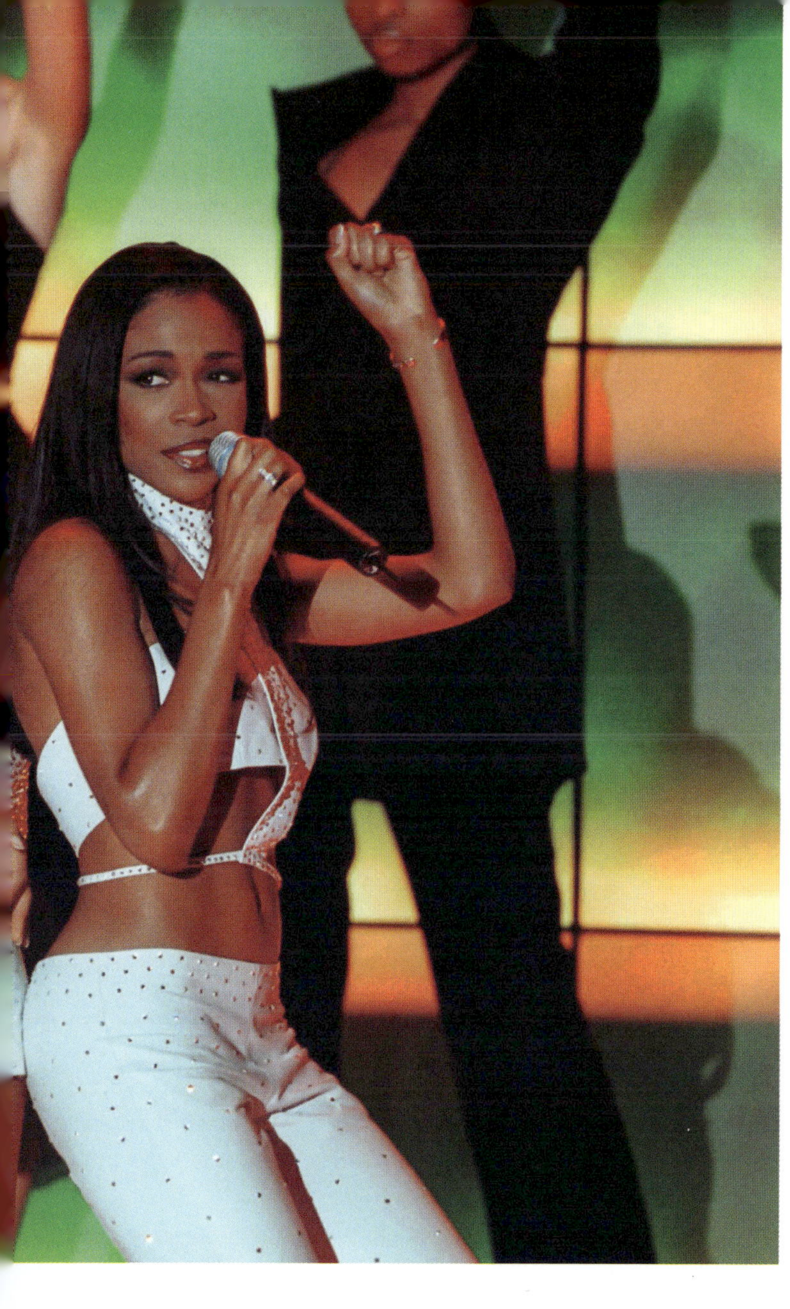

Moving to the red carpet

When you're a member of a successful R&B girl group, everyone wants you to come to their party. That's what happened to Destiny's Child. As their success grew in the late nineties, the red-carpet appearances ramped up.

In this environment, the group fluctuated when it came to their looks. They sometimes resembled what might have been more typical for a music video – different layers of leather for the MTV Awards in 1998, or matching colourful cropped tops and jeans for an appearance in 1999. By the time the final line-up was in place in 2000, there was a consistency to the looks, with a kind of glitz and glamour installed as standard, allowing these three women to look the part, whether on or away from the stage. That might mean studded leather looks or matching green dresses at the Grammys in 2001 to collect their first awards. "I can't believe we're winning a Grammy, ladies," cooed Beyoncé in their acceptance speech. She would go on to win 32, and that's only at the time of writing.

Leather queens: the first experiments on the red carpet played with texture, shape and fabric. See this bold look in 1998.

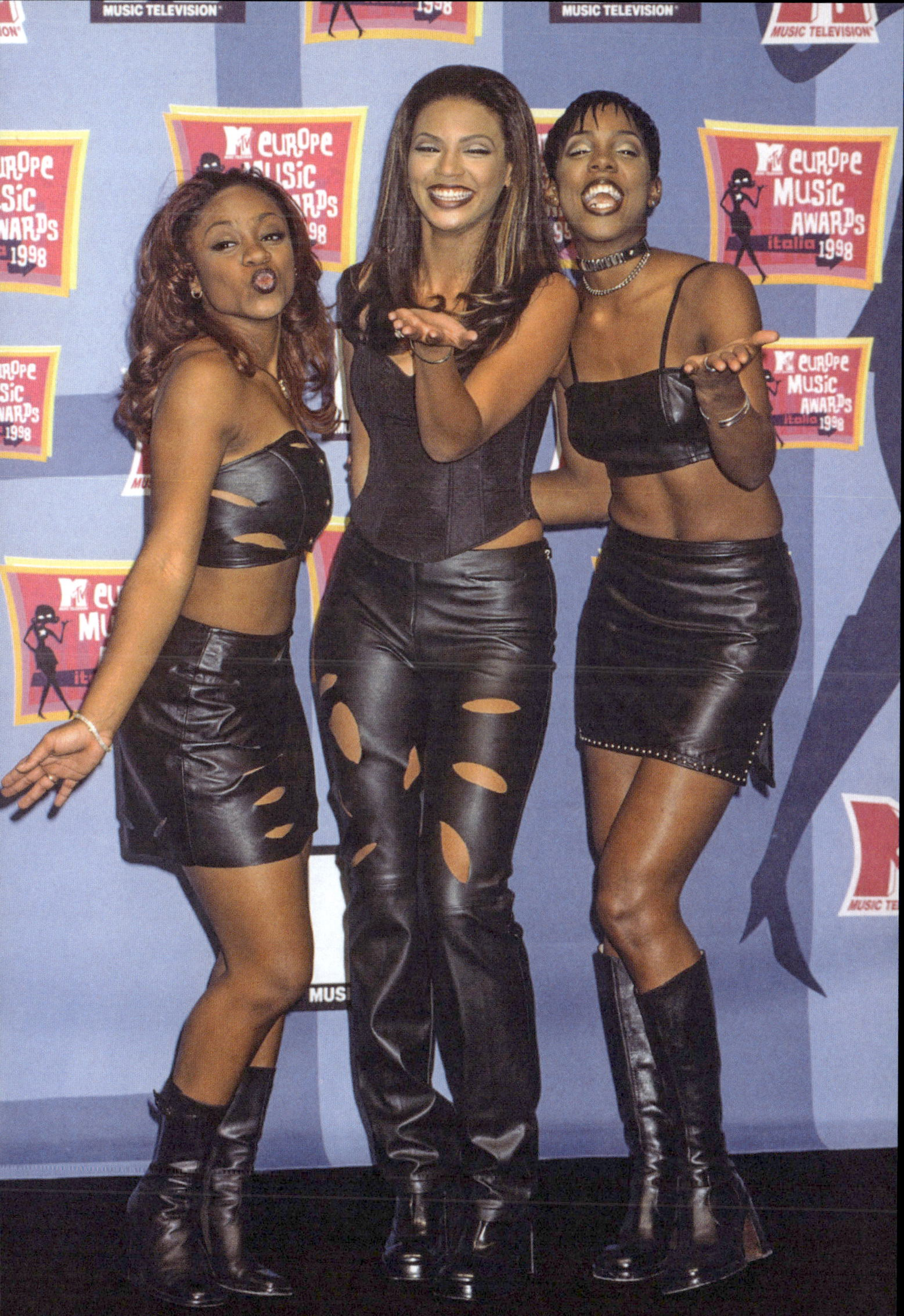
MUSIC TELEVISION®
MUSIC TELEVISION®
europe
MUSIC
AWARDS
italia 1998
europe
MUSIC
AWARDS
italia 1998
MUSIC
MUSIC TE

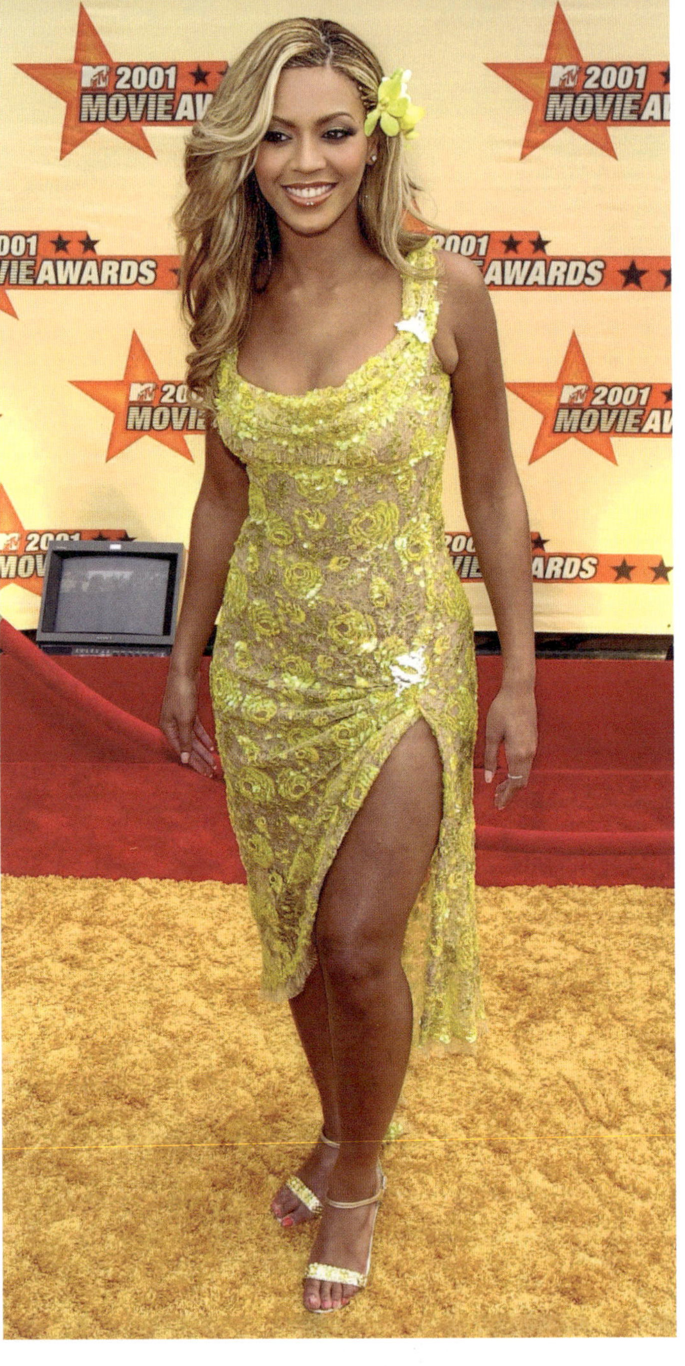

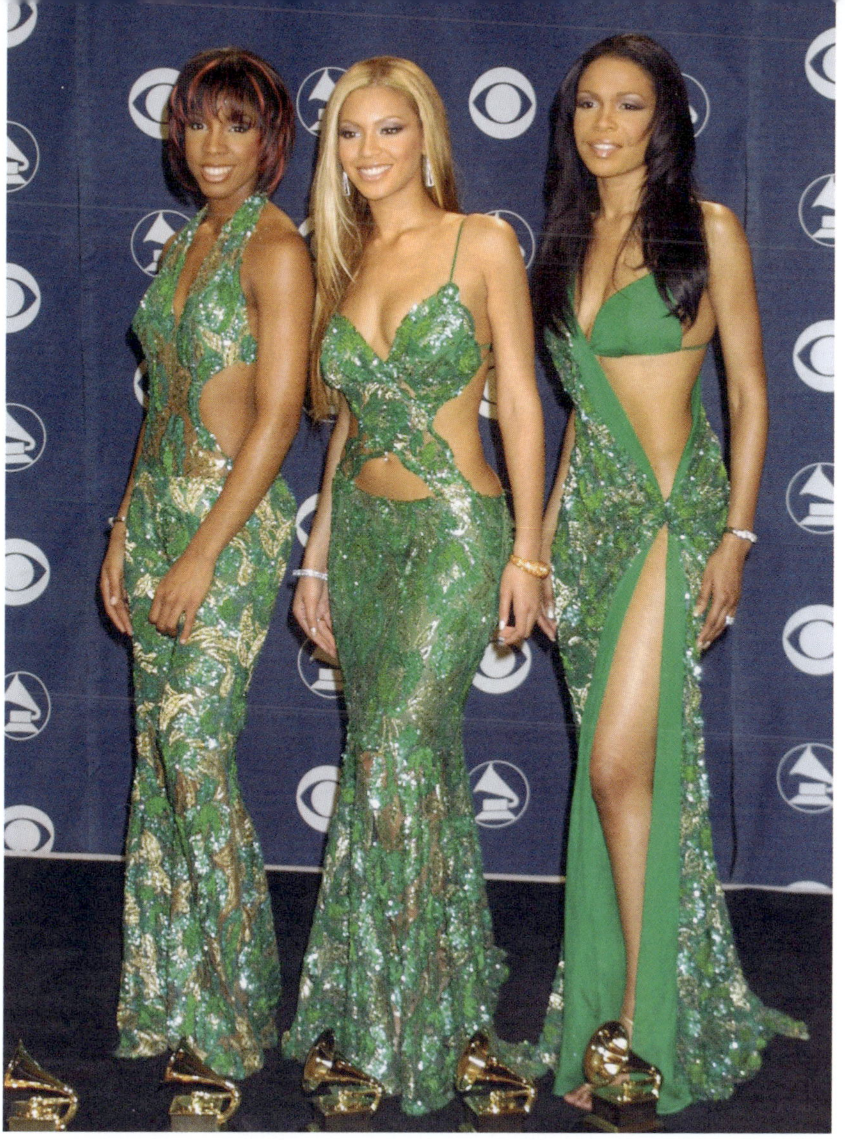

ABOVE Five Grammys and three stars: Destiny's Child bring
haute glamour to the awards ceremony in 2001.

OPPOSITE All yellow: for an early solo red-carpet appearance,
Beyoncé added playful touches like a flower behind her ear.

As the years went on, Beyoncé began attending events as a
solo act too. This started, at the turn of the millennium, with
style that had the girl-next-door glamour she championed
as part of Destiny's Child. Using yellow tones and sequins,
her appearances at film premieres and events were as sweet
as they were dazzling. See a thigh-split dress for MTV Movie
Awards in 2001, or a short sequin dress in on-theme shades of
gold for the premiere of her Austin Powers movie *Goldmember*
the following year. Still somewhat shy without her bandmates
beside her, these were the first steps toward the veteran red-
carpet star we know and love today.

OPPOSITE Golden girl: Beyoncé goes full shimmer at the *Goldmember*
premiere in 2002. Shades of gold are on theme, after all.

OVERLEAF In the middle: an appearance in 1999 showcases different
crop tops and hipster jeans. See it as inspo for Y2K dressing.

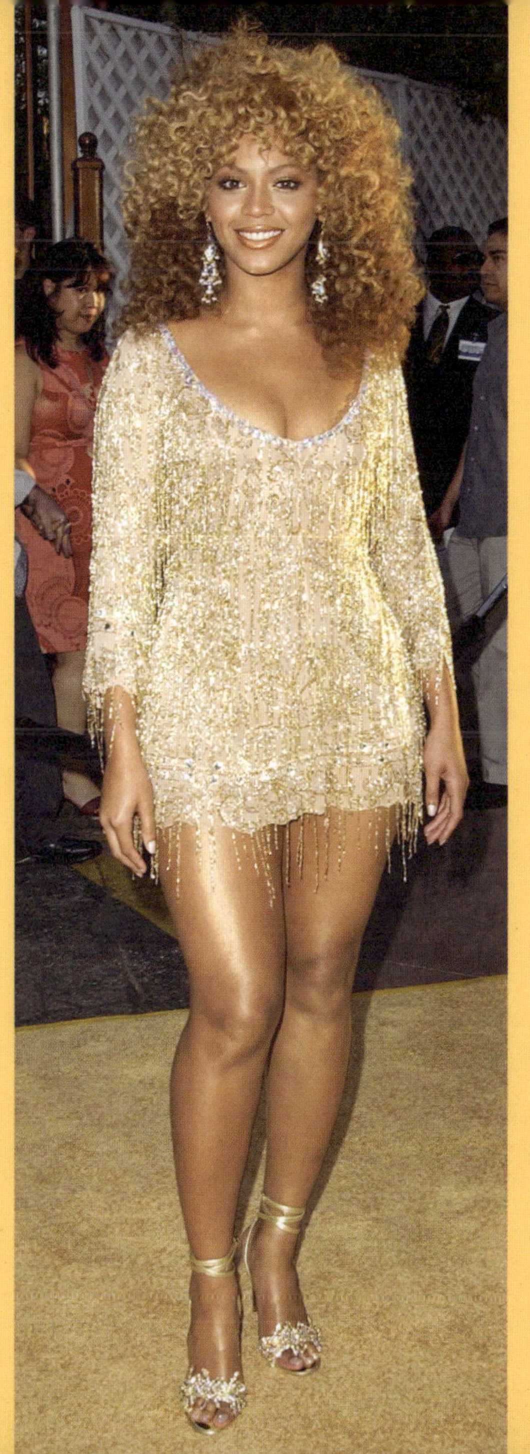

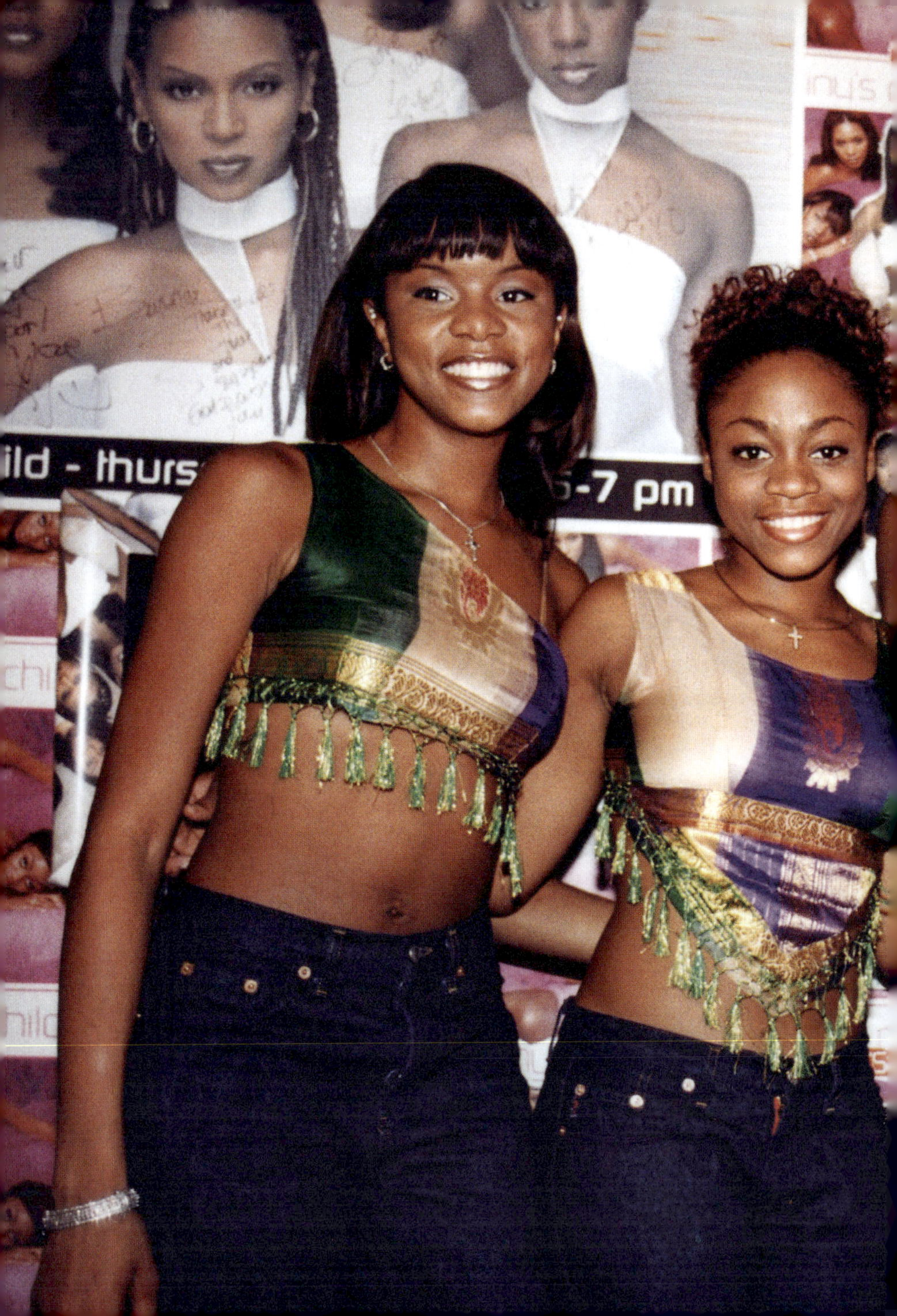
child - thurs
5-7 pm

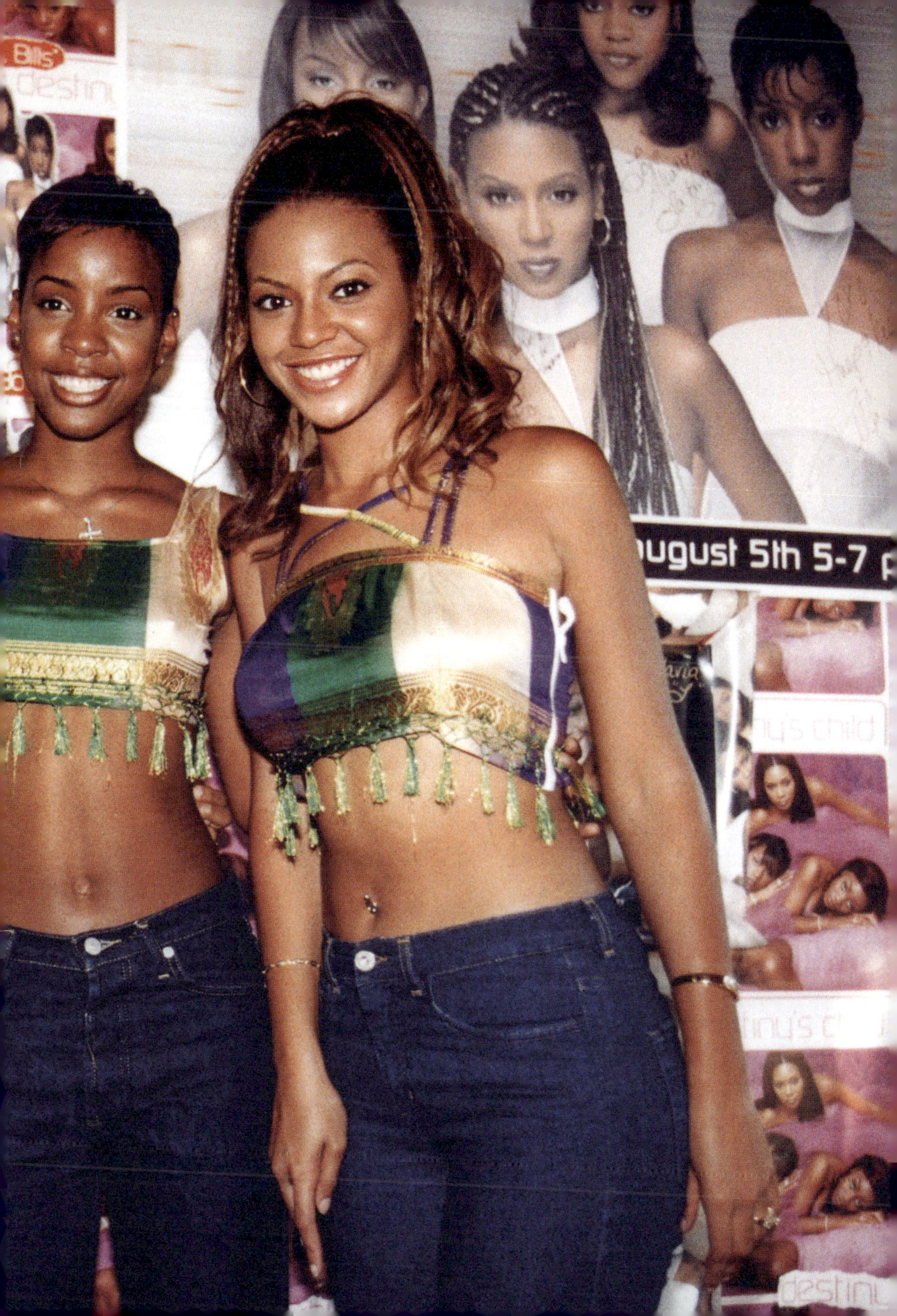

ugust 5th 5-7 p

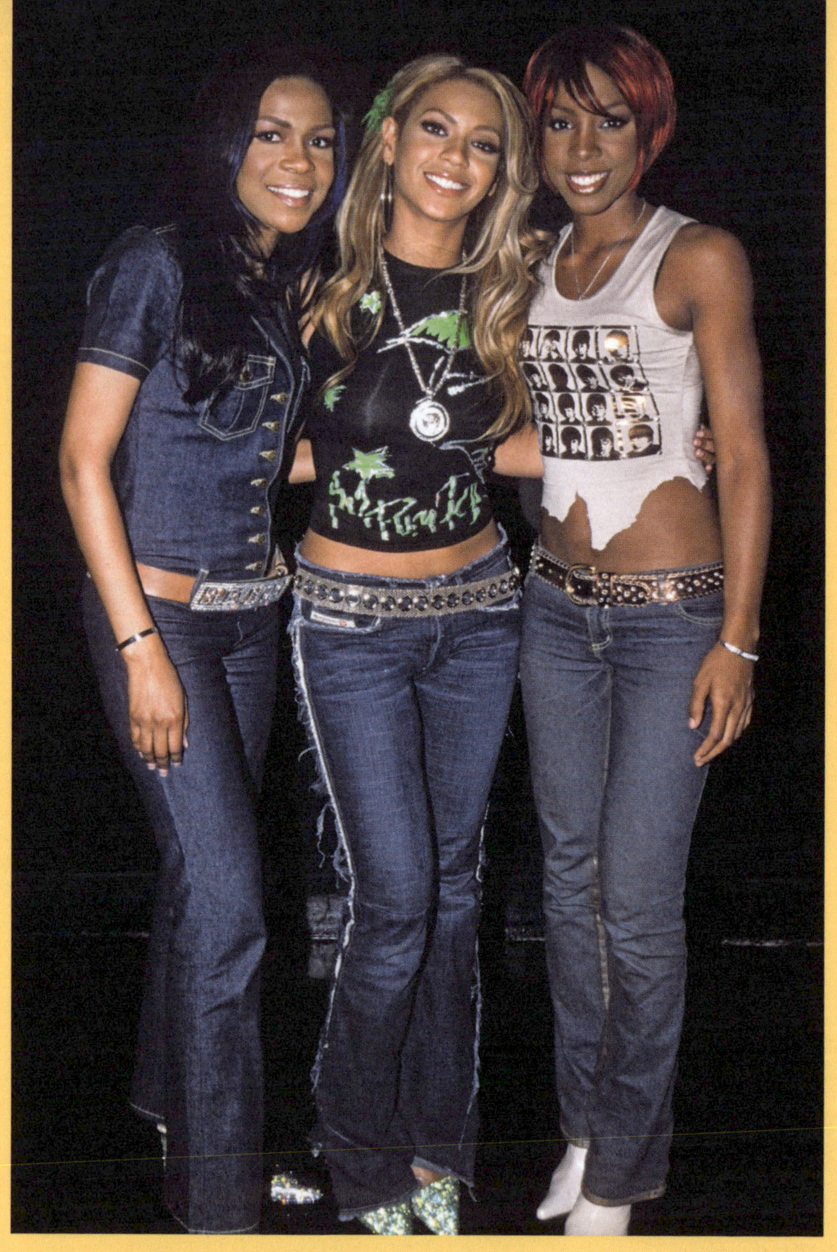

A masterclass in low-rise denim in 2001: worn with T-shirts with midriff showing and pointed shoes, the look is casual and fun at the same time.

Keeping it casual

If glamour was part of their wheelhouse, Destiny's Child were still young women in their twenties living through the nineties and early noughties. As such, they wore jeans, T-shirts and the kind of scarf tops that have inevitably threatened to come back in the 2020s.

Denim went on to become a central piece of Beyoncé's solo style and she had a grounding in it as part of Destiny's Child. The group regularly wore jeans, especially as the turn of the millennium came around – whether to movie premieres or to perform (an early performance in the UK at Party in the Park saw Beyoncé and her bandmates in those scarf tops and jeans). As befits the era, jeans were often low-slung and bootcut, the kind that young women now search resale sites for. T-shirts and hoodies, meanwhile, gave a hint of "day off" to the look.

Speaking to *The Face* in 2001, Beyoncé said the group had a rule of thumb when it came to what they wore – with a kind of PG policy for fashion: "If we feel like anyone's going to be straight staring at our boobs or butts, then, no." These casual looks underlined this, and once again, amped up their relatability.

While the trio of the final line-up wore all manner of outfits, they perhaps looked the most comfortable in more relaxed clothes – and most like their peers. These outfits signalled that these women were stars, yes, but they could have been just like me and you.

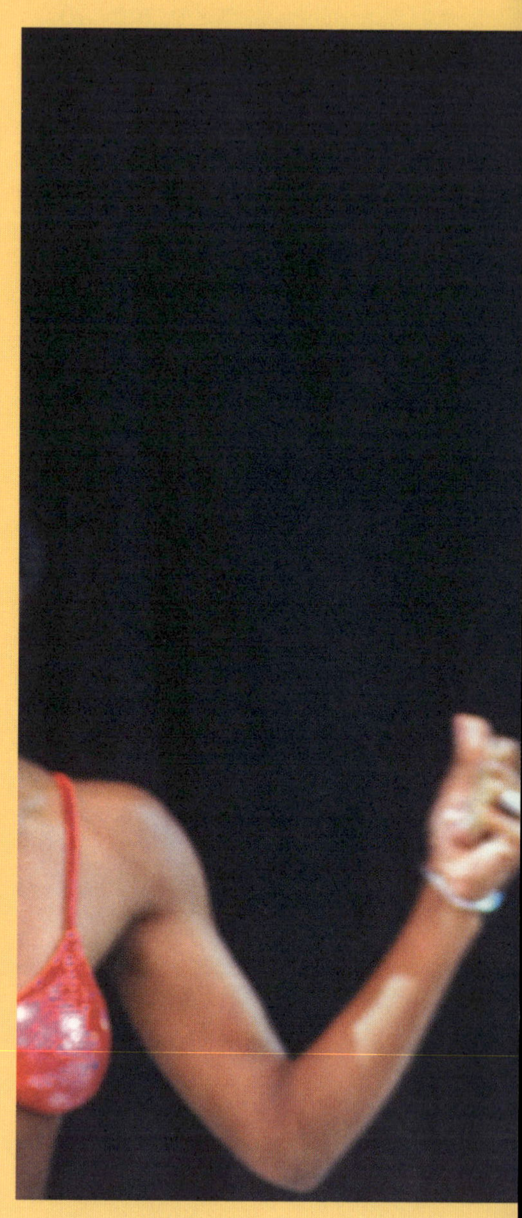

The scarf top gets a star's
seal of approval: this Beyoncé
look arguably started a trend
in the early noughties.

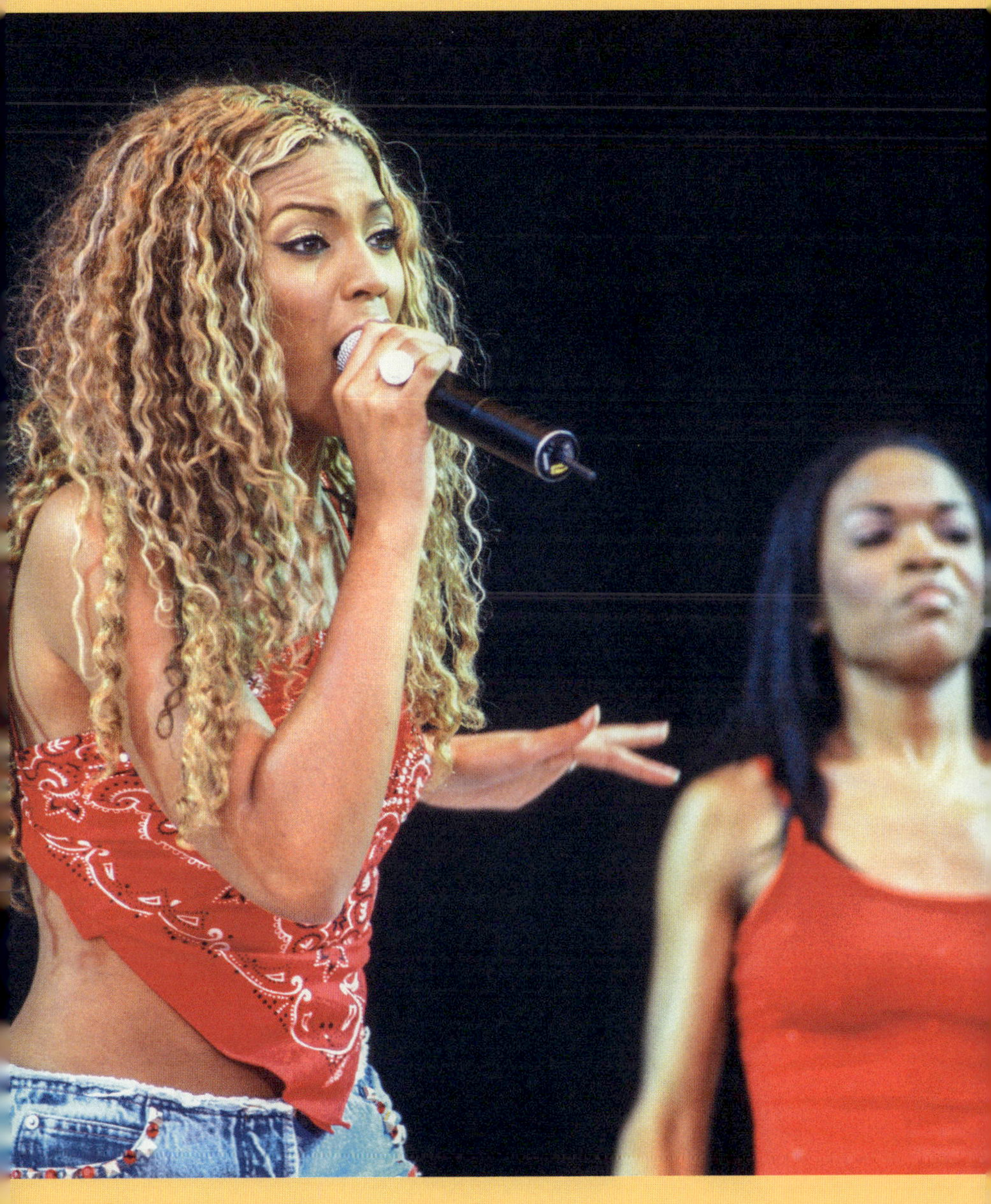

A star is born

By 2003, Destiny's Child had two critically acclaimed and commercially successful albums (*The Writing's on the Wall* and *Survivor*), three different line-ups and a tour that took in dates across Australia, Japan and Europe. The masterplan for world domination was coming together – which meant a new element: solo careers. In May 2003, Beyoncé released her first solo single proper, 'Crazy in Love'. It went to number one in the US and the UK and confirmed what everyone already knew: she was just getting started.

A solo career meant solo appearances. To promote her debut solo album *Dangerously in Love*, Beyoncé was seen more and more on the celebrity circuit. This was when her red-carpet style was shaped. Moving from the kind of dresses that might be seen on a guest at a non-celebrity wedding, she initially experimented with a kind of Disney Princess style. For her first appearance at the Golden Globes, she wore a gown with a corset-like top and tulle skirt, a shape she returned to a few times.

A princess in the making: Beyoncé makes her way in red-carpet style at the Golden Globes in 2003.

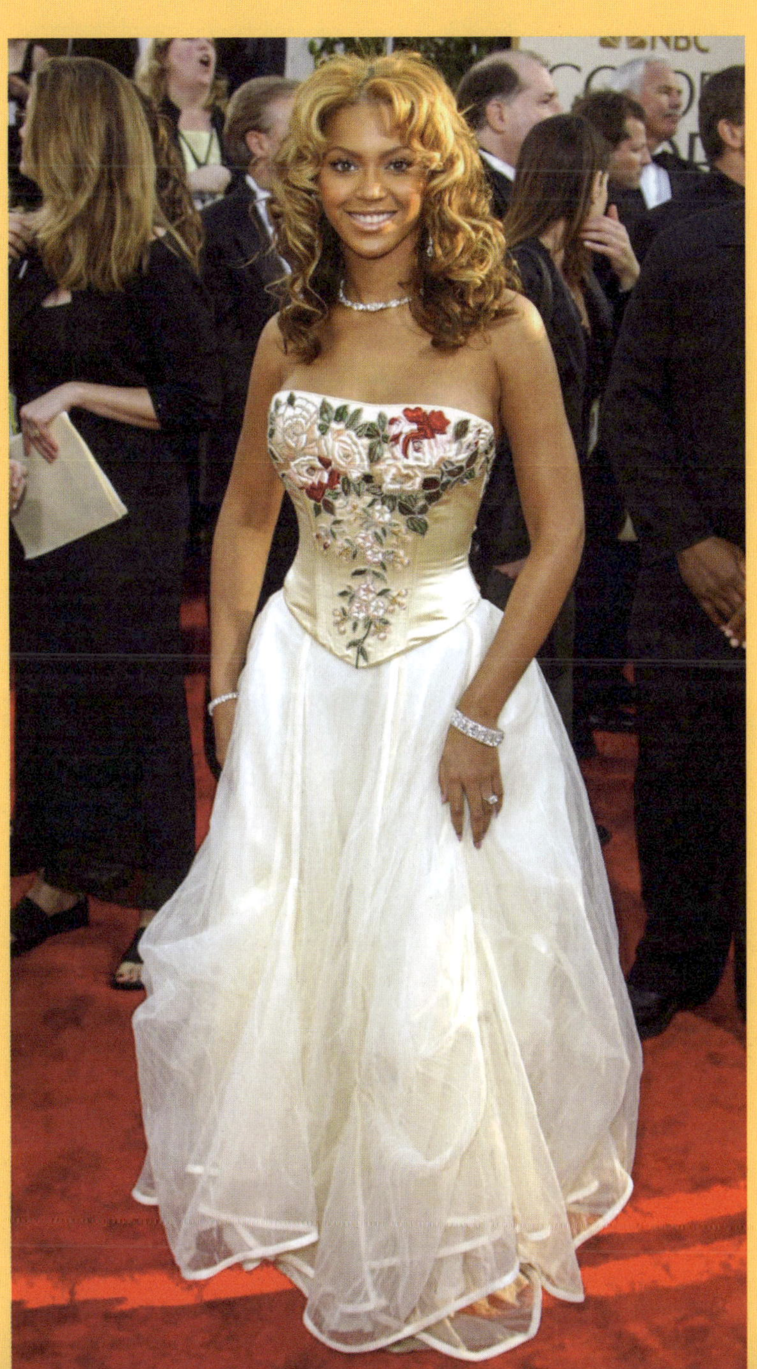

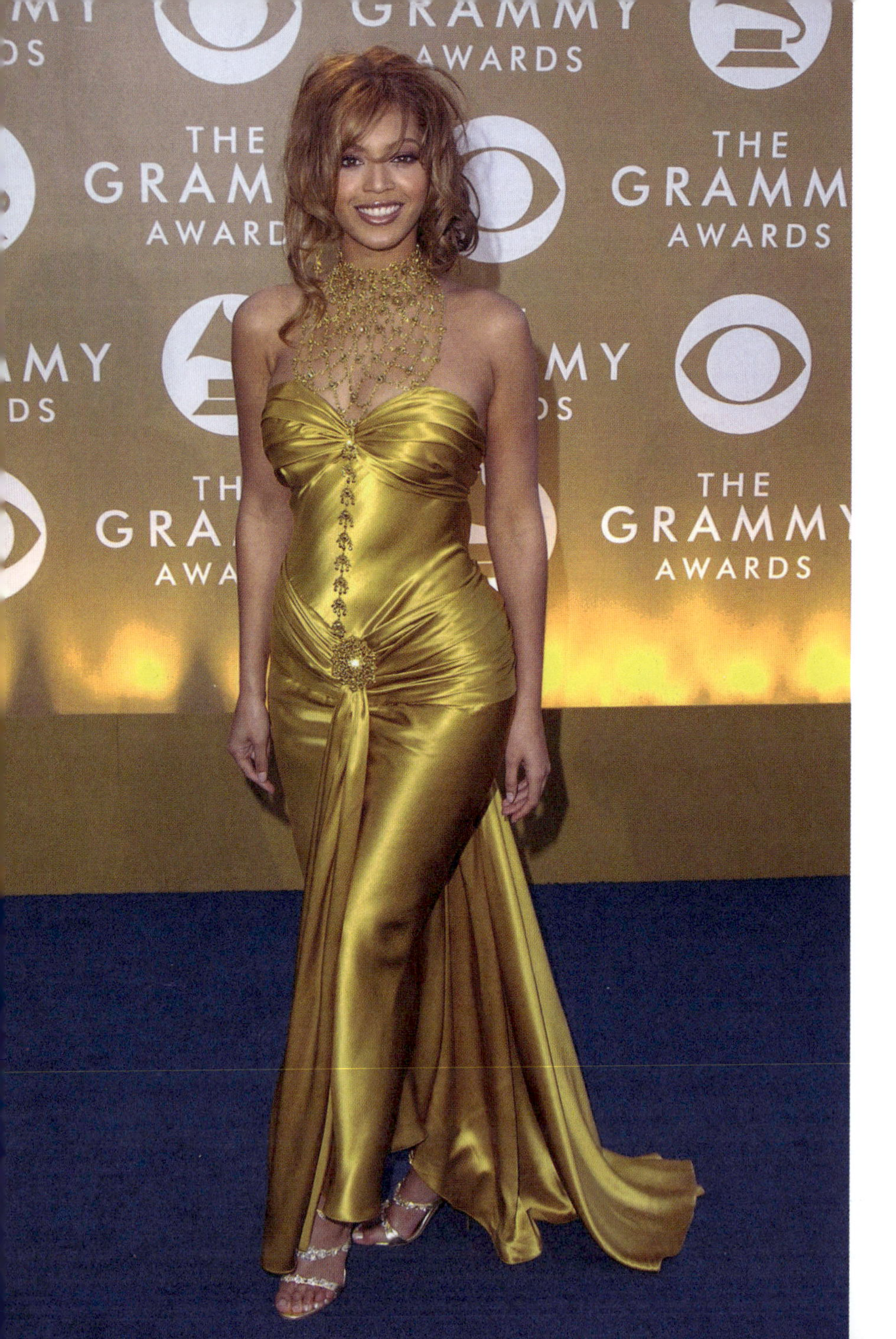
GRAMMY
AWARDS
THE
GRAMM
AWARDS
MY
DS
THE
GRAMMY
AWARDS

In an interview with *The Face* magazine in 2003, the star spoke about the "pressure" around these outfits: "It's crazy, because if you go buy clothes, you can't wear them but one time and that's the worst. You invest and it's 'ok, can't wear it again!'"

She quickly got the hang of this new world. A distinctly Beyoncé take on the red carpet began to emerge – one that combined a sense of fun with timeless glamour. Satin and velvet – old-school fabrics that the likes of Hollywood actress Lana Turner or singer Lena Horne might be familiar with – dominated. There was a full-length yellow satin dress for the Grammys in 2004 and Versace for the MTV Movie Awards.

The classic look signalling this shift came in 2005: for Beyoncé's first Oscars. An appearance just after Destiny's Child announced they would be parting ways after a tour the following year, she used it as a line in the sand. Dressed in another Versace number – this time a bustier of black velvet, accessorized simply with long earrings and a graceful Old Hollywood-worthy stance – this was a sartorial statement. Beyoncé, as we know her today, had arrived.

Satin and sparkles and undone hair: a more modern take on Old Hollywood glamour in the mid-noughties.

> *"You go buy clothes, you can't wear them but one time and that's the worst. You invest and it's 'ok, can't wear it again!'"*

BEYONCÉ ON RED-CARPET DRESSING, 2003

Picture – and pose – perfect: a polished and poised Beyoncé
in black velvet Versace at her first Oscars in 2005.

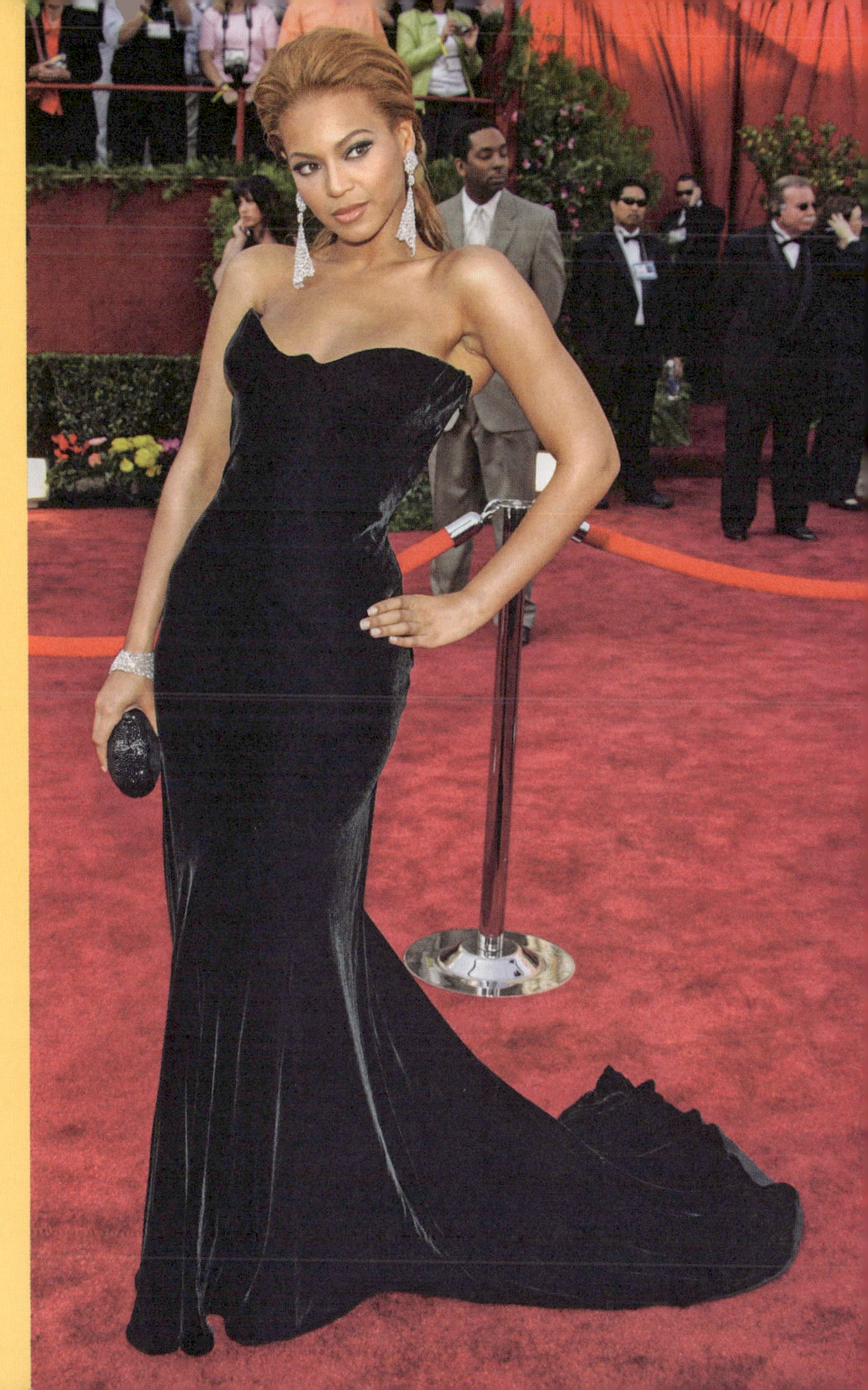

Sister, sister

In 2017, *Interview* magazine got something of a scoop – an interview with Solange Knowles conducted by none other than her big sister, Beyoncé. Through discussions of growing up in Houston, the challenges of being a woman in the public eye and heroes (Diana Ross, Minnie Riperton), the piece ends with one of the things everyone wanted to know: how Beyoncé did as a big sister. "You did a kickass job," says Solange. "You were the most patient, loving, wonderful sister ever."

The Knowles sisters are five years apart and on paper, certainly, couldn't be more different. If Beyoncé is a megastar on the radar of people around the world, Solange is more of an indie act, an early adopter, who makes experimental visuals and glassware along with music. But, despite these differences, the siblings have long been close, as images through the years demonstrate. Growing up, Solange even filled in for missing members of Destiny's Child.

Two halves: the Knowles sisters show their style in 2002. See Beyoncé's full-on glam and Solange's thrift store style.

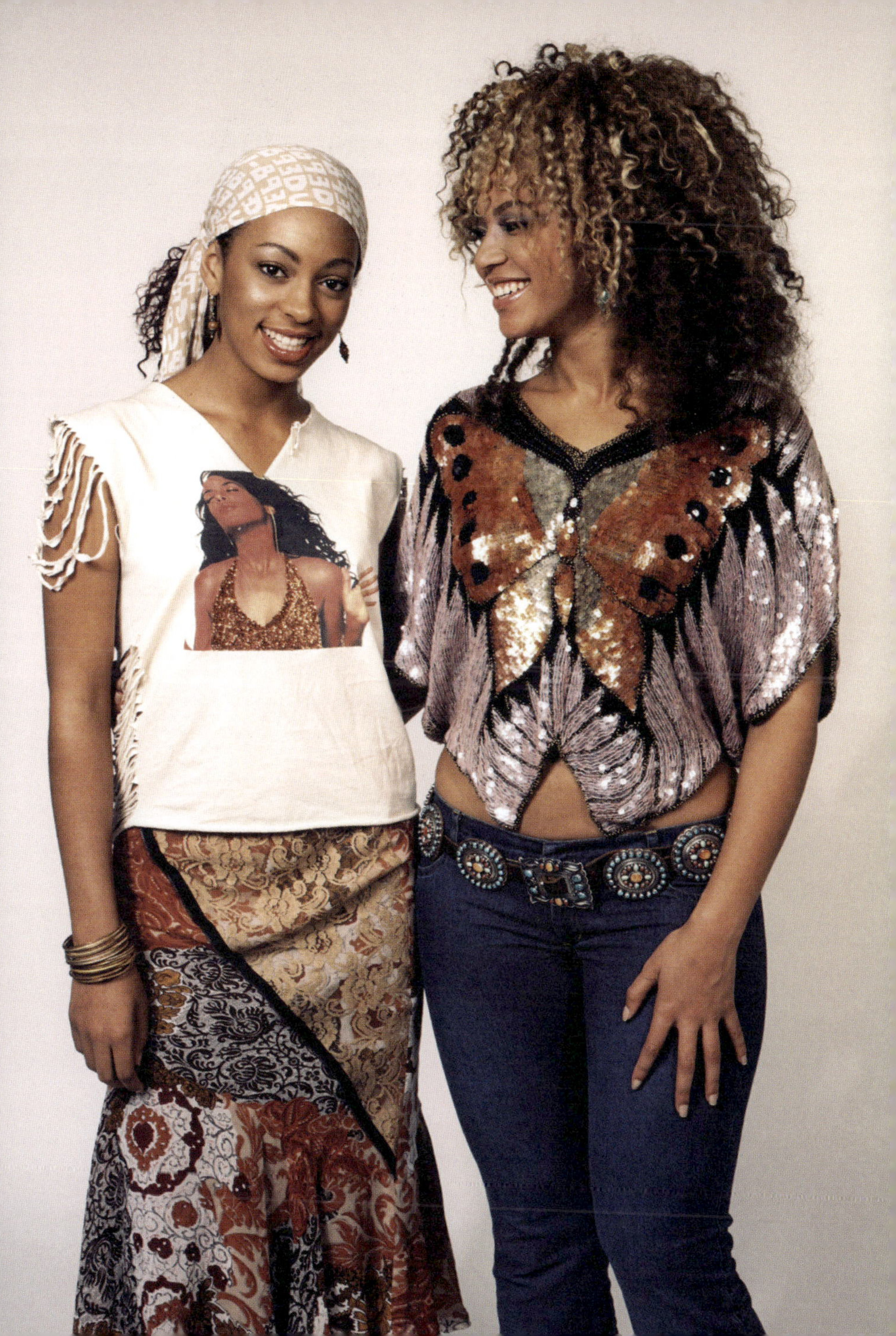

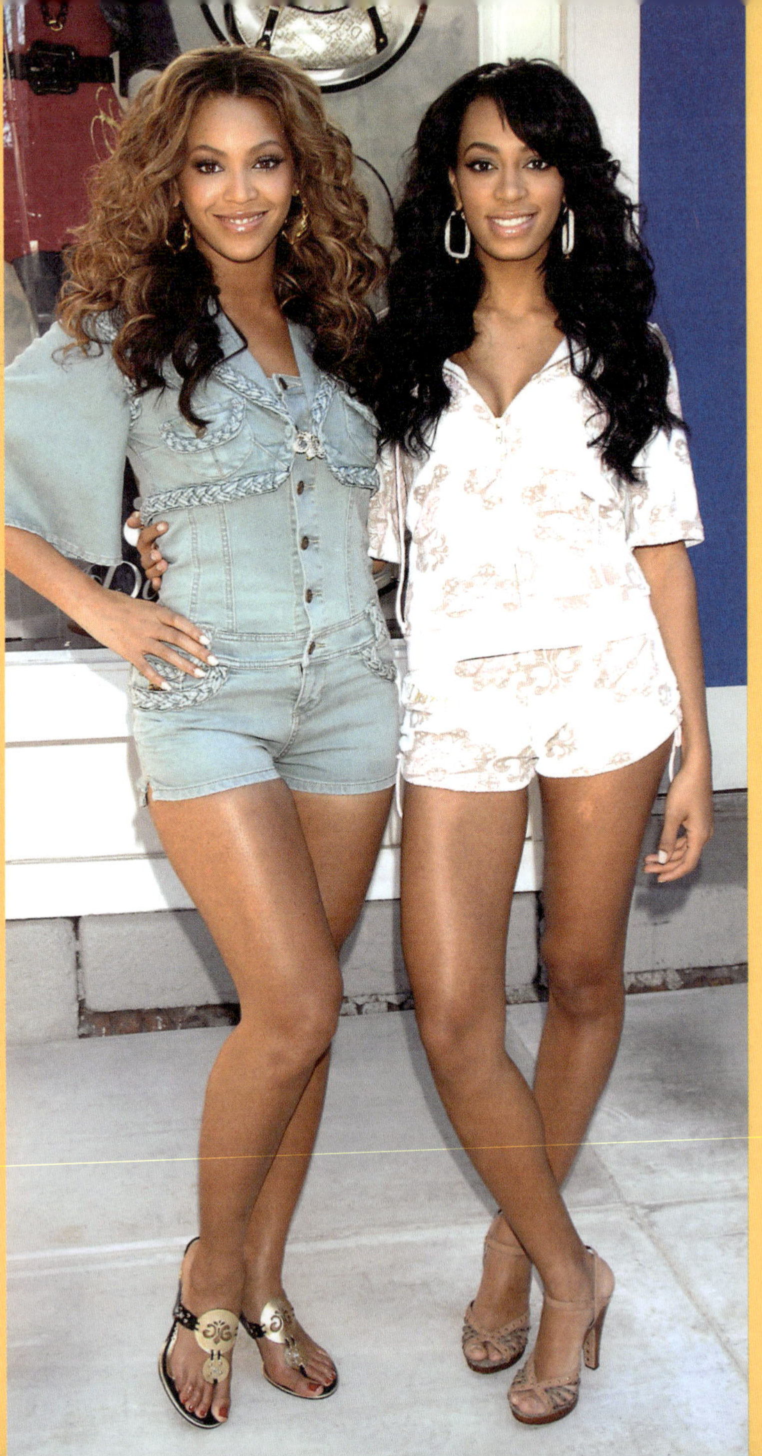

Early on in the Destiny's Child era, Solange was photographed with Beyoncé at different events. As a teenager, she already had an edge that distinguished her from her more poptastic sister – wearing an upcycled T-shirt featuring R&B icon Aaliyah on her self-titled album with a patchwork skirt, for example, or a vintage-looking red frock to a film premiere.

Of course this is a relationship that goes beyond these early years – Solange appeared in the video for Beyoncé fan classic 'Party' in 2011 and performed with her at Coachella in 2018. Her surprise appearance, with the two sisters dancing to 'Get Me Bodied' in variations of silver sparkle, was a high point. "Give it up for my sister," exclaimed Beyoncé as Solange exited the stage.

The cheerleading has continued. When Solange composed a score for the New York City Ballet in 2022, Beyoncé wrote on Instagram: "My beloved sister, there are no words to express the pride and admiration I have for you. You are a visionary and one of one."

Takes one of one to know one of one…

The sisters step out: Beyoncé and Solange promote House of Deréon designs in 2006.

Miss Tina

Destiny's Child was very much a family affair when it began in the mid-nineties. Mathew Knowles, Beyoncé's father, managed the group, while Tina, her mother, made a lot of the costumes, acting as both stylist and hairdresser. She is, therefore, singlehandedly responsible for the early iterations of the group's look. Speaking much later while accepting the CFDA Fashion Icon Award in 2016, Beyoncé described this as something of a superpower. "When I wore these clothes on stage, I felt like Khaleesi – I had an extra suit of armour."

This wasn't just a mother helping out her oldest daughter and friends. Tina knew about aesthetics – she was after all the daughter of a seamstress and the owner of a hair salon in Houston (in an interview with the *Guardian* from 2001, Michelle Williams says this is the place where she had her upper lip waxed for the first time). As such, she was able to create a look for a girl group on the rise, partly by looking to past inspirations – like the girl groups of Motown, whose glamour was even evident for those sitting in the back row. "You could see because there was a sparkle, there was a dazzle," she told the *Washington Post* in 2020. "They looked like stars. So that was the concept for Destiny's Child."

Mother and daughter: two generations of Knowleses step out on the Billboard Music Awards red carpet in 2003.

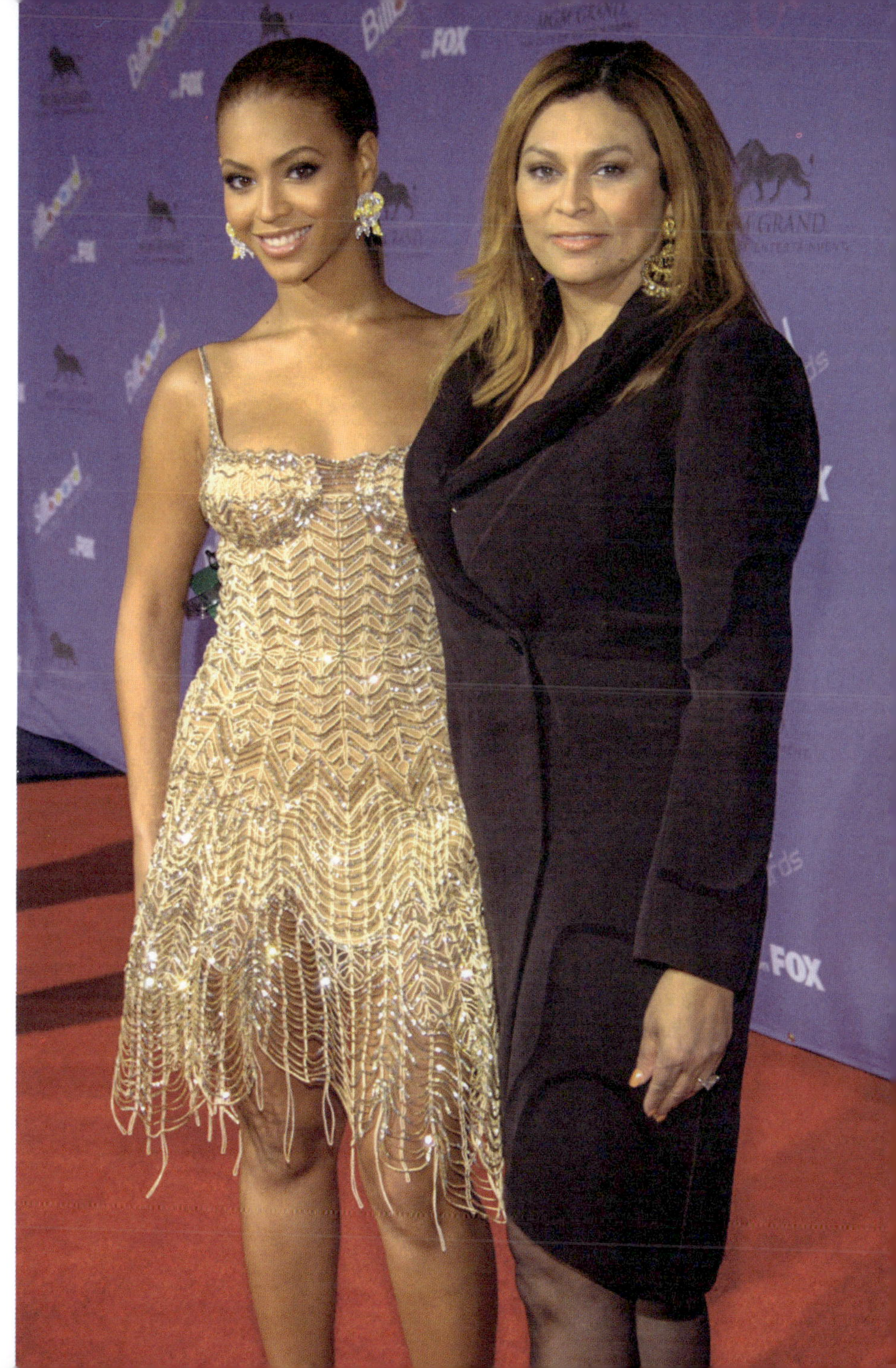

"When I wore these clothes on stage I felt like Khaleesi — I had an extra suit of armour."

BEYONCÉ, ON DESIGNS MADE BY HER MOTHER

Of course as the mother of one of the biggest stars on the planet, Miss Tina herself has become something of a celebrity herself. This started in the Destiny's Child era when she was often the red-carpet date for her daughter, with tailoring a favoured look, whether a white trouser suit or a burgundy leather skirt and jacket.

Fast forward to 2025 and she has currently over 4 million followers on Instagram and a memoir soon to be released. She also remains a crucial inspiration for Beyoncé. On 2020 track 'Savage', with Megan Thee Stallion, the star credits her savage style directly to Tina. Speaking on the *Sherri* talk show in 2023, Miss Tina revealed it was her assistant who clarified this was a compliment: "She was like, 'No, Miss Tina, that's a good thing.'"

It most certainly is.

Golden Eye

Speaking to *The Face* in 2003, at the tender age of 22, Beyoncé laid out her aspirations: "Eventually, years from now, I want to win an Oscar. A Tony. I already have Grammys…"

Grammys aside, she had recently started out on the road to Oscars and Tonys, acting first in the 2001 musical-drama *Carmen: A Hip Hopera* and then, in 2002, with Mike Myers in the Austin Powers seventies sequel, *Goldmember*. She played FBI agent Foxxy Cleopatra, complete with Afro and low-slung pants. Dressed in homage to Blaxploitation heroine Pam Grier in the 1973 classic *Coffy*, Beyoncé was helped, once again, by her mother Tina, a fan of the genre. "Every day I was transformed into this seventies queen," she said afterwards. "I looked like my mom, every picture I have seen of her."

In a feature detailing the star's involvement in the film from 2022, writer Matthew Jacobs hails it as "Beyoncé's transition from girl-group captain to singular superstar. It's when Beyoncé Knowles became simply Beyoncé." If it might sound odd to say that Beyoncé transitioned to her career as a mononymic star thanks to a noughties comedy featuring lots of retro references and a co-star with joke shop teeth, it definitely helped people see her as Beyoncé rather than Beyoncé from Destiny's Child. The look was crucial because it was unrecognizable from her Destiny's Child persona and showed a new side – as well as the possibility of the many other new sides we went on to enjoy. It also showcased an early example of the star's commitment to her curvy physique. While she has been open about dieting and training for the

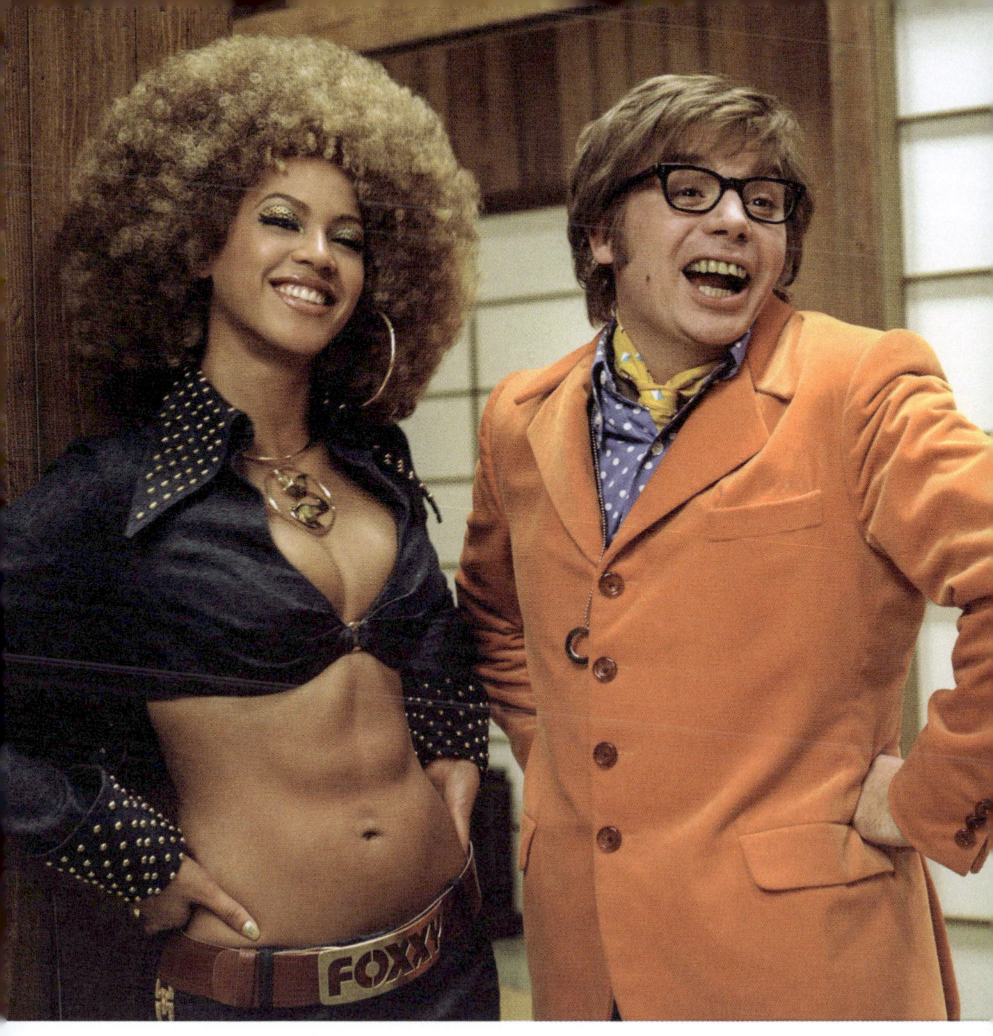

Foxxy lady: Beyoncé as a modern Pam Grier with her
Goldmember co-star Mike Myers as Austin Powers.

role, make-up artist Kate Biscoe remembered Beyoncé called
out the designers of the film's poster when it was shown to
her: "'You made me too skinny. It's not me' [she said]. Then
she did this hourglass shape. And he said, 'Okay, we'll fix that.'"

Freakum dresses to Levi's jeans

Beyoncé's Style

So blue

On 'Levii's Jeans', one of the standout tracks on her 2024 surprise country album, *Cowboy Carter*, Beyonce introduces the idea of quadruple denim. It moved the now-established idea of double denim on, but it also had a bigger fashion ripple: single-handedly increasing the stock of Levi's by 20 per cent. Such is the power of a co-sign from Mrs Carter. The connection grew later that year – when Beyoncé collaborated with the brand, recreating the iconic 1985 laundrette advert in her own inimitable style.

This might be the only time Beyoncé has dedicated a song to jeans, but denim has long been an essential component of her style. The video to 'Crazy in Love', arguably the moment that properly introduced her as a solo star in 2003, made denim crucial: a 22-year-old Beyoncé strides on screen wearing a white vest, red stilettos and a pair of J Brand denim shorts. Strikingly simple, stylist Ty Hunter said to *Vogue* in 2023 that denim's everyday quality was essential: "Everything we did prior to that was so big and so glamorous, so we wanted to strip it down into something that the kids could emulate."

Denim has since been part of a stage wardrobe, whether during the On The Run tour in 2014, or her headline appearance at Coachella in 2018. Beyoncé also, like all of us, wears denim on days off, combined with T-shirts and a ponytail. The difference? Even in clothes worn by people around the world every day she exudes star quality.

Always a pioneer: Beyoncé tries out multiple denim on a dress way back in 2002.

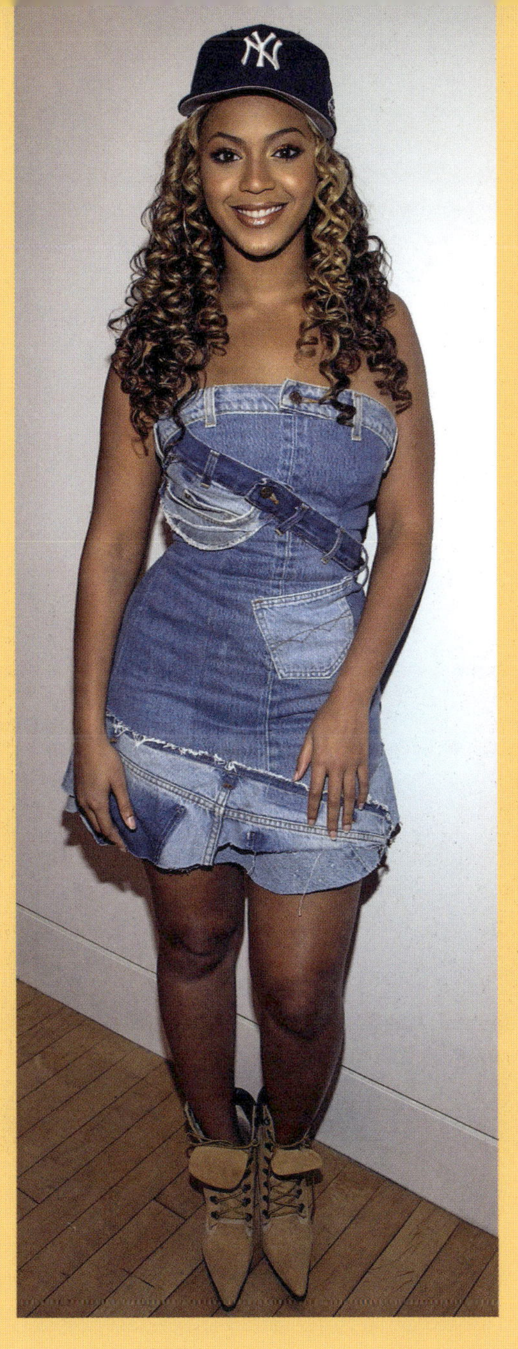

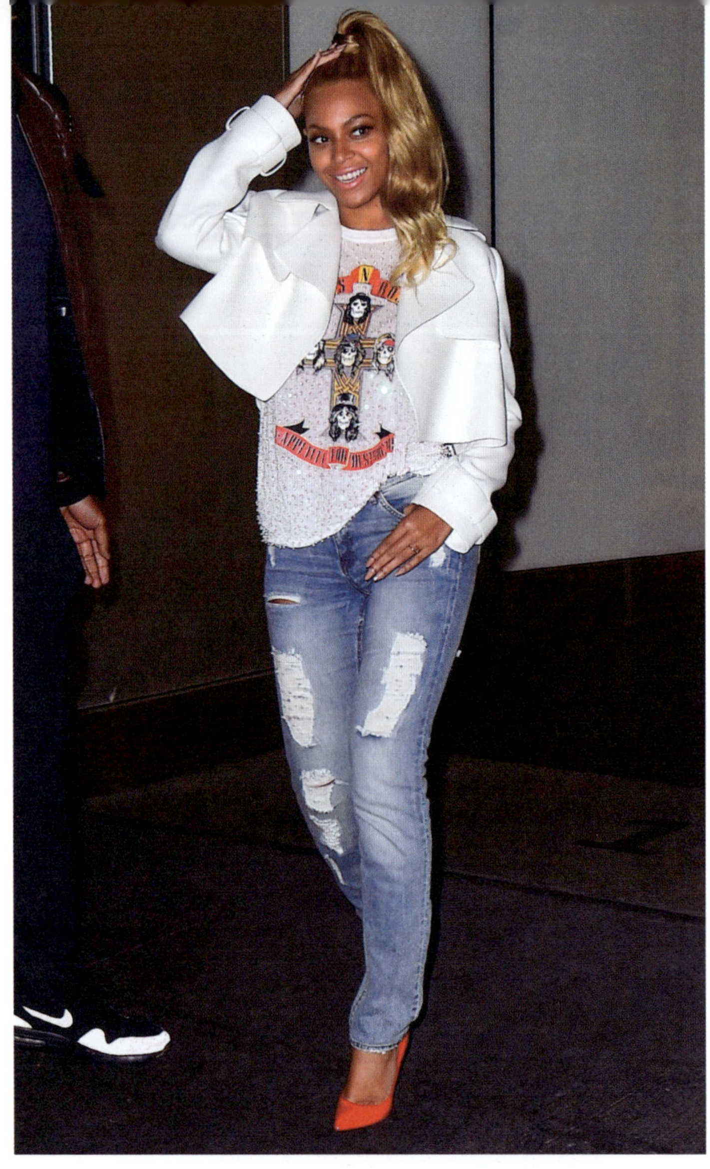

ABOVE Jeans and a T-shirt: she might be wearing ostensibly ordinary clothes but Beyoncé adds that X factor.

OPPOSITE Double denim with star power: Beyoncé takes the fabric to the stage for the On The Run tour in 2014.

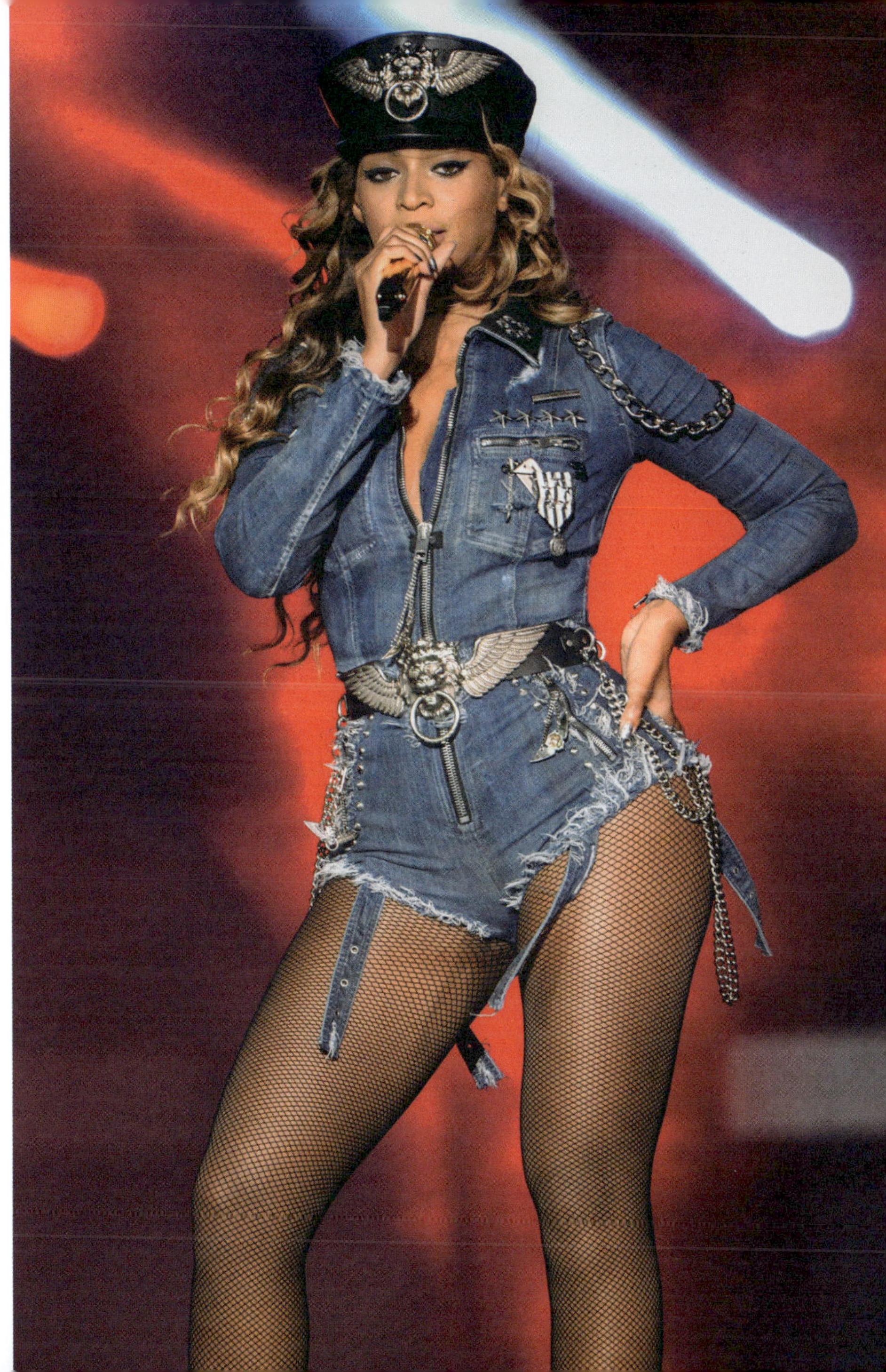

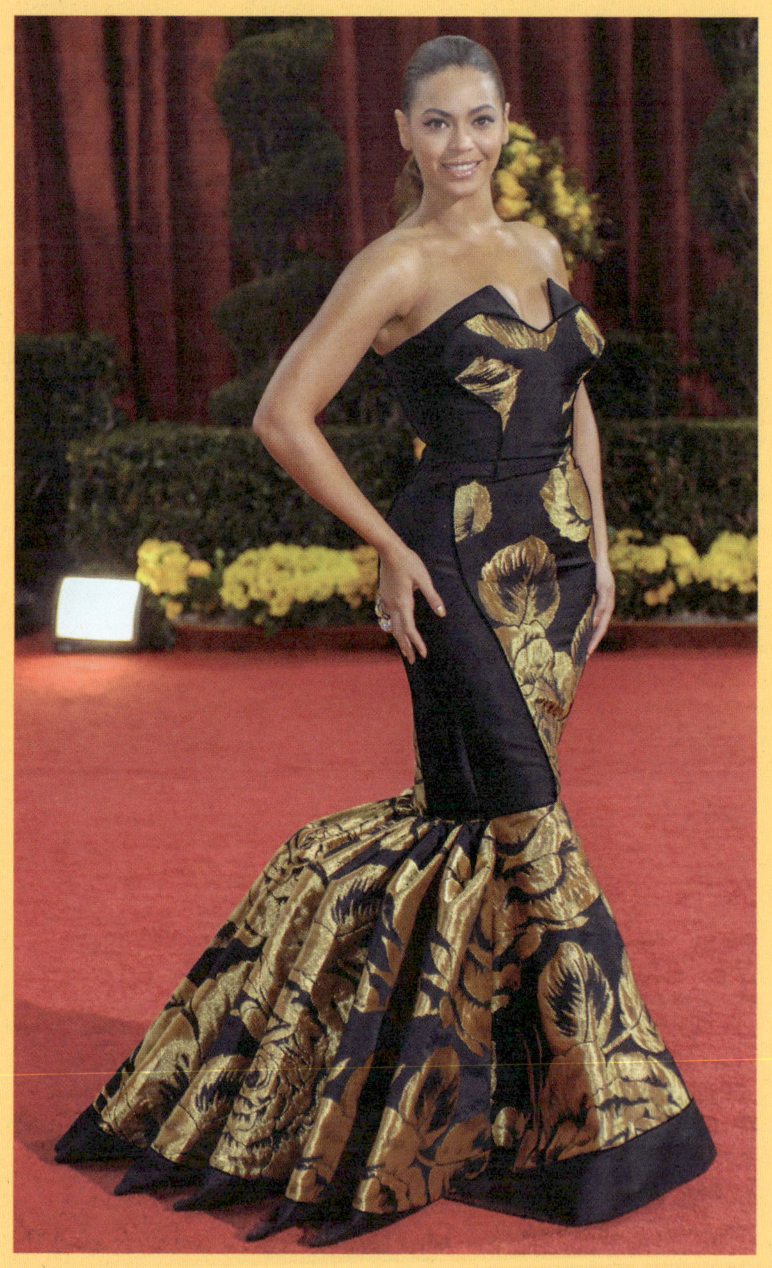

On the floor

For women, red-carpet dressing typically means full-length. While this environment was still new to her in the early noughties, Beyoncé tended to toe the line. But as the years went on, she evolved what that looked like.

Early looks fitted a specific format: a corset-style top with a longer skirt, sometimes bringing an underwear-as-outerwear edge. A change came in 2009, at the Oscars, when a different kind of elegance entered the frame. Wearing a black and gold strapless gown with a mermaid train designed by her mother, it was effortlessly paired with a low ponytail and simple eyeliner flicks. The combination of the ultra-glamorous gown and almost natural make-up ushered in a new era.

Portrait of a star: an Oscars look for 2009 cemented Beyoncé's interpretation of long lengths for the red carpet.

Over the years, Beyoncé's take on full-length red-carpet dressing has never been cookie cutter. Instead, there's always contrast or something surprising. That might be oversized sleeves at the Oscars in 2020, or a cut-out dress for a Tidal launch in 2017. Sometimes it's simply a showstopper, as with the gold Dolce & Gabbana dress chosen for the launch of the Atlantis hotel in Dubai in 2023.

One of several outfits worn to perform and attend the event, the gold design showed just how Beyoncé has disrupted the idea of full-length. Consisting of metal breast plates, a chainmail panel and a gold opera coat, slits at the side went up to the star's hips – an idea that would no doubt shock Old Hollywood traditionalists. But combined with simple curled hair and low-key make-up, there was something of the modern Venus about it. It was certainly very far away from those first looks from the noughties.

OPPOSITE Always put-together, never predictable: the cut-outs on Beyoncé's dress add a sexy spin on full-length. The ponytail is a playful touch.

OVERLEAF Pure gold: Beyoncé leans into her goddess side with gold waves on hair and dress, for a hotel launch in 2023.

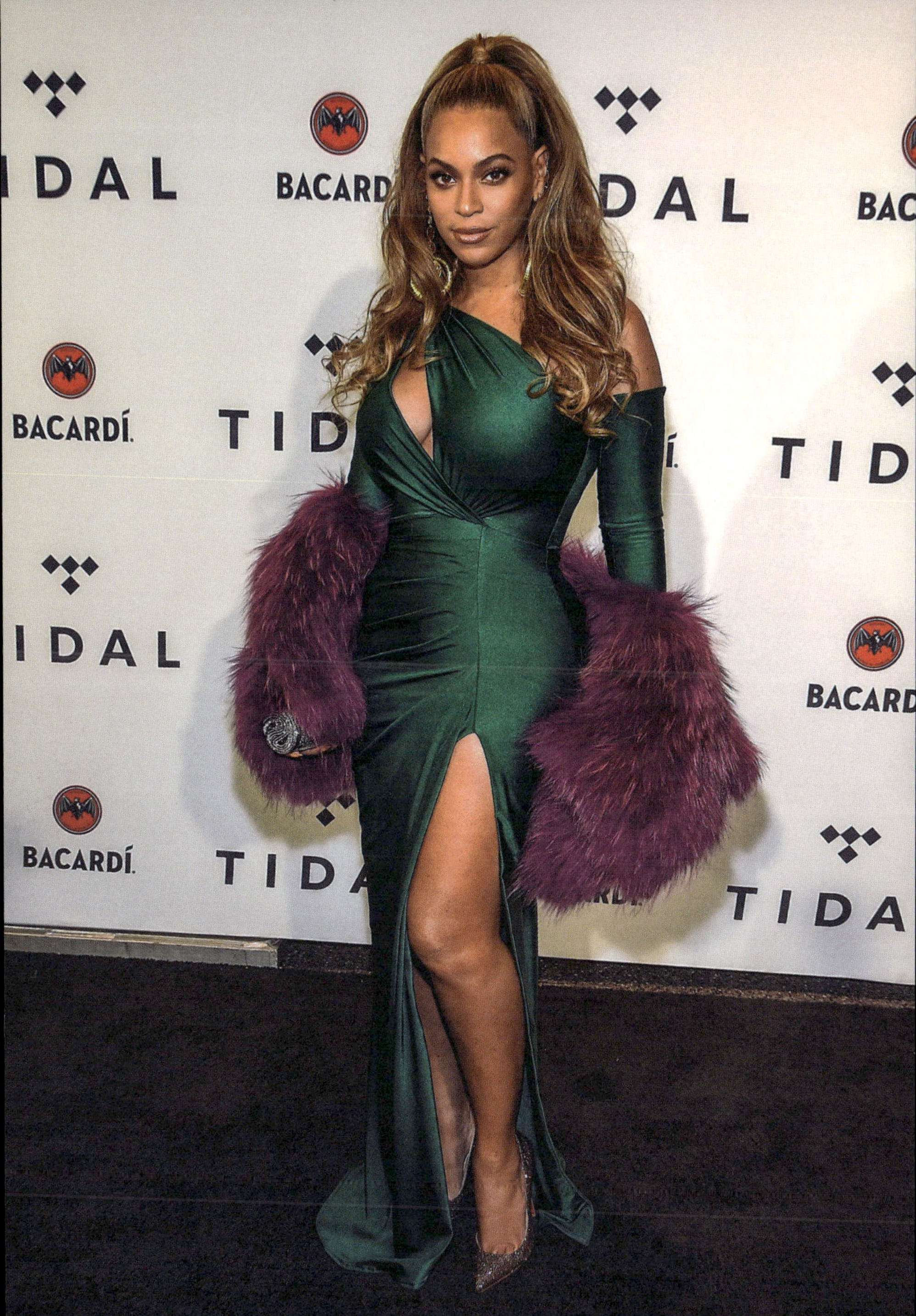

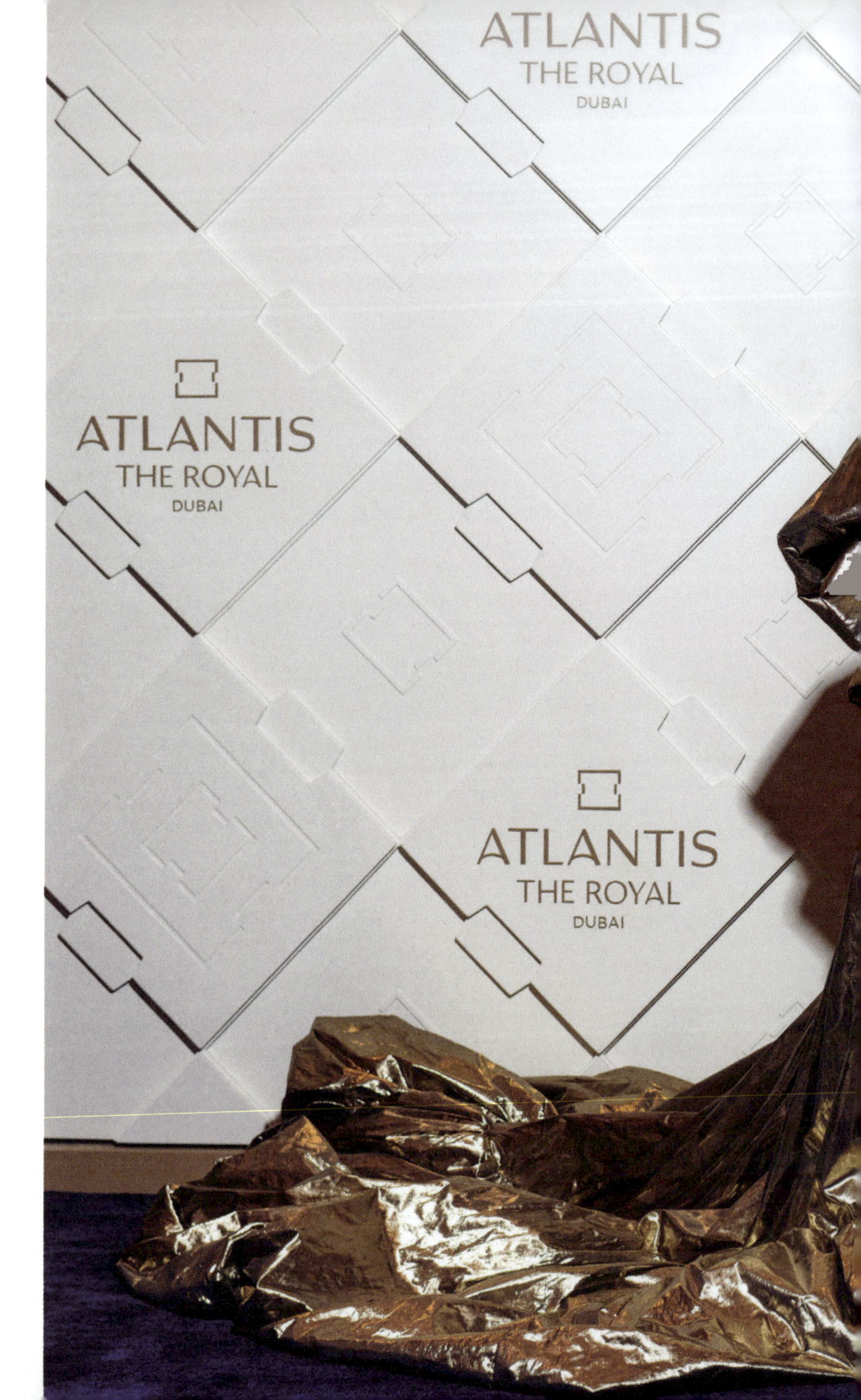
ATLANTIS
THE ROYAL
DUBAI

ATLANTIS
THE ROYAL
DUBAI

ATLANTIS
THE ROYAL
DUBAI

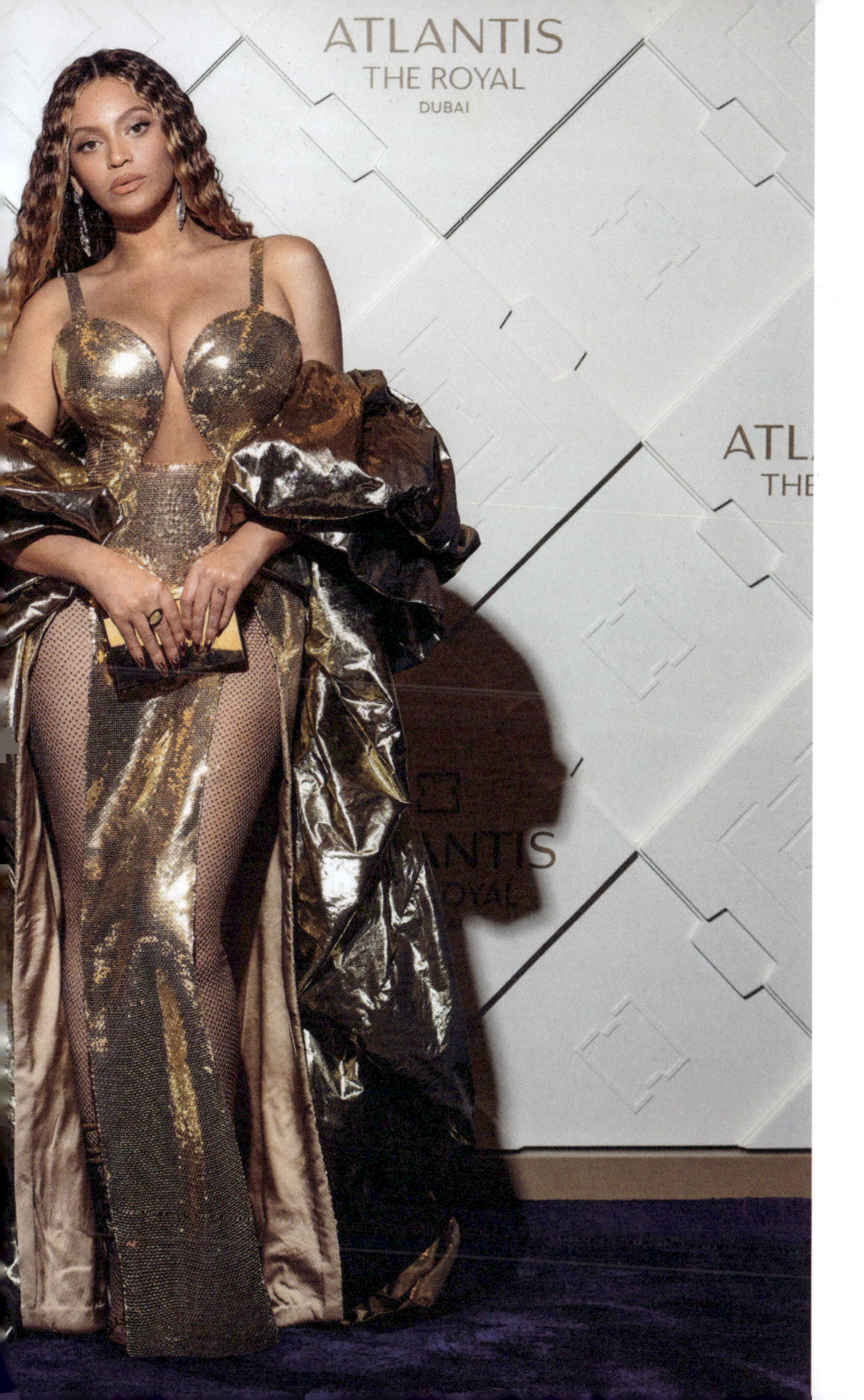
ATLANTIS
THE ROYAL
DUBAI
ATL
THE
ANTIS
ROYAL

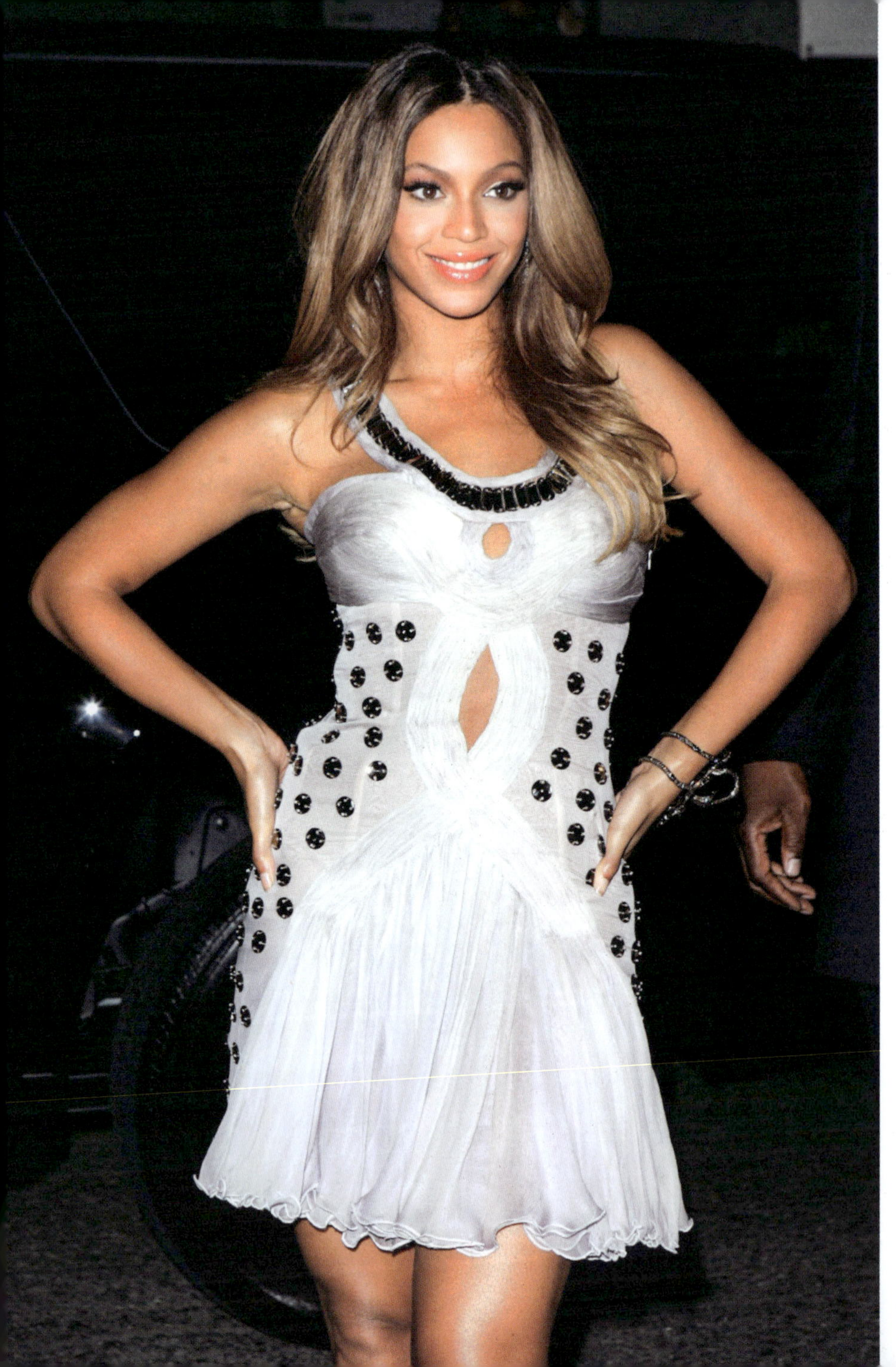

In black and white

When it comes to colour combinations, the virtues of black and white were pointed out long ago by none other than the legendary designer Coco Chanel: "I have said that black has it all. White too," she declared. "Their beauty is absolute. It is their perfect harmony."

Beyoncé, for one, was paying attention to her fashion history. If the star has never been pinned down by a colour scheme across her career, the use of black and white is consistent and works well for her, partly because it provides a kind of graphic impact that is hard to beat. As a seasoned pro, that factor is going to appeal.

Happy birthday: Beyoncé keeps it classy in black and white for her celebrations – and album launch – in 2006.

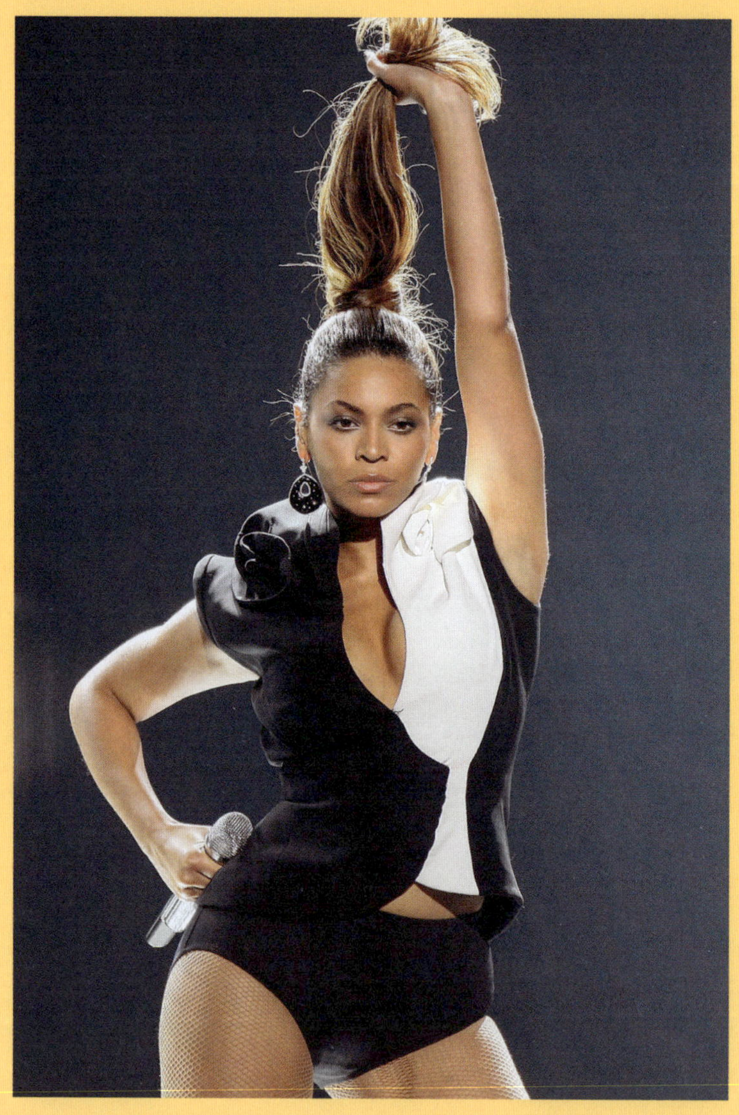

ABOVE Making an impact: black and white worn on stage
for the American Music Awards in 2008.

OPPOSITE Chic and star-worthy: Beyoncé waves to fans while
wearing a black and white hood and sunglasses in 2024.

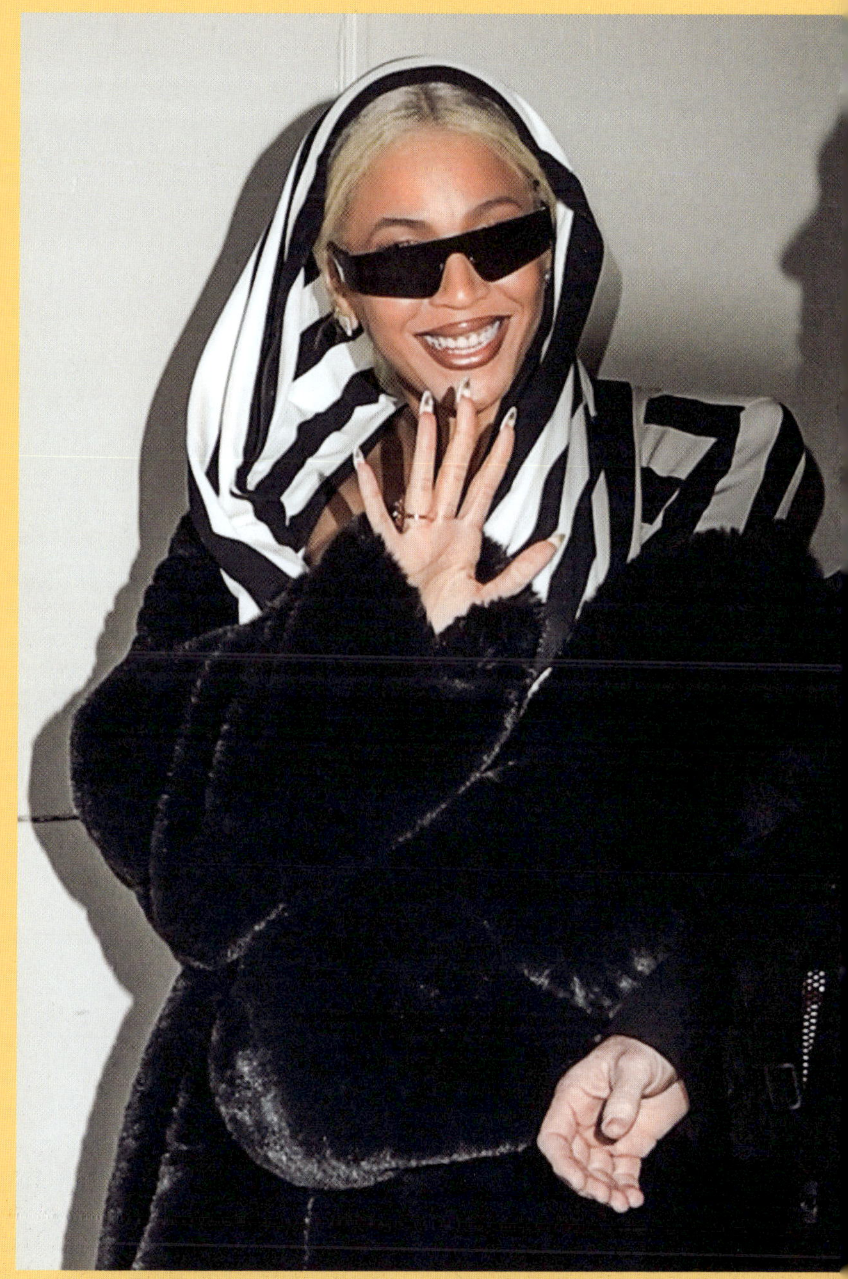

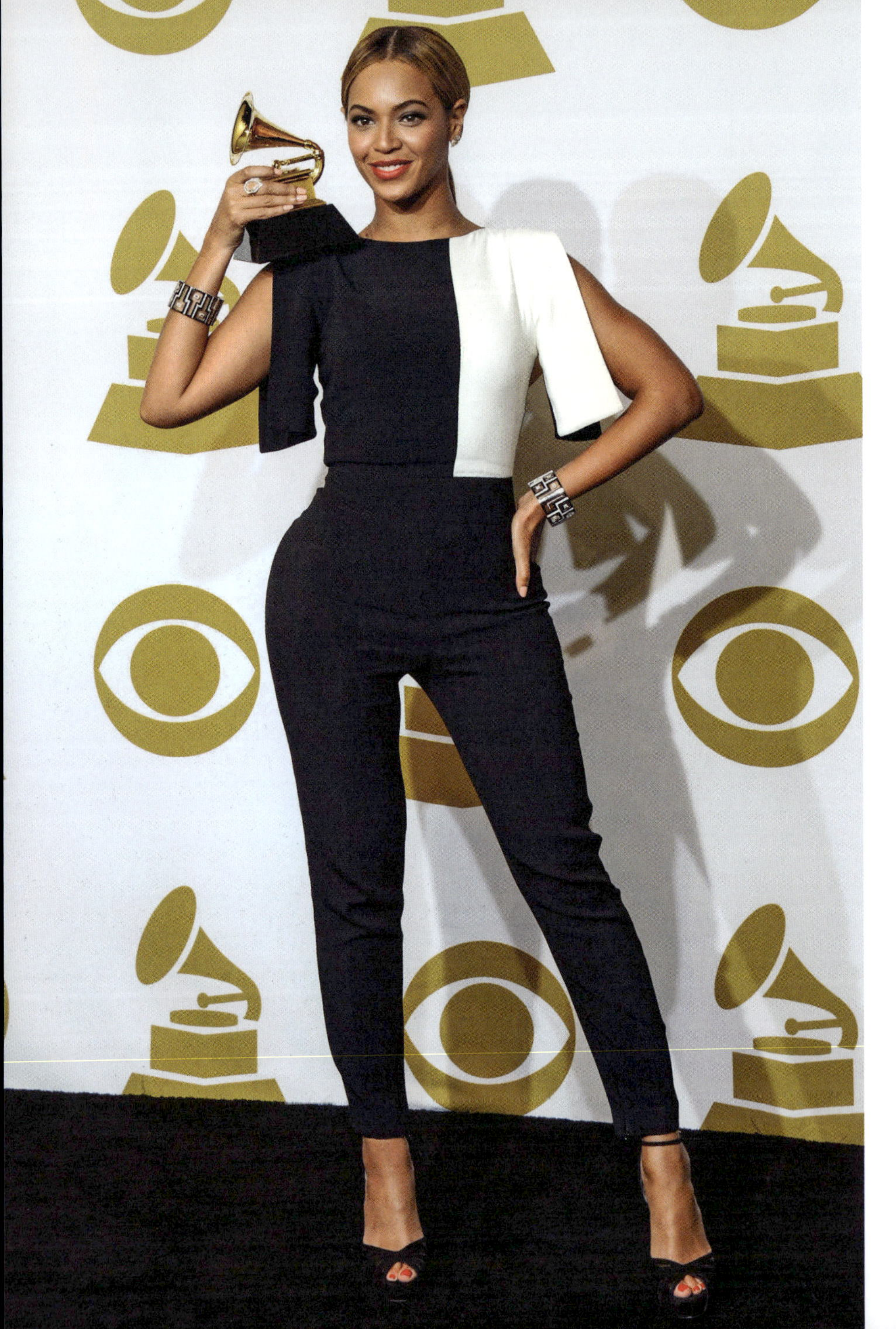

Her black and white outfits began in earnest post-Destiny's
Child, possibly as a sartorial palette cleanser from group
dressing, which tended toward colour and glitz. Notably,
Beyoncé wore a white dress with black detailing to celebrate
the release of her second album, *B'Day*. It was appropriately
released on her 25th birthday in 2006, the first since the
Destiny's Child split in February of that year. To celebrate,
she looked Chanel-approved: sophisticated and youthful
all at once.

The colour combination has returned over the years and
provides a lesson in how it can work as an easy win. Beyoncé
has worn black and white for stage appearances (at the
American Music Awards in 2008) and on the red carpet. She
wore a black jumpsuit with white panelling to accept yet
another Grammy – Best Traditional R&B Vocal Performance
for fan favourite 'Love on Top' – in 2013. Combined with red
lipstick and a simple low ponytail, it brought out the best
in this classic colour combo. The looks keep coming too –
Beyoncé now wears black and white on and off-duty, showing
the two shades together still have Chanel's absolute beauty
but they are also absolutely versatile.

Black, white and gold: the best way to celebrate a Grammy
win in 2013? Wear a striking monochrome jumpsuit.

Feeling herself

From the release of 'Naughty Girl' in 2003, it was clear that Beyoncé was not shy when it came to talking about sex. This has continued across her eight solo albums. See songs that might qualify as NSFW including 'Rocket', 'Blow', 'Partition' and 'Drunk in Love' – right through to the potentially blush-making 'Bodyguard' on *Cowboy Carter*.

This sex-positive attitude comes through in what she wears too, particularly as she moved from teenage years in Destiny's Child to become, as they say, "grown and sexy". She even dedicated a song – 2006's 'Freakum Dress' – to dresses that wow. The term is now one understood through her fanbase and beyond.

An early take on the naked dress trend: on stage with Destiny's Child in 2005.

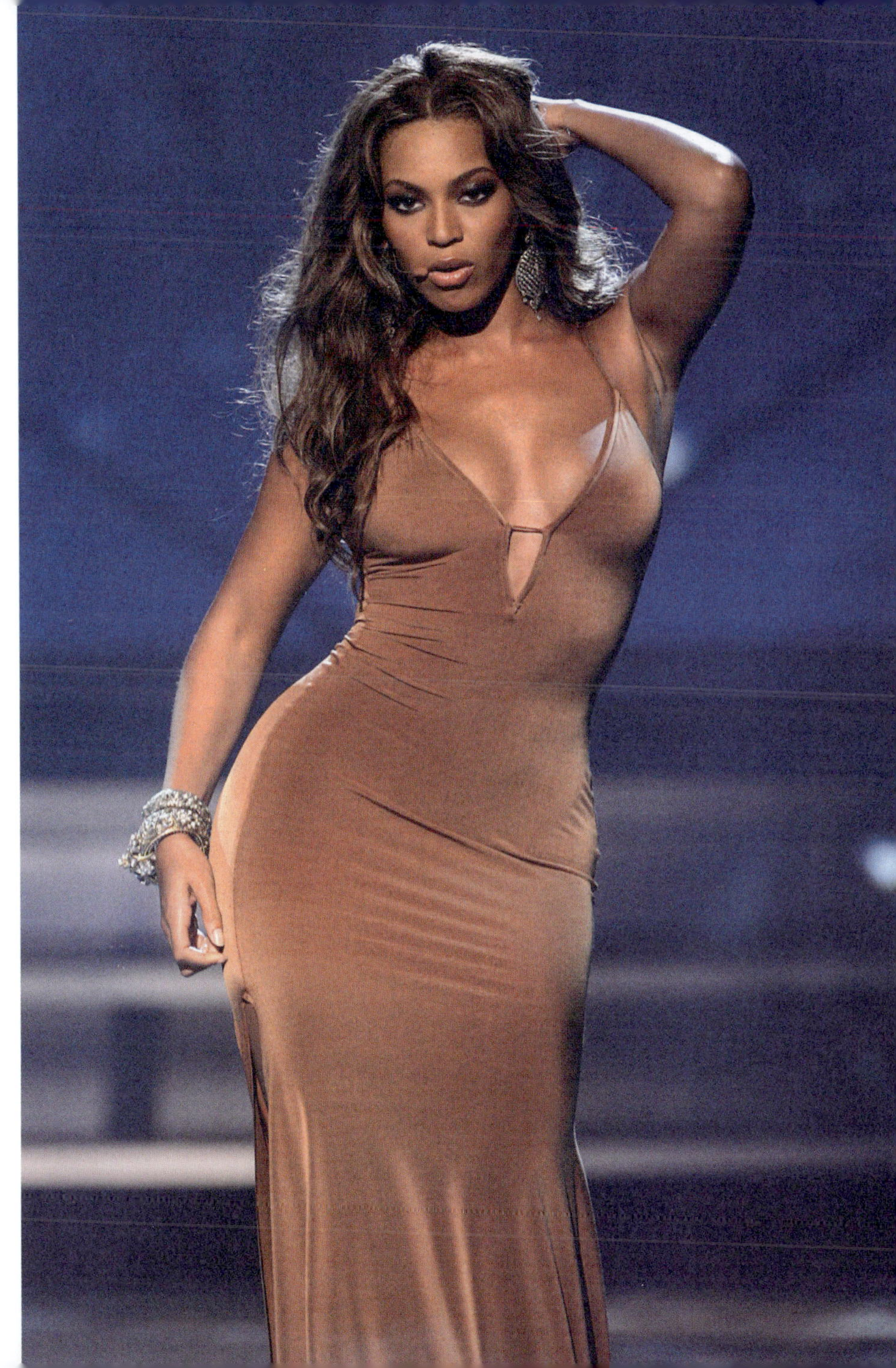

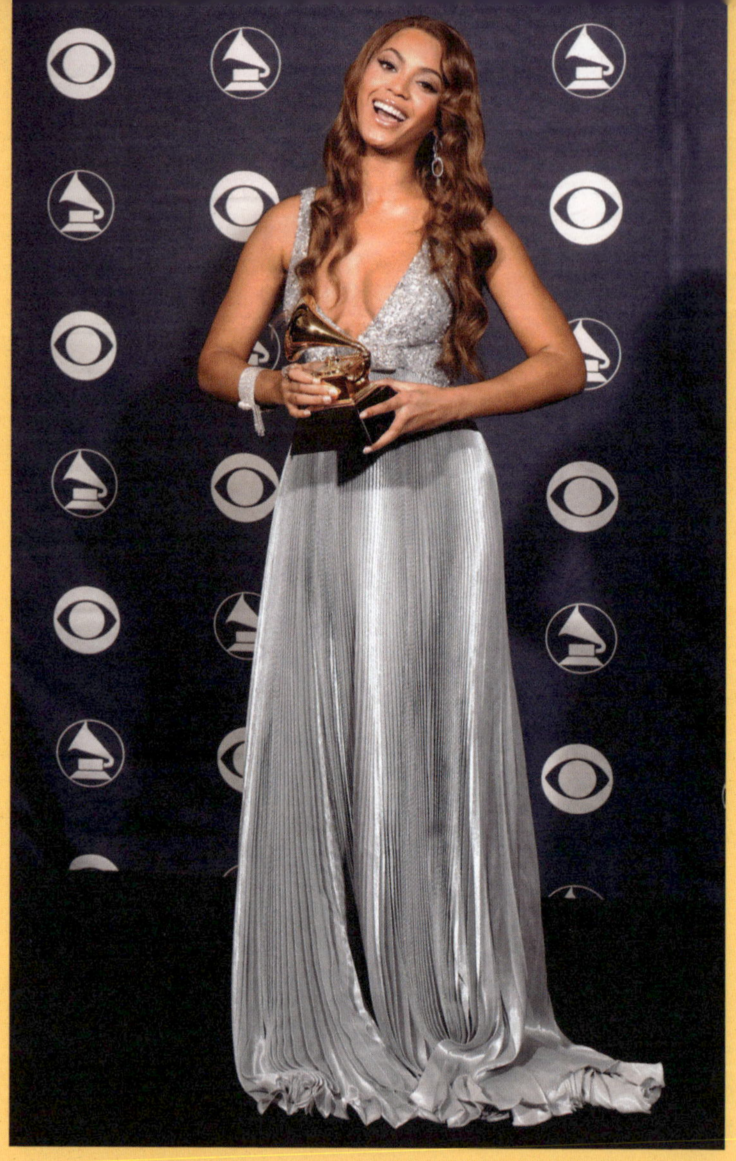

ABOVE Seduction in silver: Beyoncé brings underwear-as-outerwear to the Grammys red carpet in 2007.

OPPOSITE Miaow: leopard boots, bodysuit and matching mask bring on-stage impact in 2018.

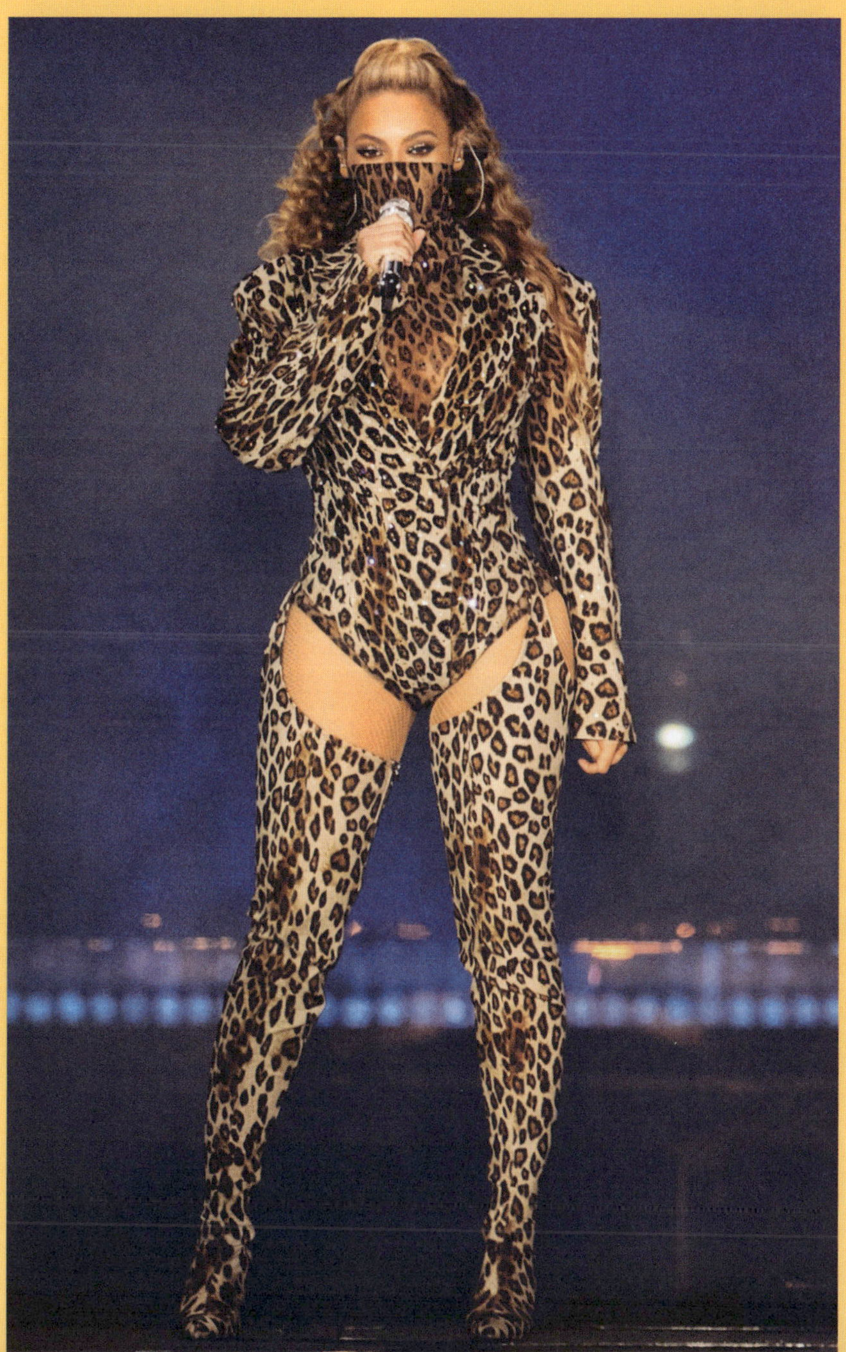

There's a staggering range of looks that Beyoncé uses to
express this part of herself. Performing at the BET Awards
in 2005, all of Destiny's Child wore matching bodycon
skin-coloured gowns, pre-dating the modern concept of
naked dressing by almost 20 years. Other dresses have the
feel of lingerie, even when rendered in party-ready silver.
More recently, she has reinvented the idea of underwear-
as-outerwear with her unique take – suspenders worn with
boots and a bodysuit, for example. In an interview with *Vogue*
in 2018, she articulated her thinking: "I think it's important
for women and men to see and appreciate the beauty in their
natural bodies," she said.

Even with the variation, Beyoncé's take on seductive style
always leads back to one fabric: lace. The association with
women's underwear since the eighteenth century and its
reveal-yet-conceal nature means the fabric has long been
tied to sex appeal. Beyoncé draws this out in new ways. See
a now-classic Grammys outfit from 2014, utilizing white lace
to dramatic effect. While, at first glance, it looks like Beyoncé
is naked underneath, designer Michael Costello told the *Los
Angeles Times* she was anything but: "I added this nude mesh
overlay to the fabric to give it the illusion of skin," he said.

Sexy but classy is the Beyoncé rule of seductive dressing.

Lace, in place: a playful and distinctly classy idea
of sexy dressing at the Grammys in 2014.

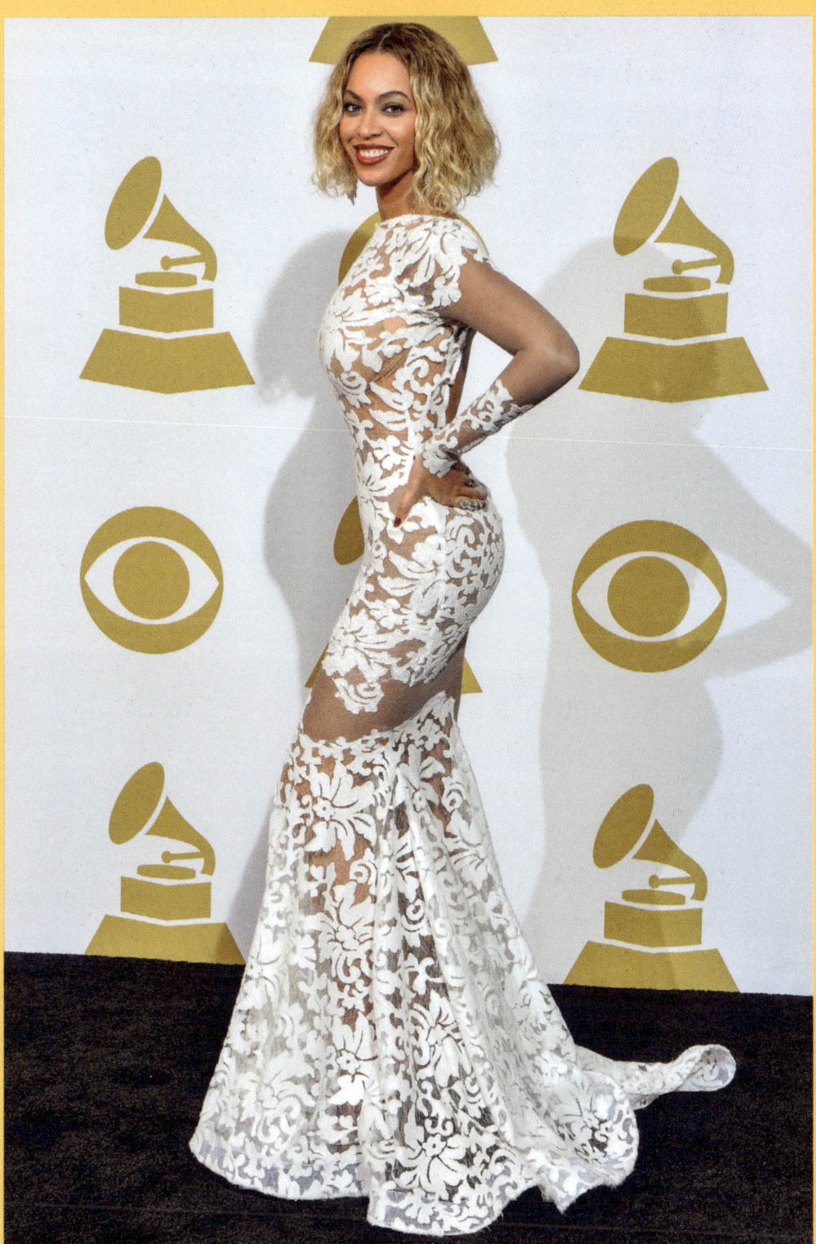

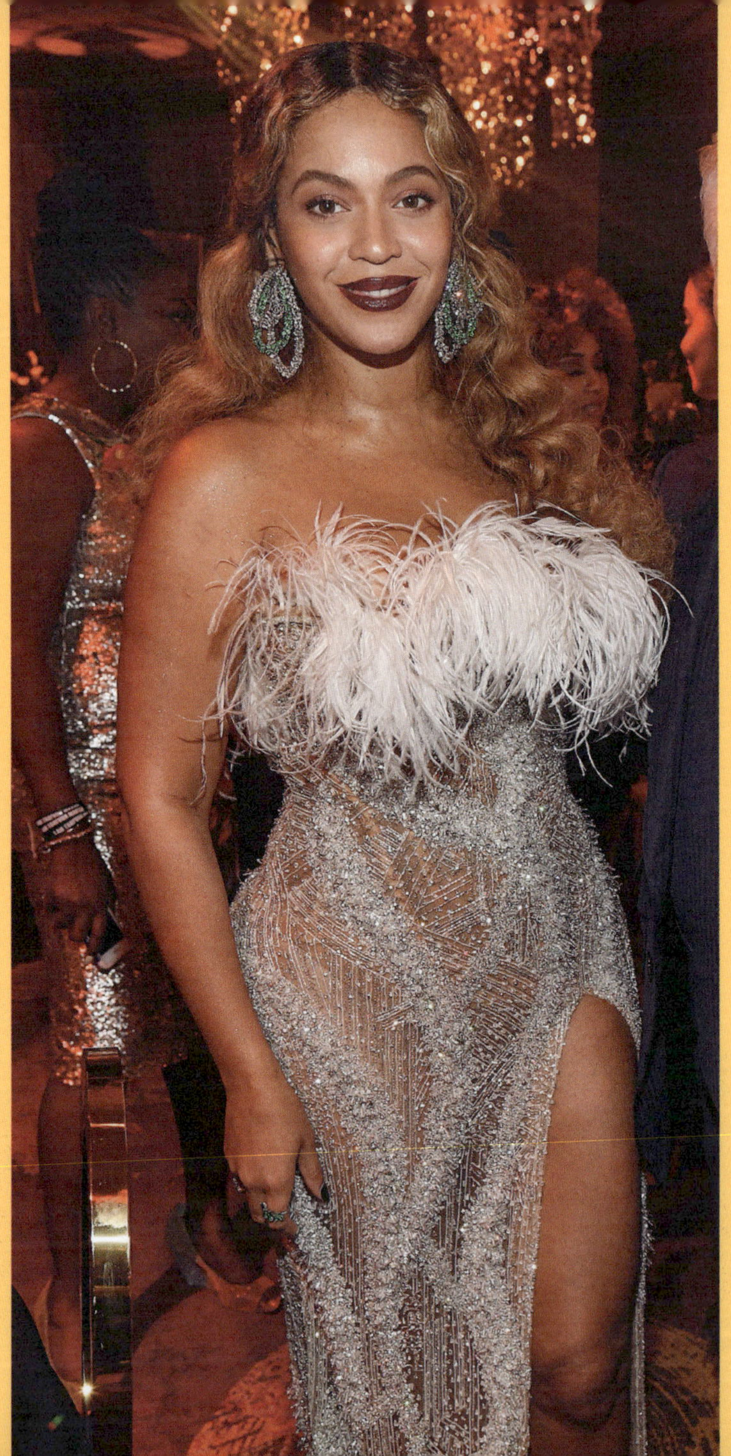

"I think it's important for women and men to see and appreciate the beauty in their natural bodies."

BEYONCÉ

Feathers and sequins: a time-honoured classic combination for after-dark dressing, Beyoncé takes the look for a spin in 2019.

Sports day

If lots of school-age children spend their time on sports fields throwing, kicking or hitting a ball, Beyoncé was far too busy preparing for megastardom. Girls Tyme, the original precursor to Destiny's Child, began when she was eight.

But, if she did not have a sporty childhood, the star has consistently returned to sport as a style trope, playing with the uniforms of American football and basketball, as well as (like many of us) wearing the hoodies and sweats of resting athletes, on or off-duty. That's not to mention her association with sporting events – whether watching basketball or performing at that highlight of the American football calendar, the NFL Super Bowl.

An early – and charming – way to do sportswear: Beyoncé repurposes an American football jersey to a Bardot-style top.

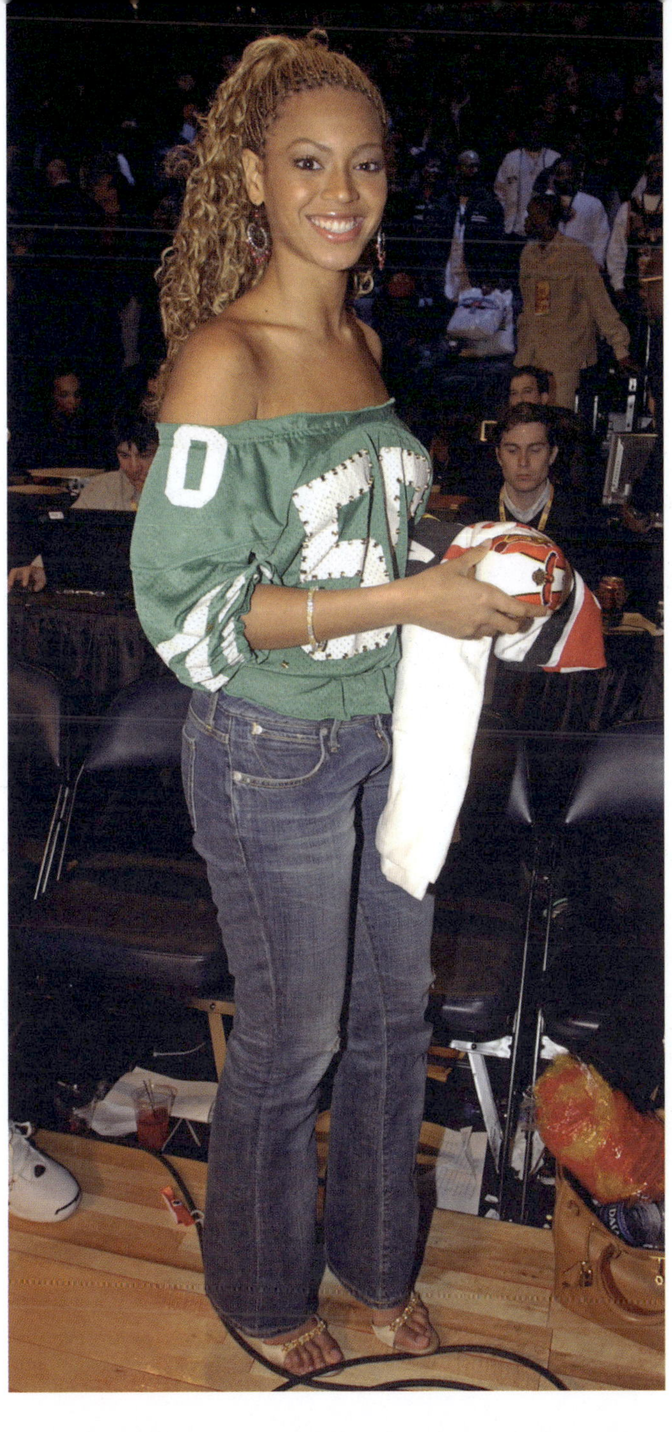

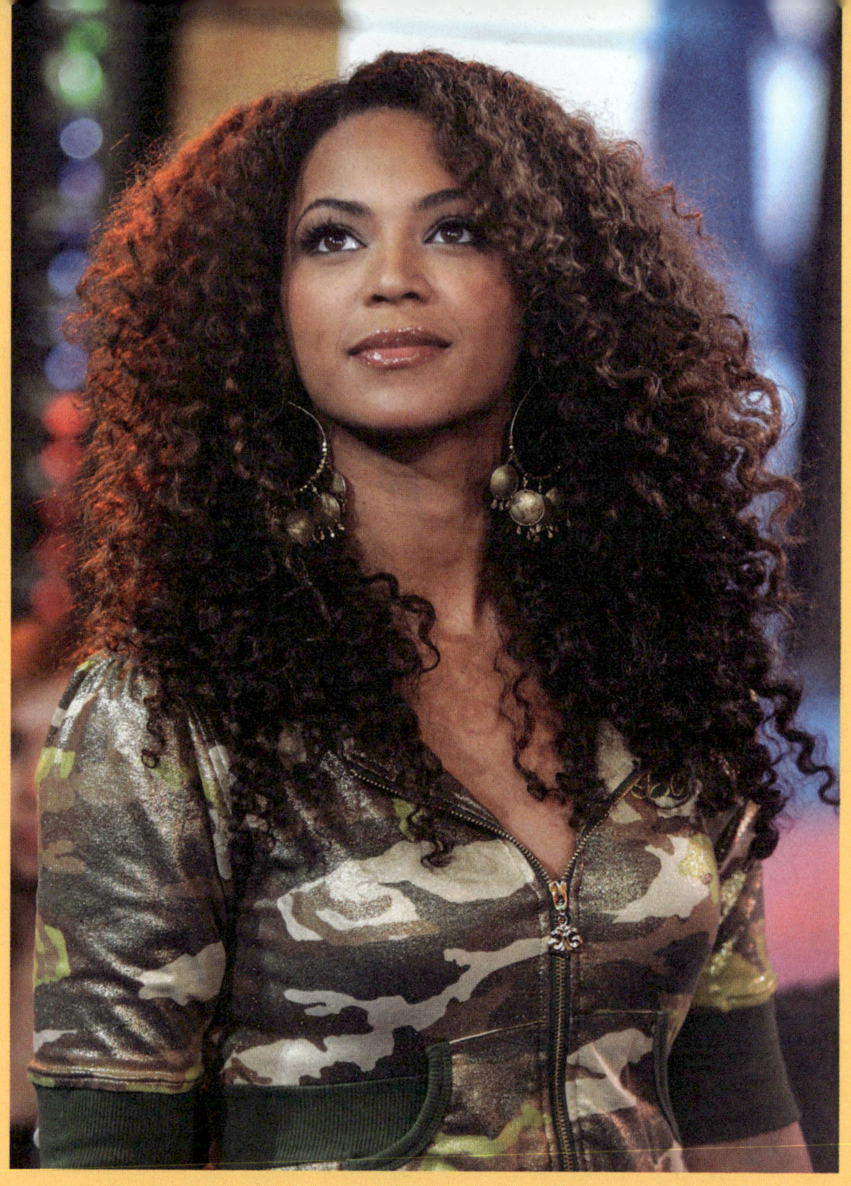

ABOVE Keeping cosy: even superstar Beyoncé is not averse to the charms of a hoodie. Here's an early look at the item, on MTV TRL in 2007.

OPPOSITE Sportswear, but not as you know it: Tom Ford's sequinned football jersey was just the thing for a stage performance in 2014.

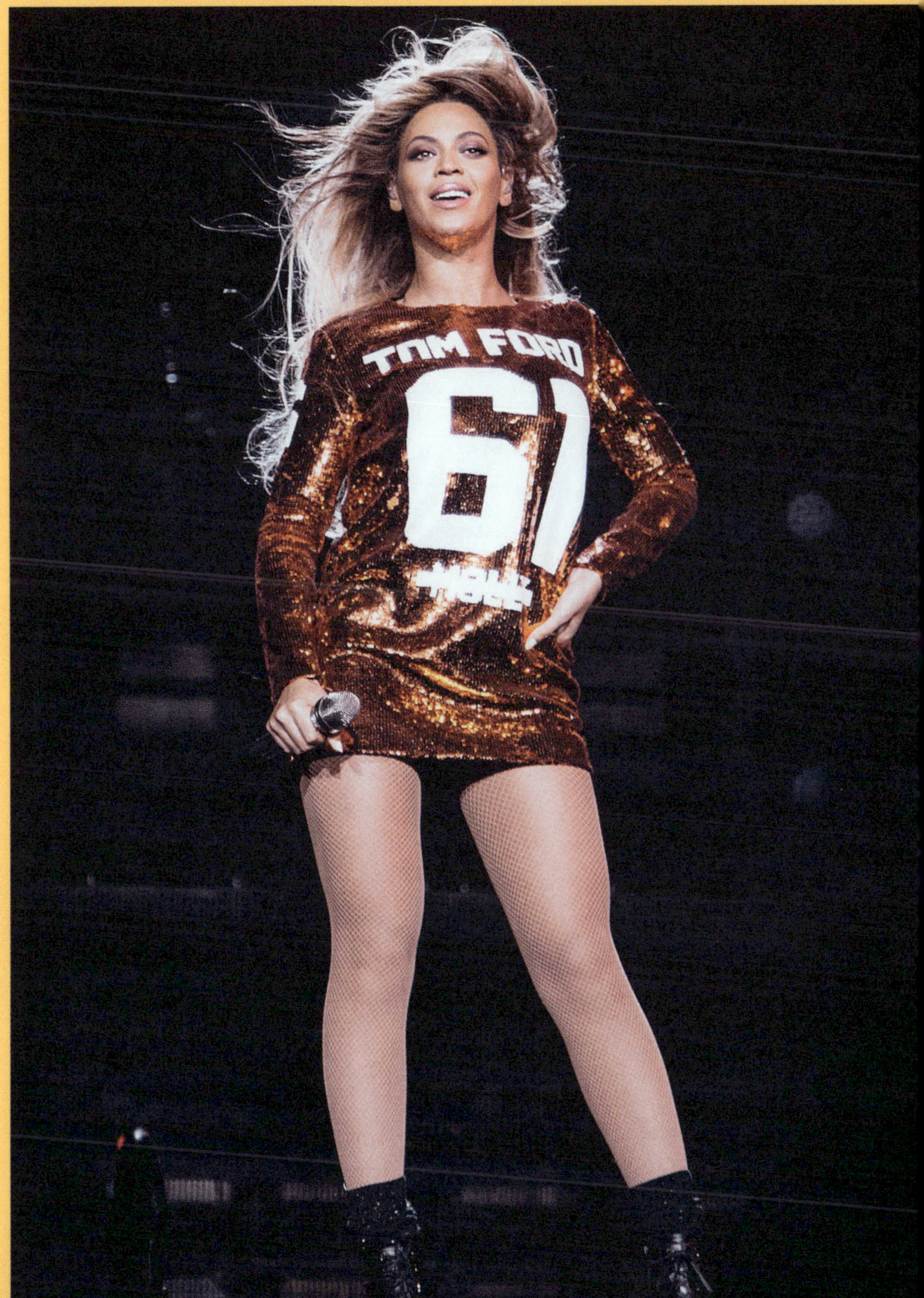

TOM FORD
61
HELL

Beyoncé's best sporting looks come, naturally, from the uniform of the MVP – whether that's a star quarterback or a shooting guard in basketball (Michael Jordan's position, FYI).

This ranges from a classic American football T-shirt redesigned in sequins by Tom Ford, worn on stage in 2014 or a bodysuit based on the jersey worn by Houston Rockets all-star James Harden in 2015.

It was the latter that was taken to heart by the sporting world. Two years later, rumours began that Beyoncé would be investing in the Rockets when the team was up for sale. While that did not transpire, basketball is clearly a favourite in the Carter household, across genders. After college team the South Carolina Gamecocks won their National Collegiate Athletic Association (NCAA) third title in eight years, coach Dawn Staley became the first Black woman to retain the title. Beyoncé sent her flowers.

She's a fan: Beyoncé shows her love for the Houston Rockets in her own inimitable way.

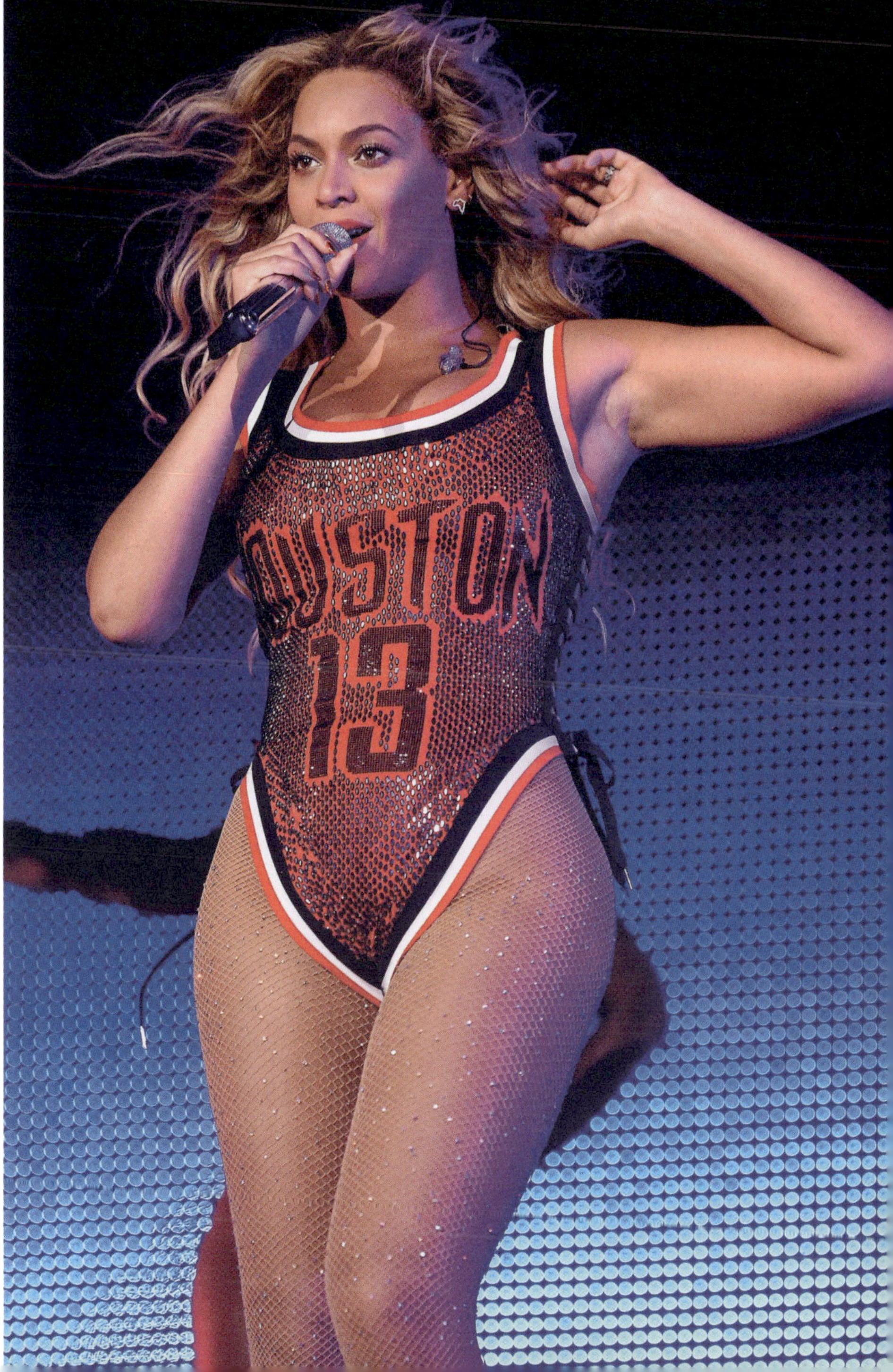

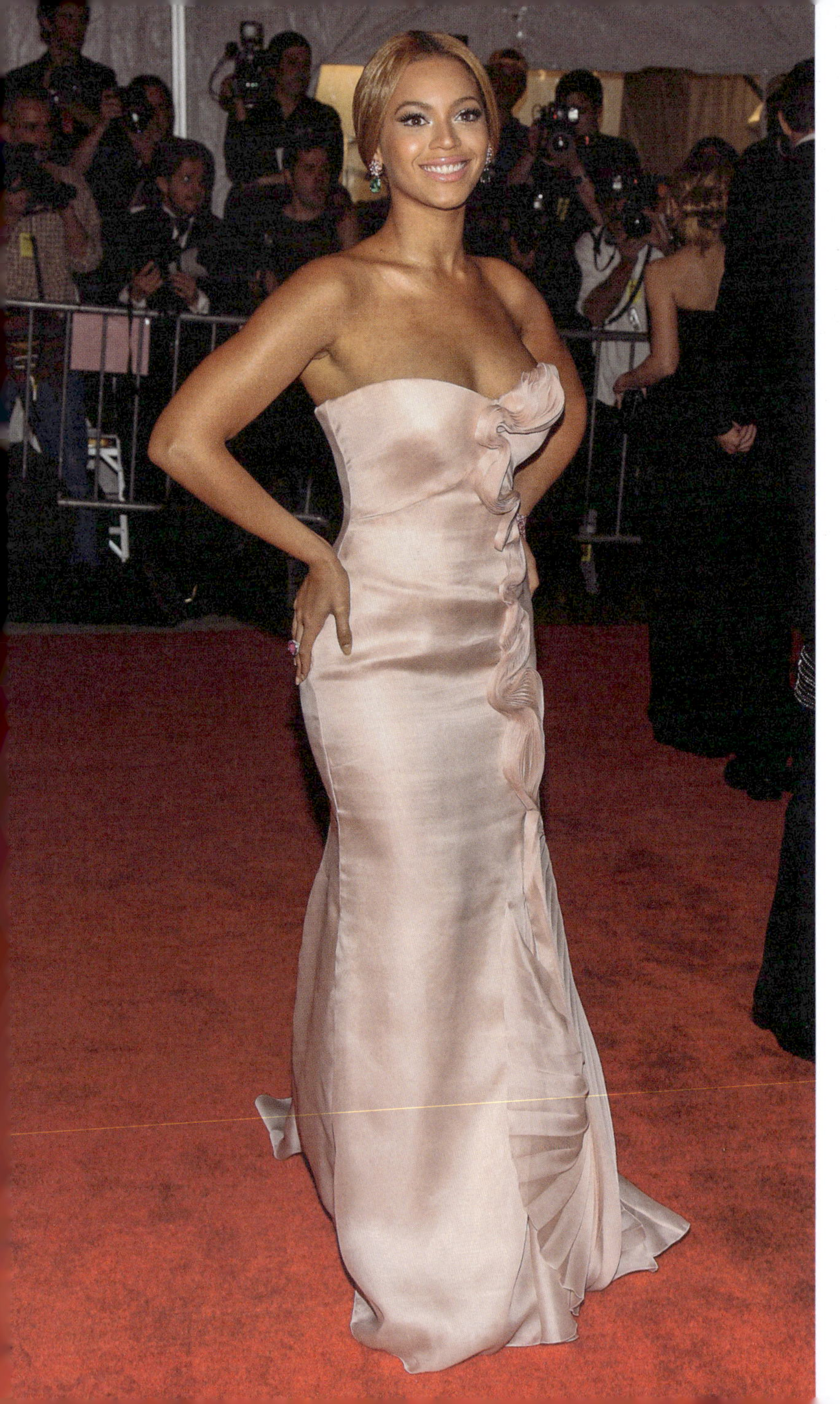

Meeting the Met

The Met Gala is often called "the Oscars of fashion". Taking place on the first Monday of May since 1948, it began as an event to raise funds for New York's Metropolitan Museum of Art. But, in the twenty-first century, it is now more known as the place for stars to showcase their most "fashion" looks, taking loose inspiration from themes ranging from secret gardens to the notion of camp.

Beyoncé has, to date, attended the Met Gala seven times. Her debut was in 2008, when she wore a relatively low-key Armani/Privé strapless blush dress. 2012 was when she began to ramp things up, wearing a creation made by Riccardo Tisci, then creative director at Givenchy. Ascending the now-familiar red stairs – the backdrop to other celebrity moments like Rihanna's meme-worthy "omelette" dress in 2015, or Kim Kardashian's controversial "Marilyn" dress in 2022 – the back of the dress was the showpiece. Entirely see-through lace surrounded by feathers, it – as *People* magazine wrote later – "gave new meaning to the term 'rear view.'"

Baby's first Met Gala: a blush pink gown and groomed up-do was the right combination for 2008.

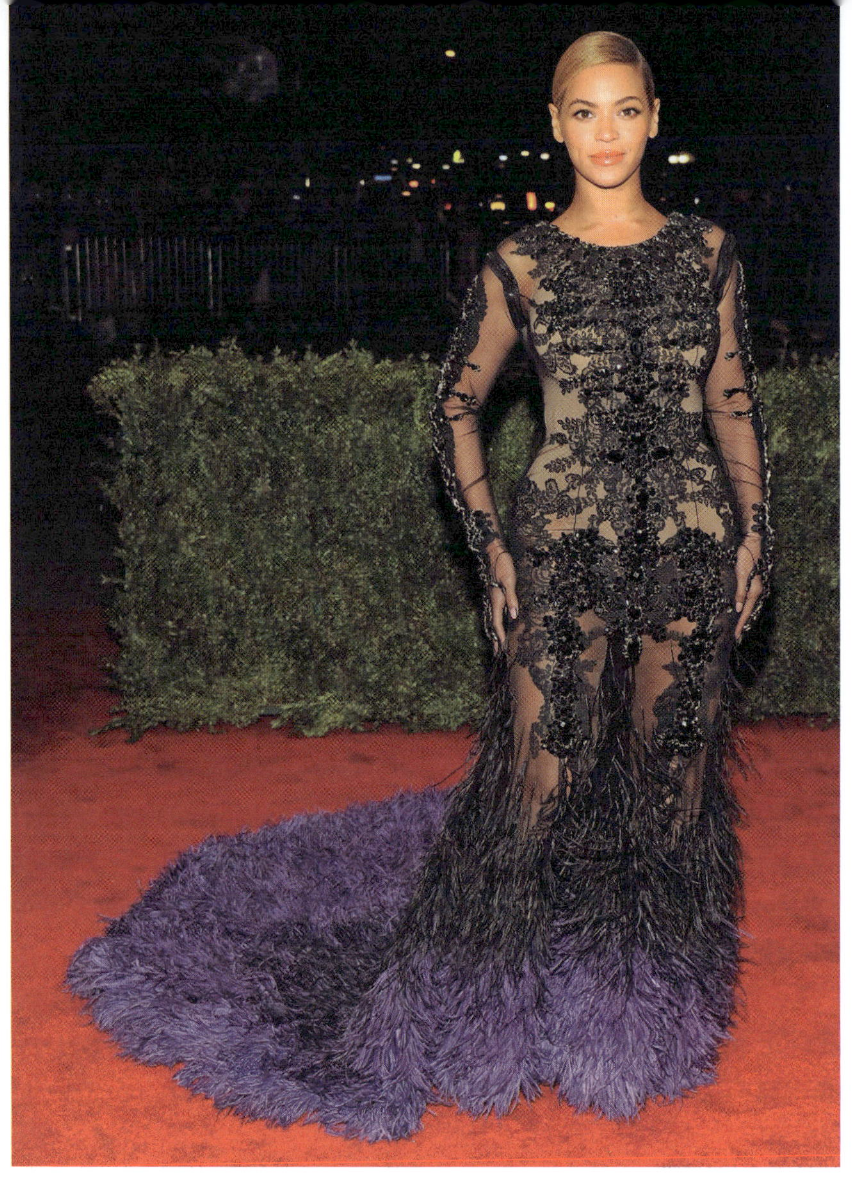

ABOVE Look both ways: a dress that worked from whatever angle. Beyoncé made jaws drop with this stunning Givenchy creation in 2012.

OPPOSITE Made for walking: matching your boots to train is an A-list move. See Beyoncé's outfit for the Met in 2013.

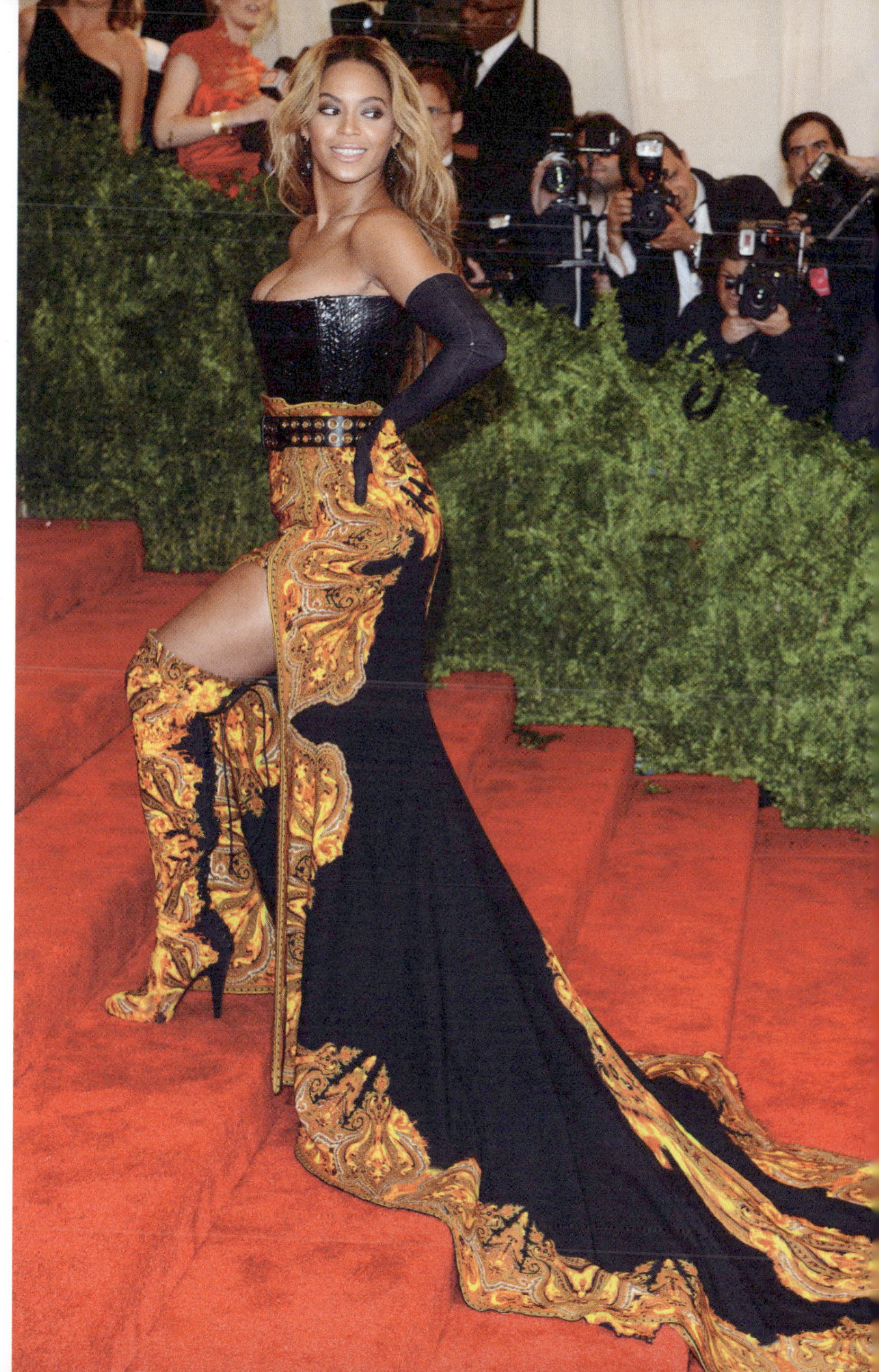

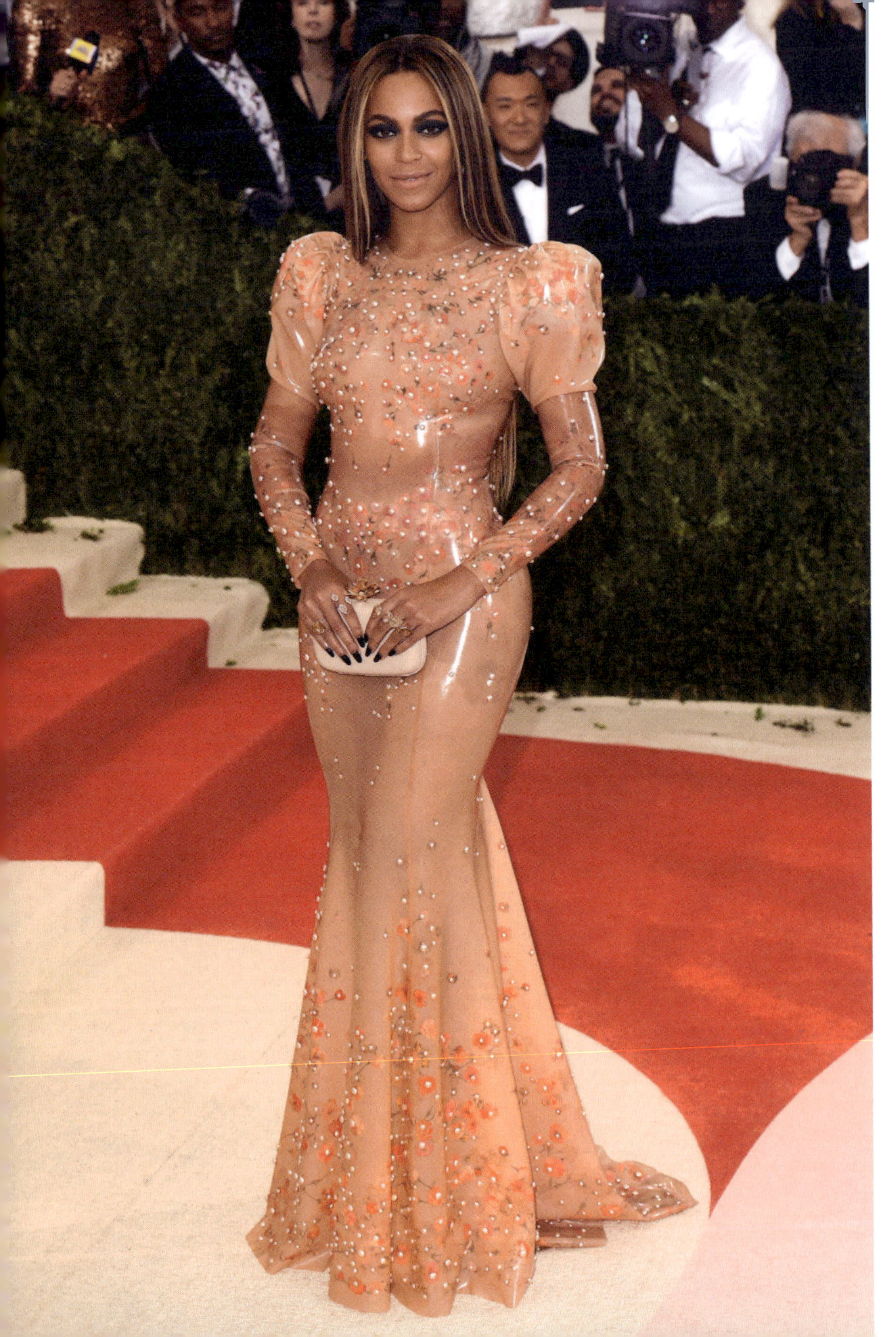

Since then, Beyoncé's appearances on the Met Gala red carpet have shared a purpose. Whatever the theme, she has used it as a showcase for her most experimental looks, be it an even-more-see-through lace dress in 2015 or her last appearance in 2016, wearing a full-length latex gown. Made by Tisci again, it was fitted by "the Baroness", a woman more usually serving the fetish community in New York. Speaking to *Vice* after the Met Gala, said Baroness noted the contrast was key: "The styling of her dress was very conservative. It was classic in its hourglass shape and everything. I'm hoping that people seeing [it] will see that latex isn't what you think it is."

There's no doubt Beyoncé's outfit will certainly help the cause.

A different kind of shine: Beyoncé experiments with latex for the 2016 Met Gala. Her last appearance to date, she went out in style.

It takes two

At the start of the 2002 track '03 Bonnie & Clyde', Jay Z famously asks Beyonce if she's ready. She was, of course. She was born ready.

This was the fans' introduction to one of the most powerful power couples of our time. The duo first met around the millennium and were friends before they started dating, eventually going public in 2004. Always private about their relationship, they married in 2008, in a private ceremony with only 40 guests in attendance at Jay-Z's New York penthouse; the rest of us didn't know about it until years later. Always secretive (even through the rumour mill around *Lemonade*'s relationship narrative in 2016), they still kept us hooked – partly through a masterclass in couple style.

OPPOSITE Casual, and cool: Beyoncé and Jay-Z do court-side chic, complete with matching chains, in 2012.

OVERLEAF An after-dark look: for a boxing match in 2015, Jay-Z and Beyoncé went for his and hers suiting.

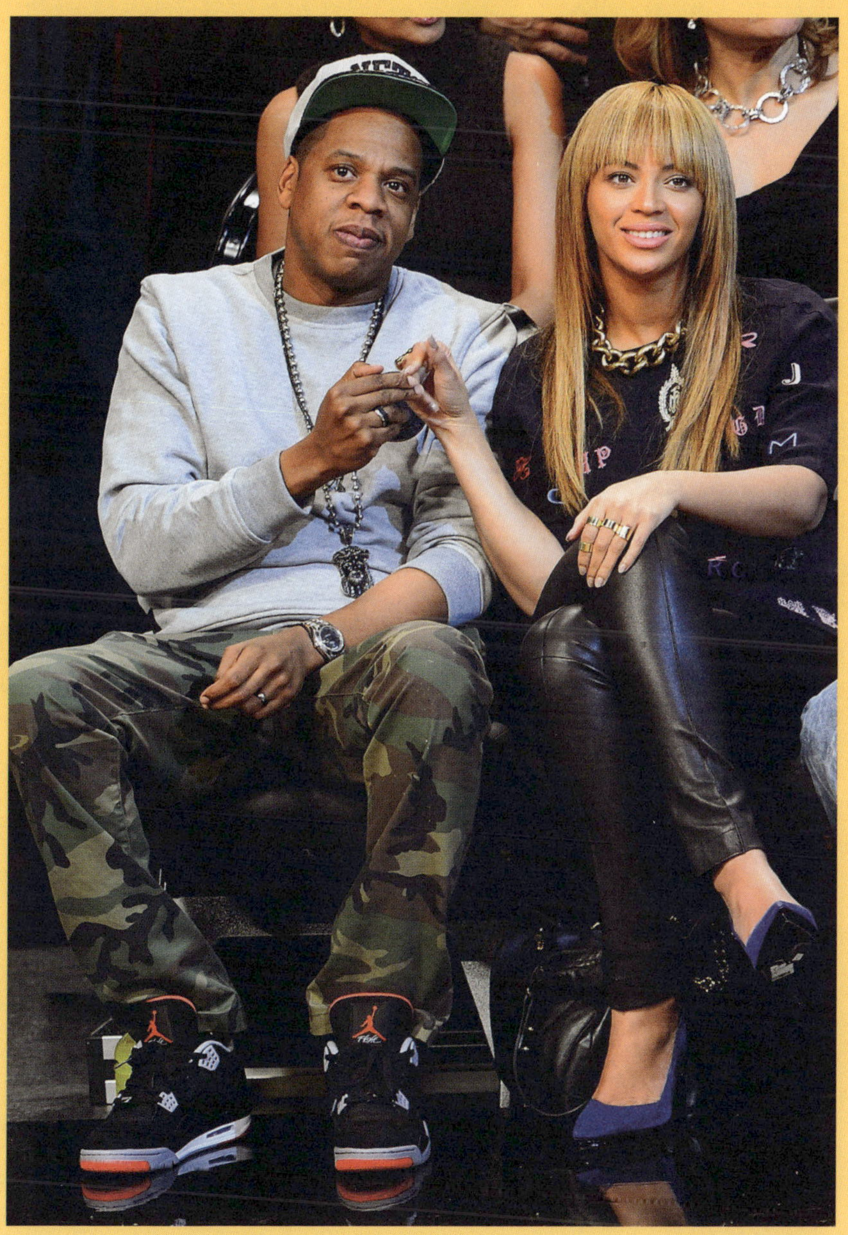

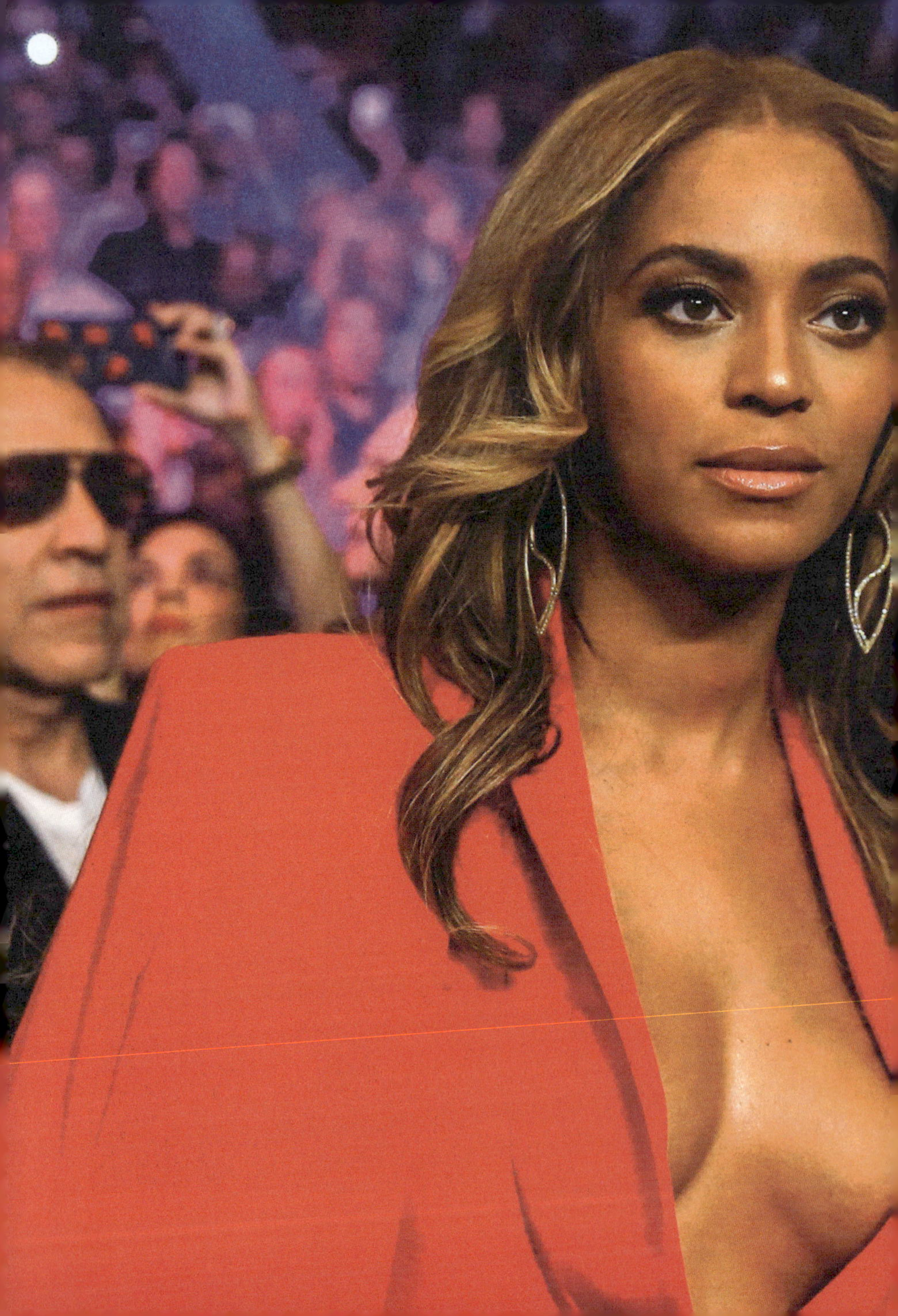

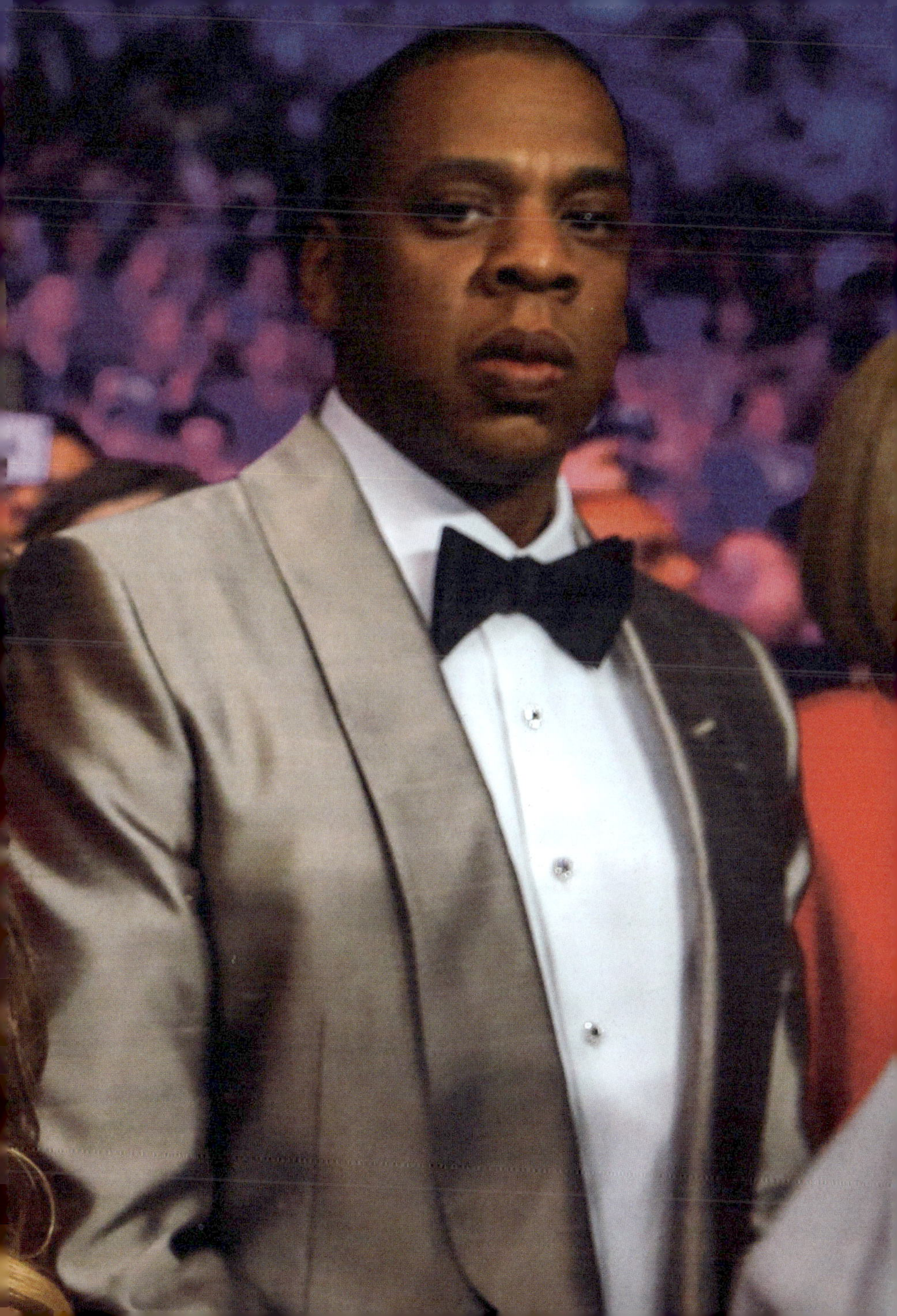

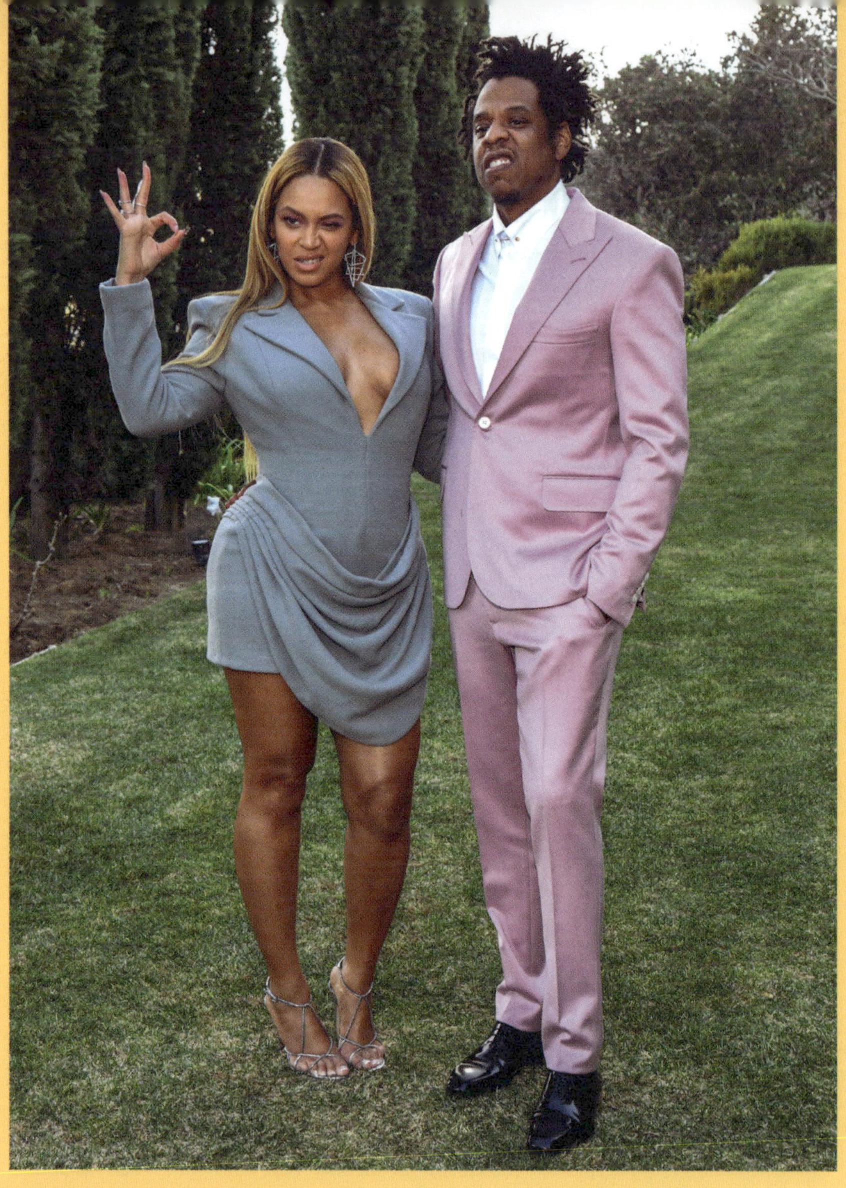

ABOVE Pastels, with a wink: couple style is all about complementary colours. In 2020, that meant green for Beyoncé and pink for Jay-Z.

OPPOSITE Evening glamour: Beyoncé and Jay-Z at a birthday party for a pre-controversy Sean Combs in 2019.

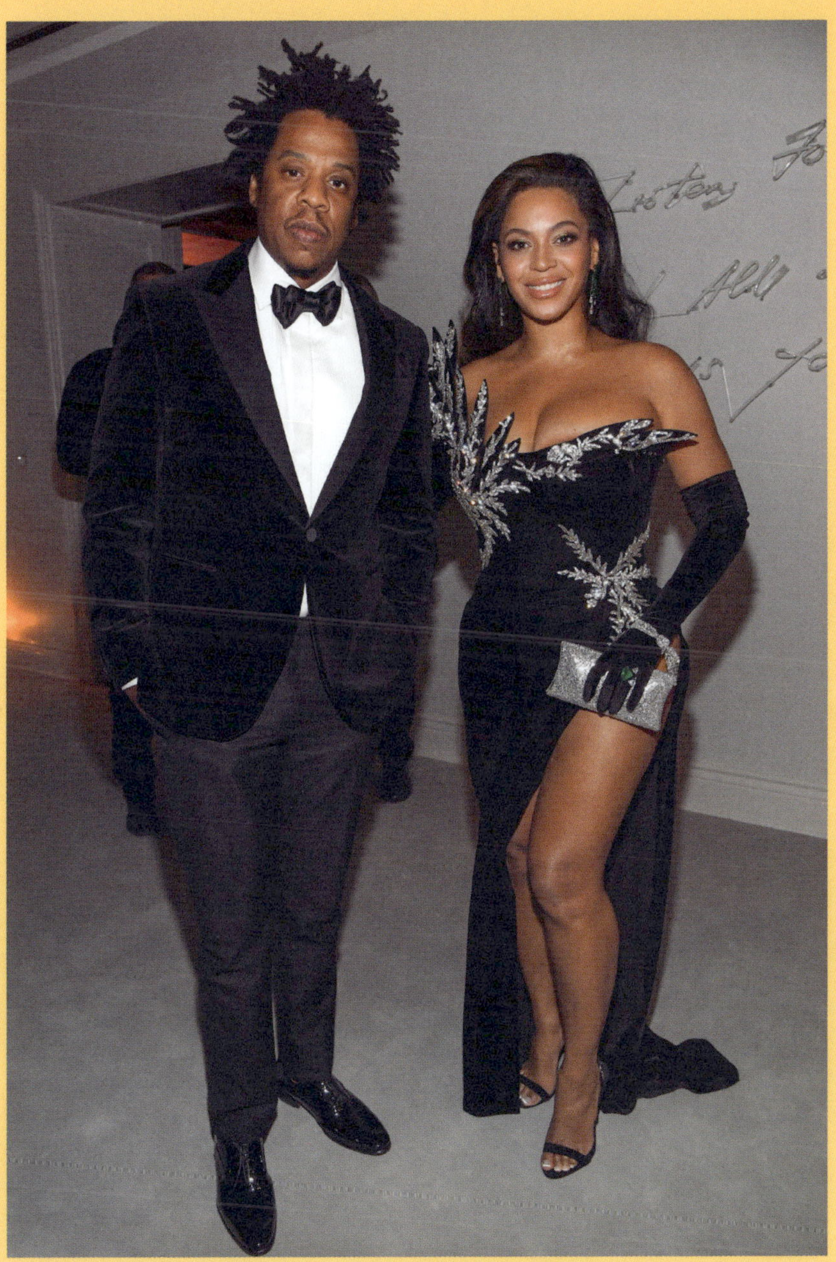

"*My rock.
My best friend.*"

BEYONCÉ ON JAY-Z

Sometimes they excel by using contrast – Beyoncé's innate glamour compared with Jay-Z's crisp casual outfits, as seen at basketball games. There are also the red-carpet appearances, with Jay-Z in a classic tux accompanying Beyoncé in a full-length gown. It was likely this kind of look that scored the pair the campaign with high-end jewellery brand Tiffany in 2022. But, as collaborators as well as partners and parents, the duo also star in videos together and they tour together. Notable moments include 'Apeshit' from their 2018 album *EVERYTHING IS LOVE*, filmed inside the Louvre, with the couple in contrasting pastel coloured suiting, or two On The Run tours in 2014 and 2018. Outfits chime here too – whether with US symbolism like Jay-Z's stars and stripes T-shirt and Beyoncé's cowboy hat, or her white lace with his white sportswear.

Speaking at the iHeartRadio Music Awards ceremony in 2024, the star paid tribute to her husband, calling him, "my rock. My best friend." It's clear that they still have the playfulness that was there from the start – judging by recent photos of the two of them dressed in those complementary tones, attending parties, hopping on the bullet train in Japan and holidaying on boats.

Twenty-odd years, one scandal and three children in, they remain ready, just like '03 Bonnie & Clyde' said, long ago.

OVERLEAF All white on the night: tour costumes for the On The Run tour updated a matching but not matching formula.

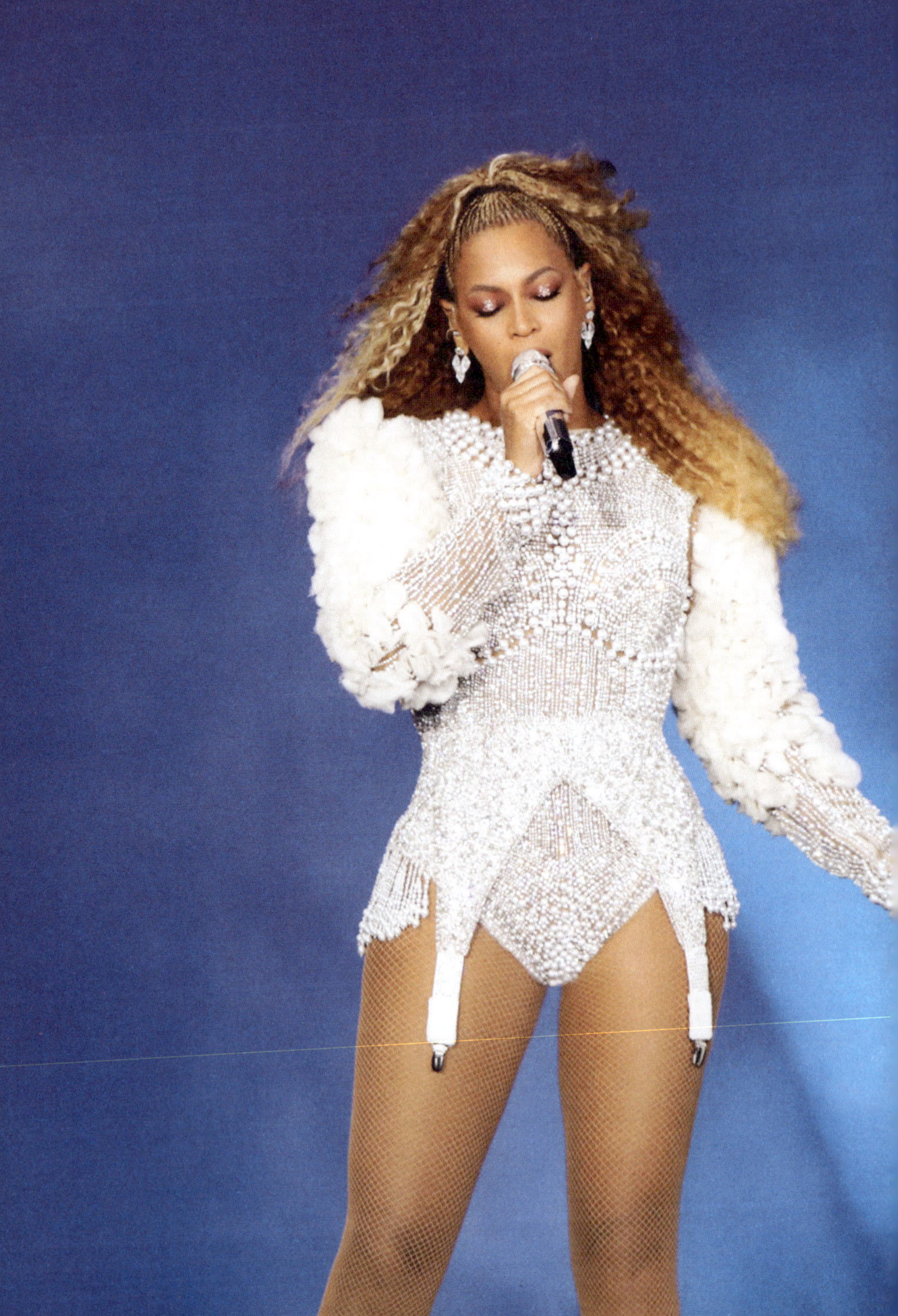

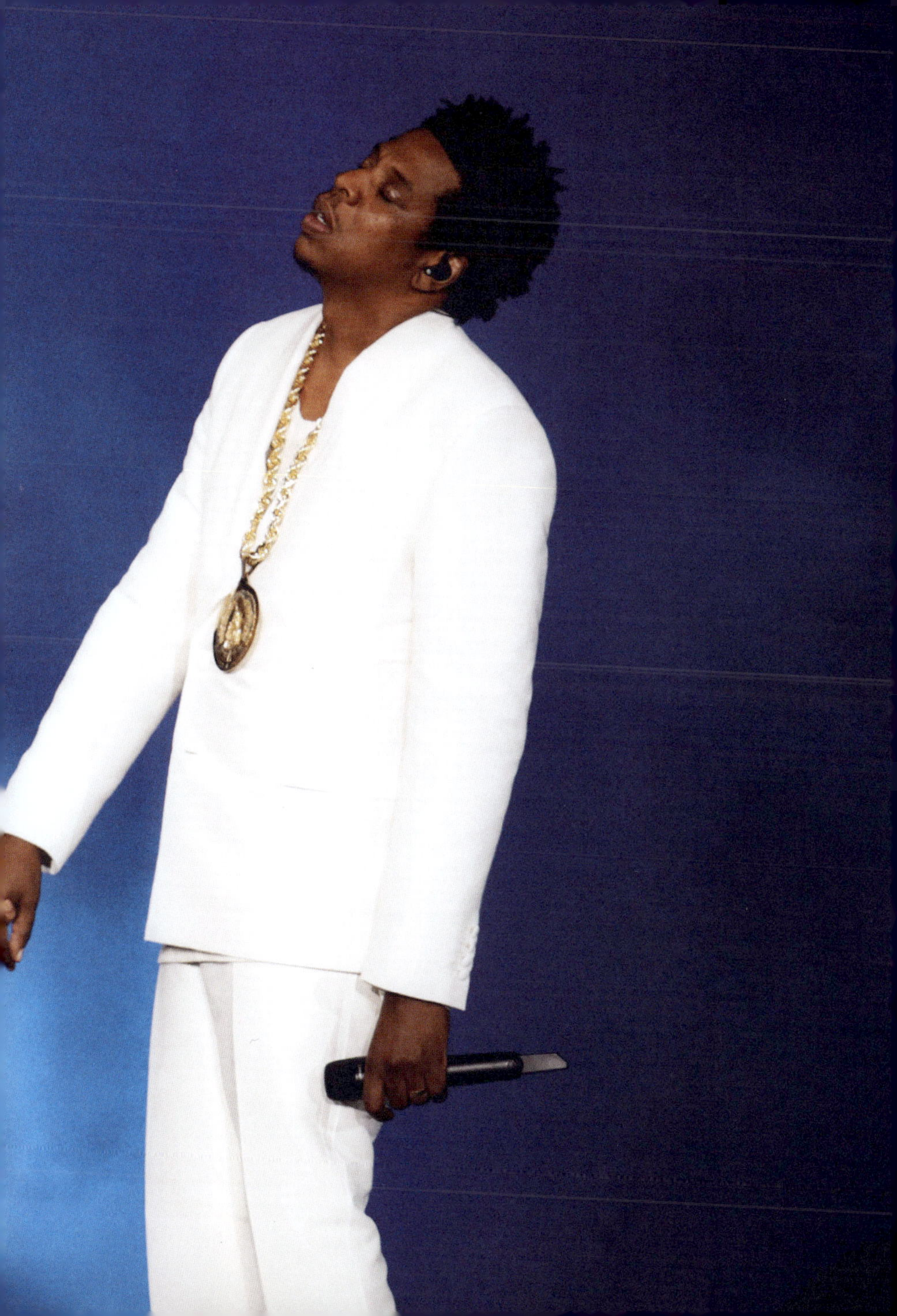

Giving mother

When Beyoncé announced she was pregnant in August 2011, she gained a Guinness World Record – with the news generating the highest number of Tweets per second ever, 8,868 to be exact. From that point on, the star's pregnancy with her first daughter Blue Ivy was watched with interest from fans and the media, whether through red-carpet appearances or in the video for 4 classic, 'Countdown'.

This was followed, of course, by the epic announcement on Instagram of her pregnancy with twins in 2017. Photographed sitting in her underwear, wearing a veil, on a bed of flowers, it recalled classical imagery celebrating motherhood but also became the most liked post of the year. This pregnancy was highly watched too – from an appearance at the Grammys in a bump-revealing red sequinned gown by Peter Dundas to a birth announcement image of newborn twins Rumi and Sir, featuring another veil and a flowing gown.

Two Grammys and one bump: a fine way to celebrate a double win at the awards ceremony in 2017.

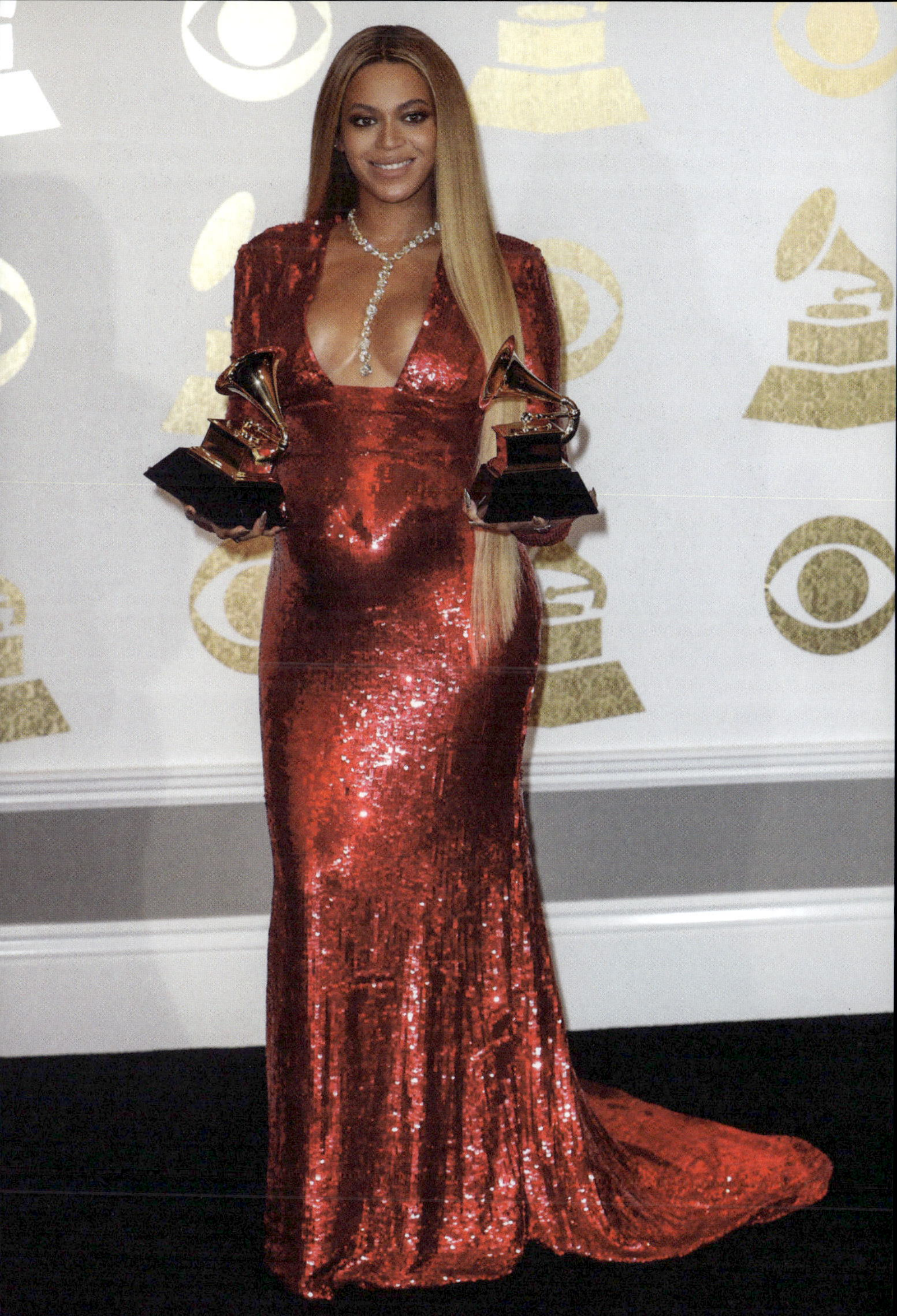

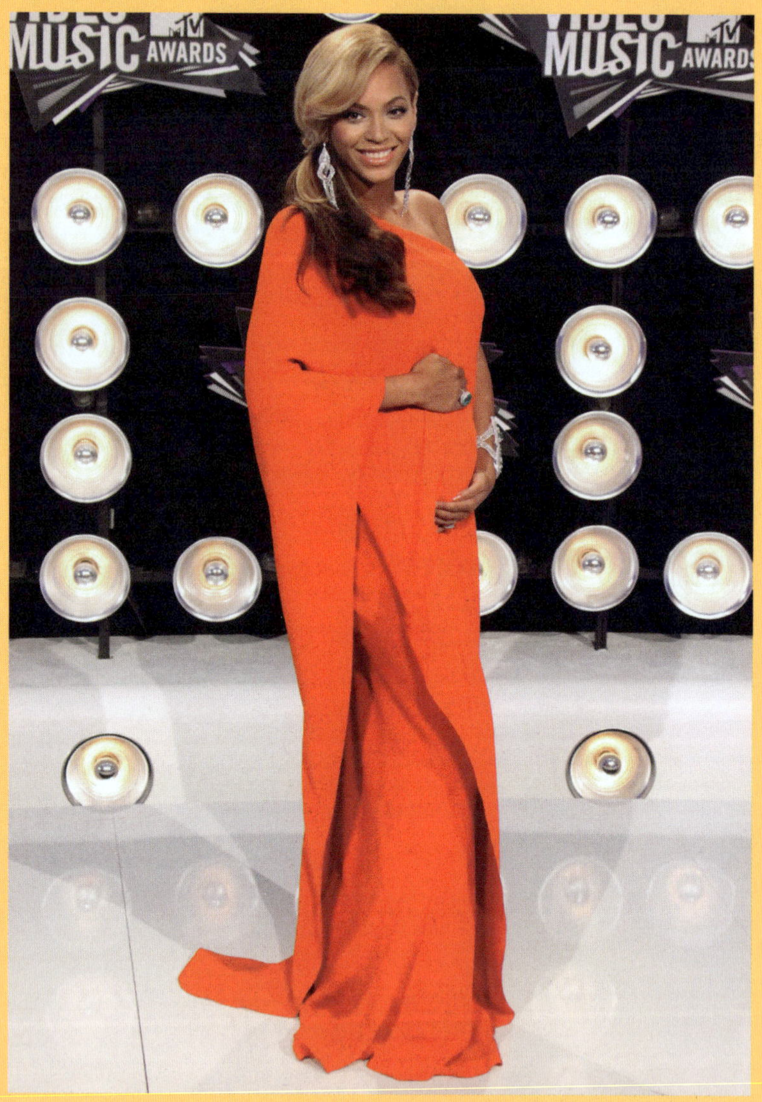

ABOVE Lady in red: Beyoncé cradles her baby bump at the MTV Video Music Awards (VMAs) in 2011, starting a new wave of pregnancy style.

OPPOSITE A cool mom, not a regular mom: a burgundy jumpsuit, sharp fringe and even sharper stilettos is a chic combo, even with a stroller.

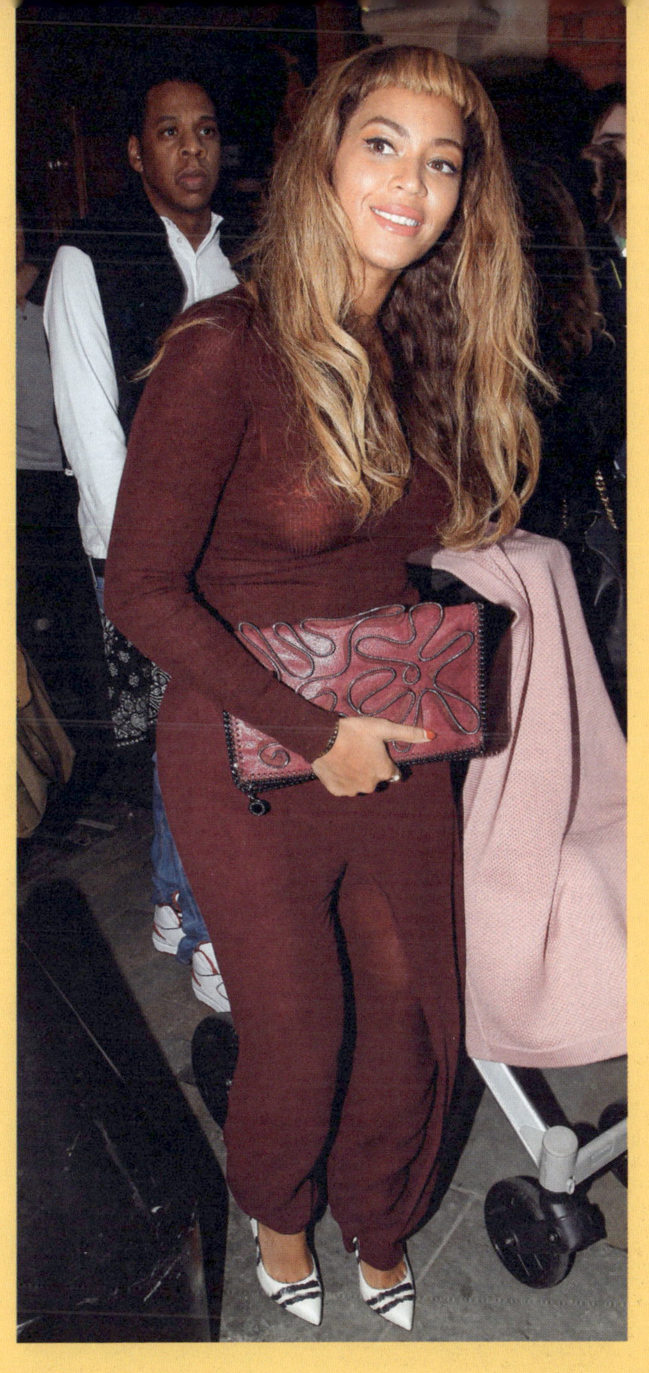

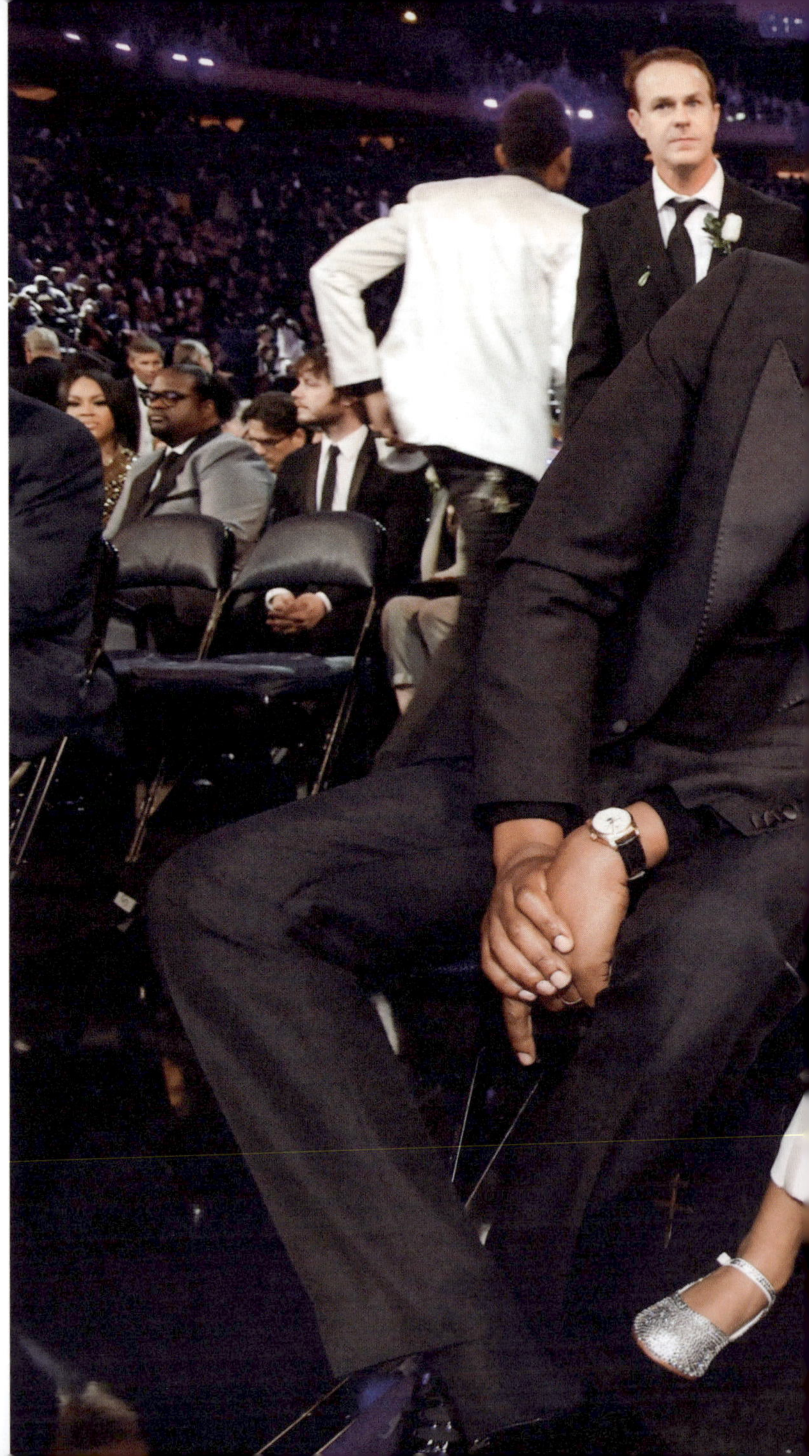

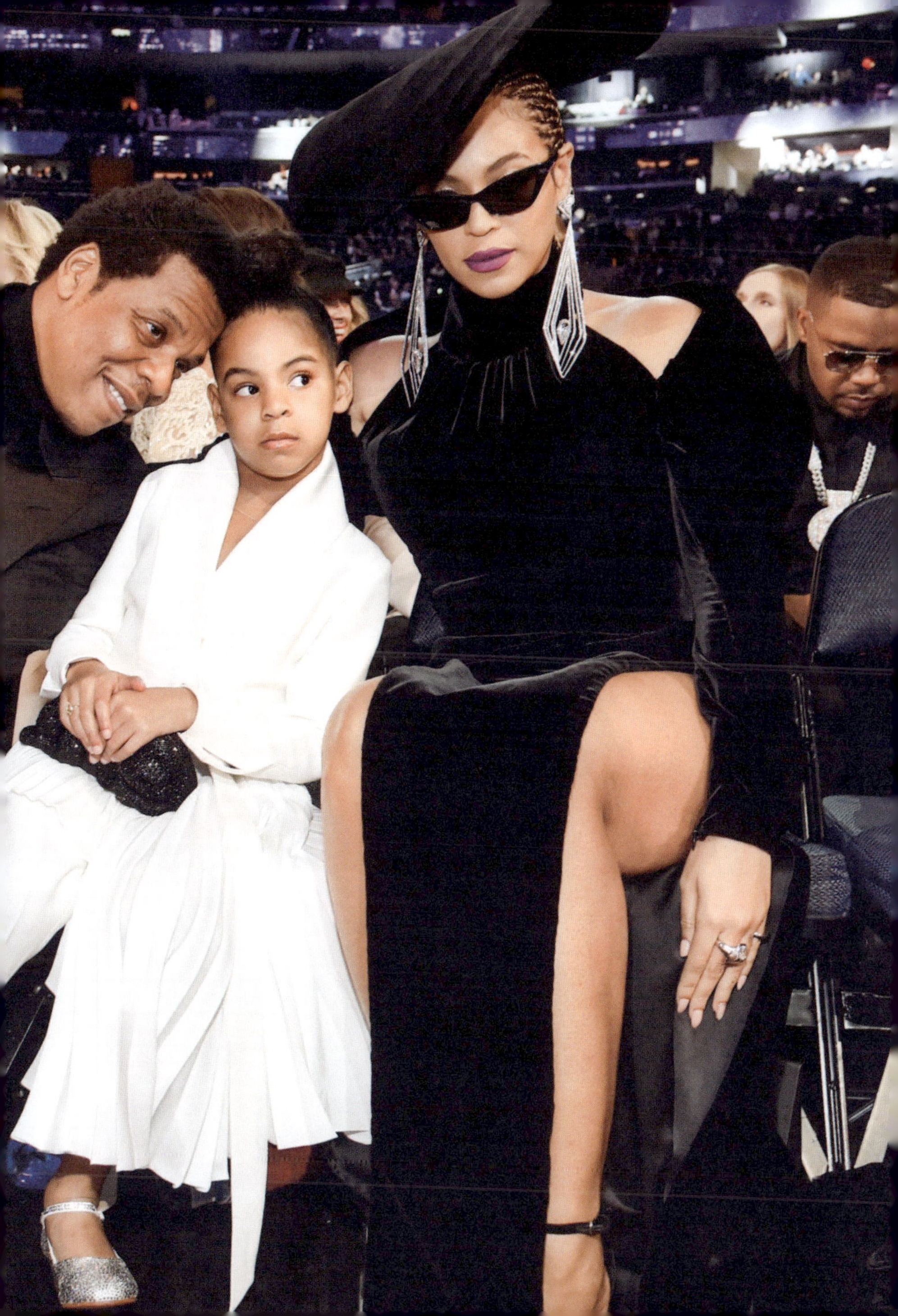

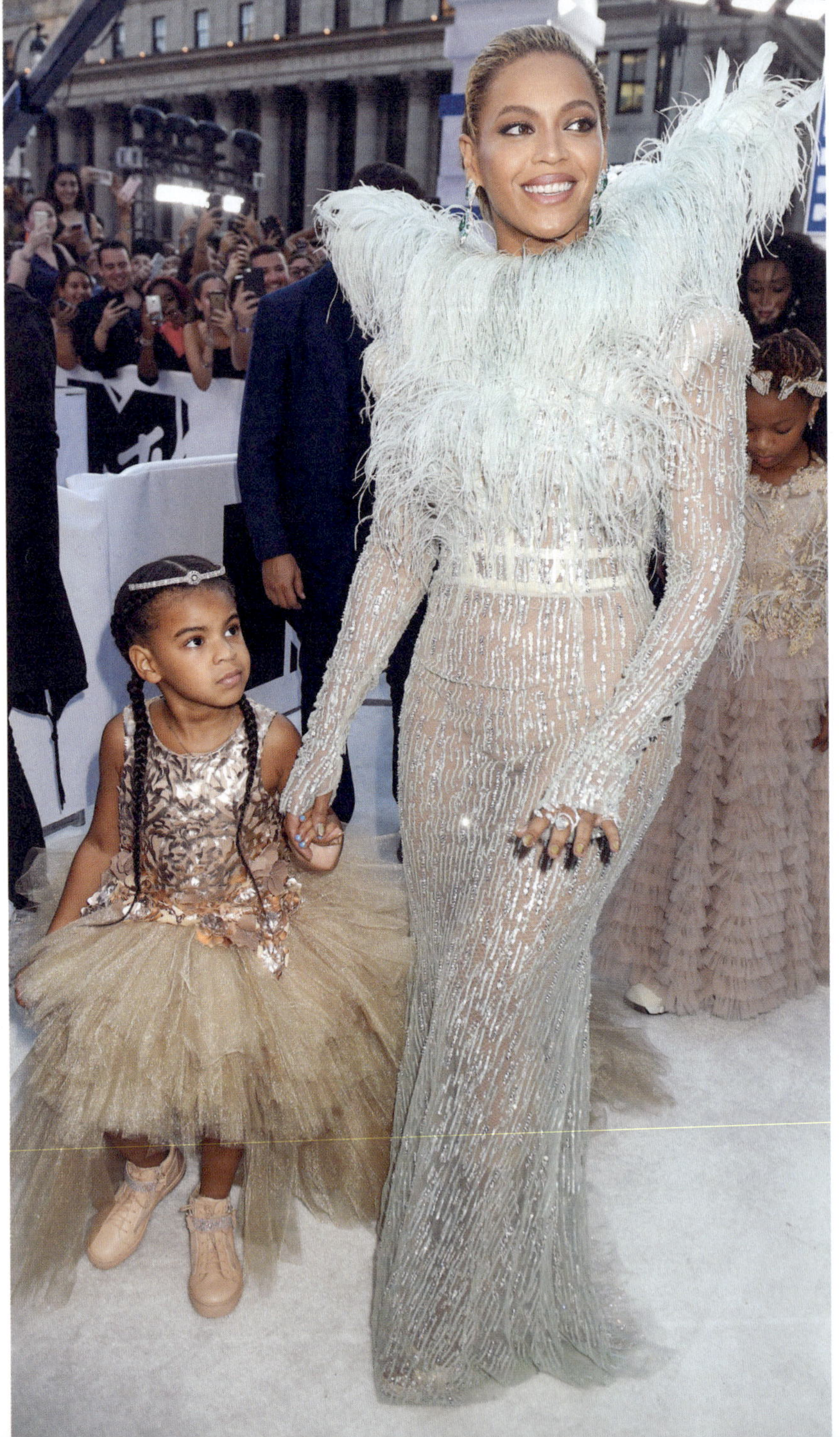

Beyoncé was quick to bring Blue (as she became known) along to events – the little girl was adorable as a four-year-old in matching tulle when attending the MTV Video Music Awards in 2016. She's continued to accompany her very famous parents to events, with the spotlight inevitably turning on her, now quite literally.

The 11-year-old appeared as a dancer, alongside her mother, on 2023's Renaissance tour, despite the inevitable scrutiny that her parents bring. "Blue comes up fighting against all the negativity that was put on her just because she was our kid," Beyoncé says in the film *Renaissance*. "She was ready to take back her power." Blue Ivy is also getting ready for her close-up. Appearing at 12 on stage alongside Jay-Z at the Grammys in 2024, wearing a Vivienne Westwood frock, the next generation of the Knowles-Carter dynasty has arrived.

PREVIOUS A family affair: Blue Ivy has style in her genes. See a visit to the 2018 Grammys with her parents, aged six.

OPPOSITE Heart-meltingly cute. a four year-old Blue Ivy almost outshines her mother with sequins and matching tulle in 2016.

"Blue comes up fighting against all the negativity that was put on her just because she was our kid. She was ready to take back her power."

BEYONCÉ

The shape of things to come: a 12-year-old Blue Ivy takes to the stage at the Grammys, wearing Vivienne Westwood.

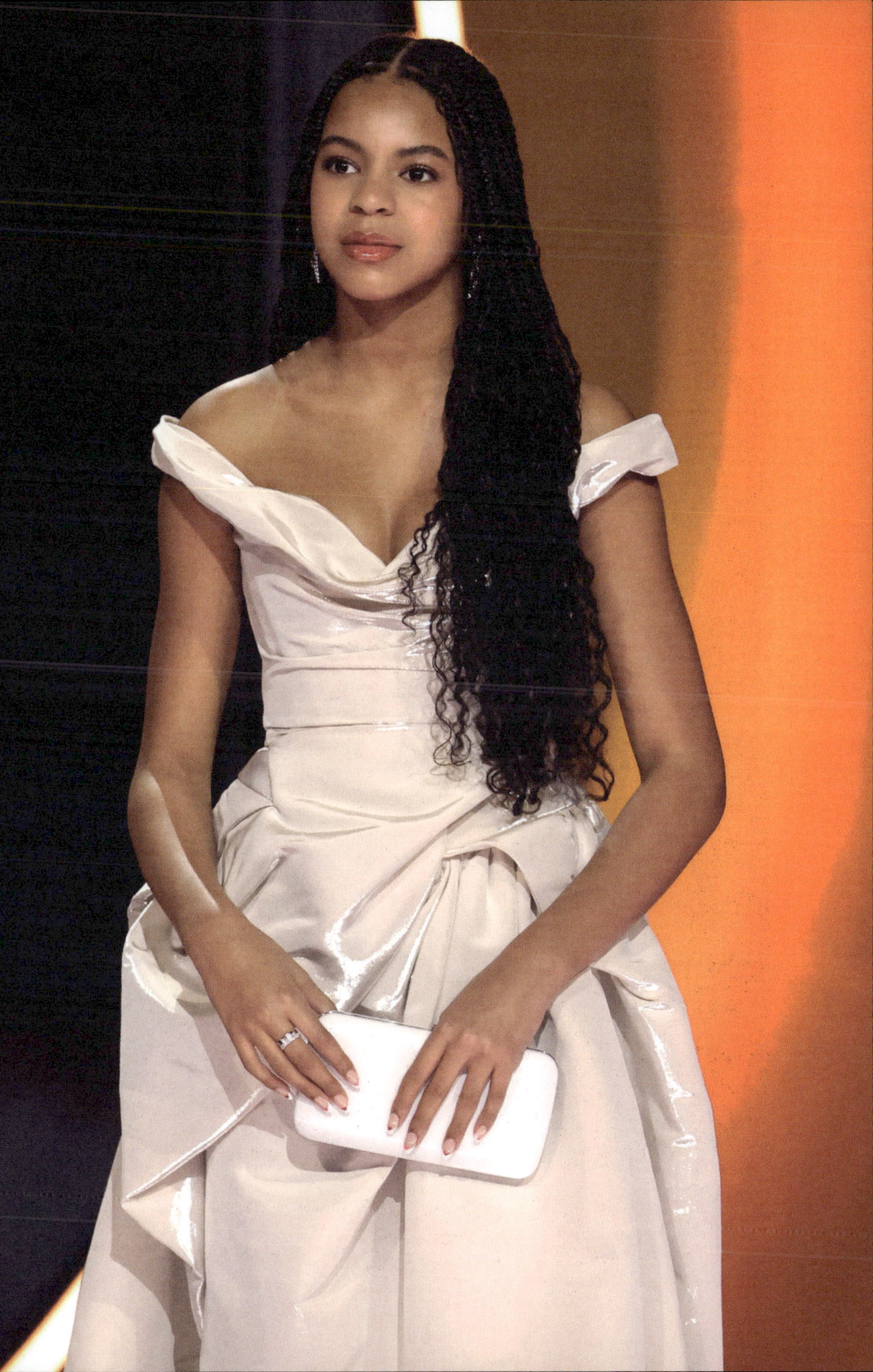

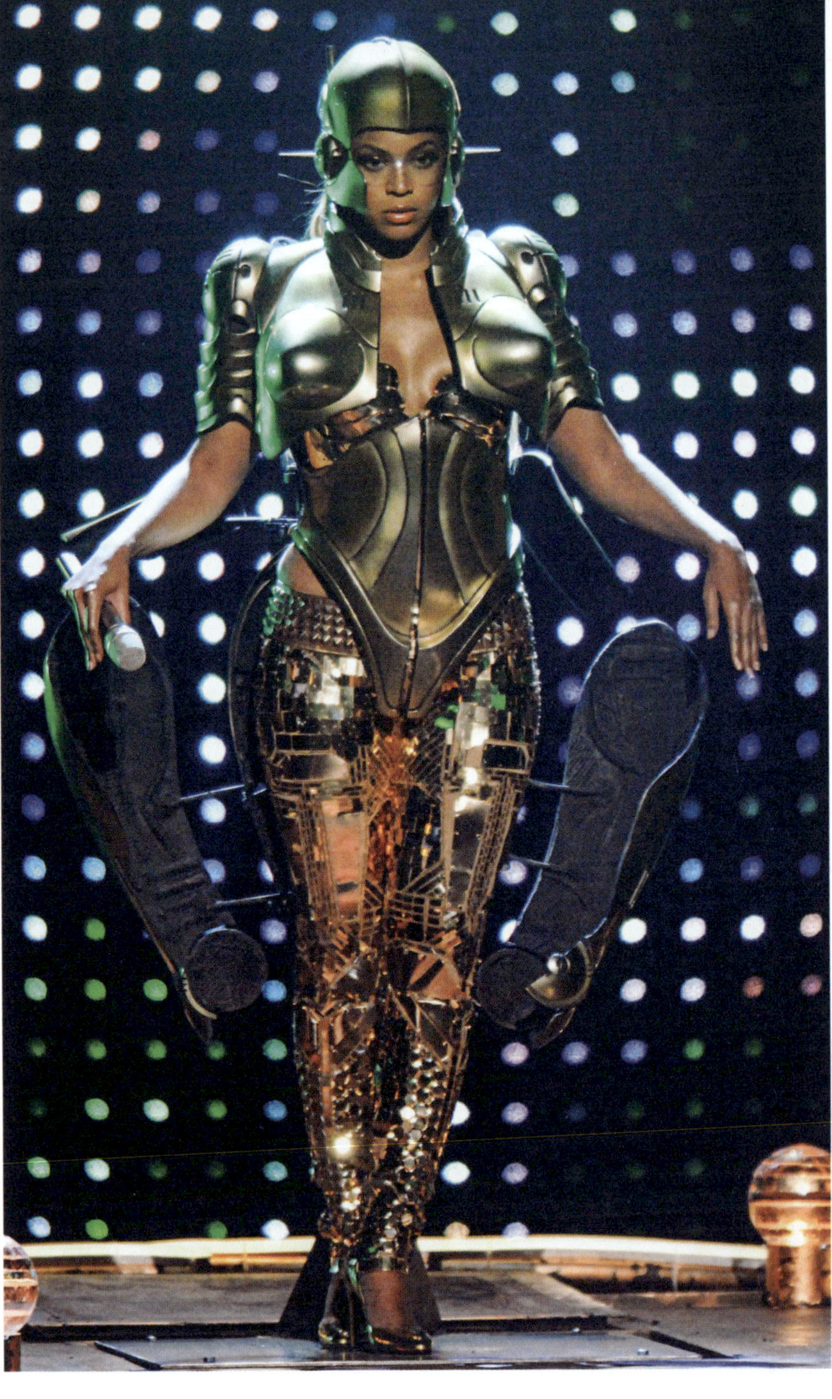

Future facing

When Beyoncé took to the stage for her Renaissance tour wearing an outfit that turned her from megastar to cyborg and then promptly performed 'Cozy' with two robot arms as backing dancers, it was hailed as one of the best moments of the tour and potentially a comment on the looming spectre of AI. But, in actual fact, the star has been invested in a futuristic idea of aesthetics long before ChatGPT was even an option when composing a college essay.

To perform 'Get Me Bodied' at the BET Awards in 2007, she resembled a beautiful robot in an outfit that looked like Maria, otherwise known as the *Maschinenmensch*, the character from sci-fi classic, Fritz Lang's 1927 *Metropolis*. Aptly, she was ahead of her time with this reference – predating similar imagery on Janelle Monae's *The ArchAndroid* by three years.

OPPOSITE *Metropolis*, reimagined for the twenty-first century: Beyoncé's vision of the 1927 film, for the BET Awards in 2007.

OVERLEAF Ringing it: the famous robot hand, worn for a performance in 2009, took the futuristic look stratospheric.

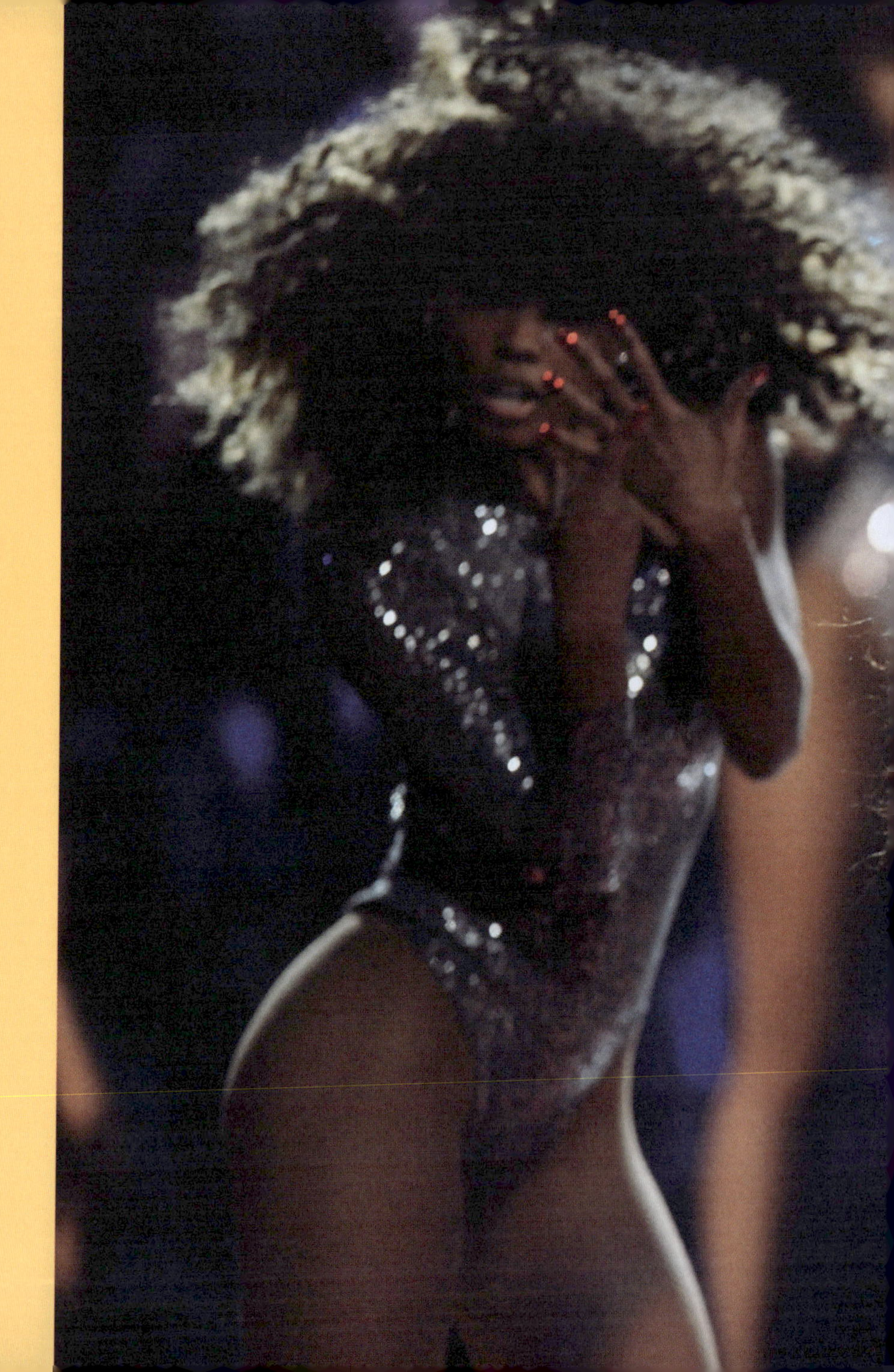

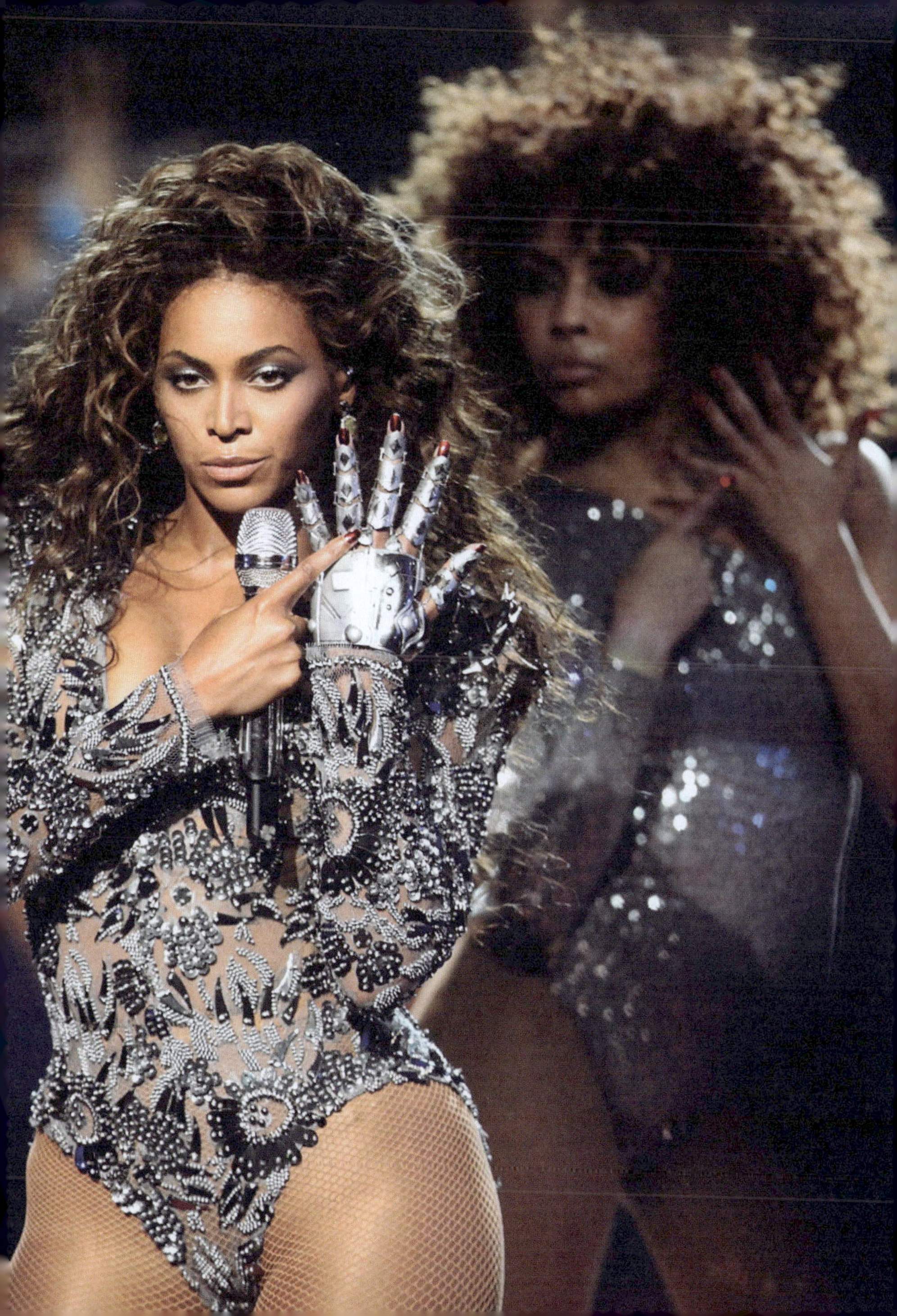

Both women have been hailed as referencing an Afrofuturism aesthetic – the term for the ways that the Black experience has been explored through sci-fi references. First defined in 1993, the idea dates back to artists like experimental jazz musician Sun Ra in the sixties and George Clinton's Funkadelic – complete with mothership – in the seventies.

When Beyoncé is involved, these references have a megastar reach. The robot hand she wore to perform the famous 'Single Ladies' dance in 2009 went viral as the move spread throughout the world.

Writing about Afrofuturism as seen in the work of artists ranging from Beyoncé to Donald Glover to Flying Lotus in the *Guardian* in 2018, Lanre Bakare said the aesthetic "symbolised the revival of a genre in which strangeness and blackness not only co-exist but are impossible to separate." Beyoncé, as one of the biggest Black stars on the planet, perhaps identifies with this point of view – whether she's wearing a robot costume or not.

A subtle cyborg: Beyoncé takes the futuristic look to the stage for a Tidal concert in 2015.

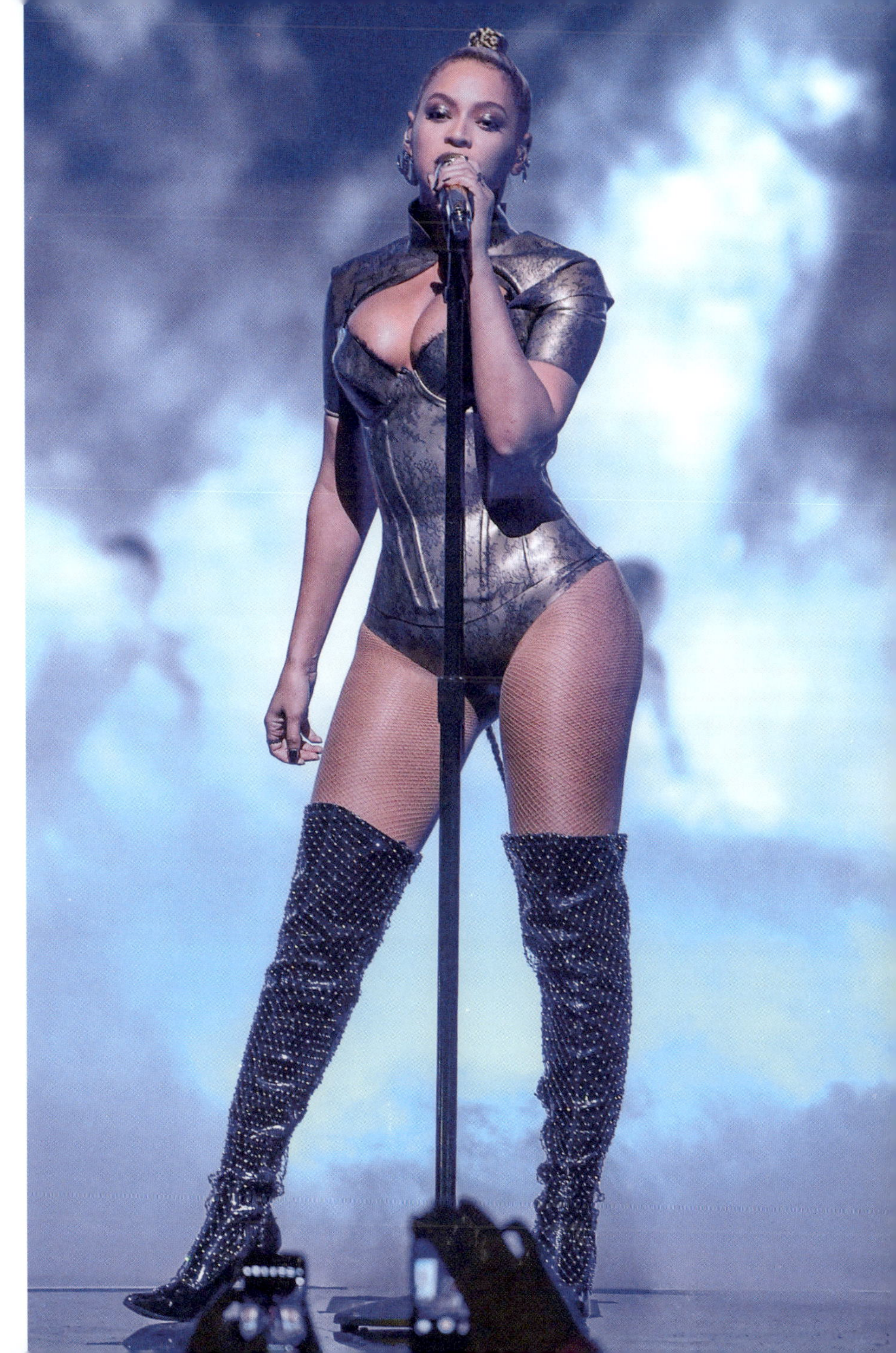

(Black and) yellow

Anyone with half an eye on the world of Beyoncé will be well aware that her fan army is referred to as the Beyhive, with the bee emoji often deployed on social media to express support for the star. This may perhaps go some way toward explaining why the object of their adoration is a particular fan of yellow, a colour known to attract these stripy flying creatures.

Beyoncé has worn the shade for decades, from appearances straight out of Destiny's Child to various awards ceremonies. She wore Stephane Rolland chartreuse satin to accept the BET Award for Best Female R&B Artist in 2012, a golden goddess gown by Vietnamese designer Nguyen Cong Tri for the London premiere of *The Lion King* in 2019 and a highlighter shade by her label Ivy Park to perform at the Oscars in 2022.

OPPOSITE Smooth satin: a beautiful chartreuse shade was the perfect choice for the BET Awards in 2012.

OVERLEAF A neon army: Beyoncé and her backing dancers bring the colour to the Oscars, wearing her Ivy Park label in 2022.

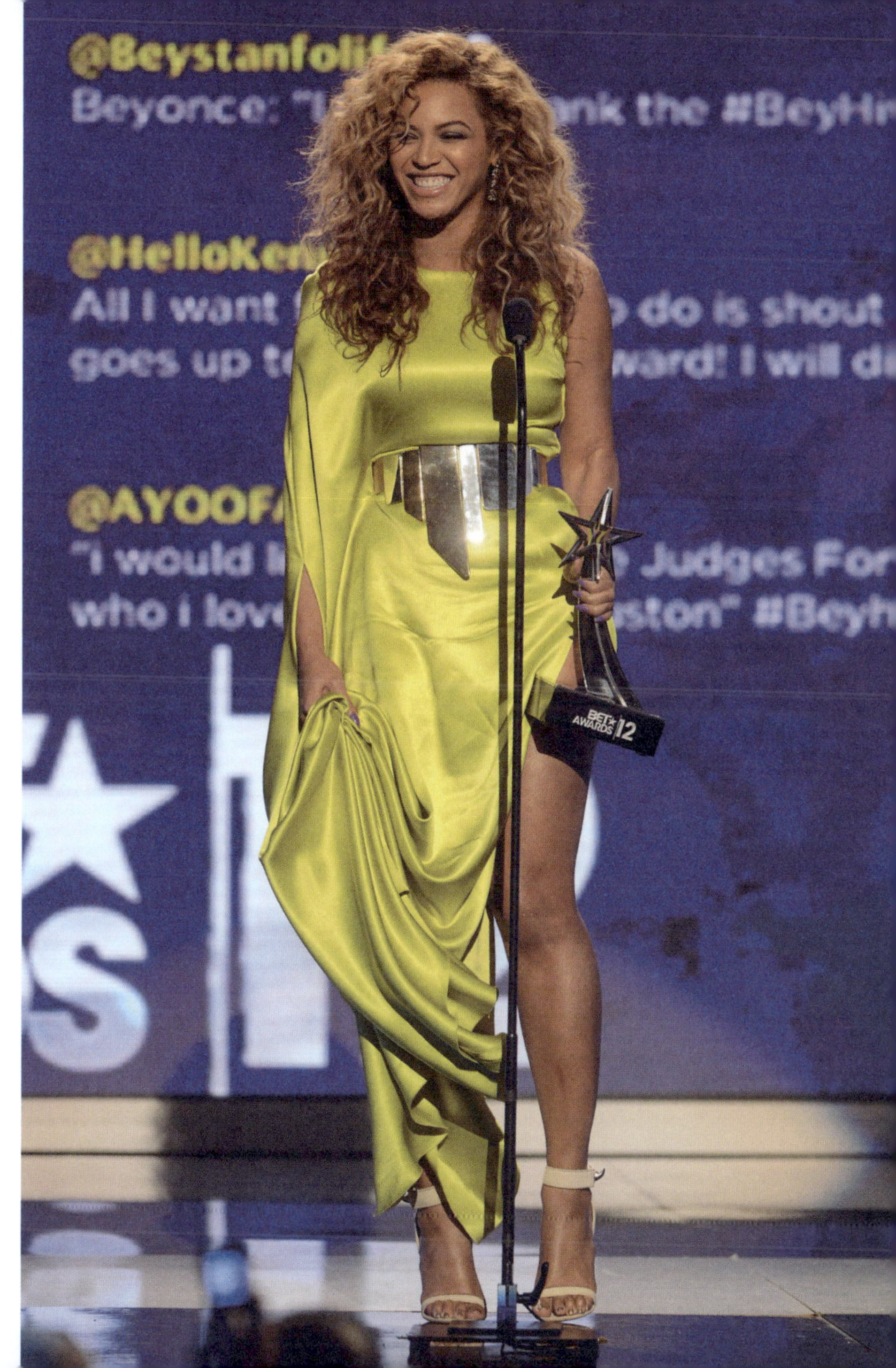

@Beystanfolif
Beyonce: "I ank the #BeyHi
@HelloKen
All I want do is shout
goes up to ward! I will d
@AYOOFA
"I would Judges For
who i love ston" #Bey
BET
AWARDS 12

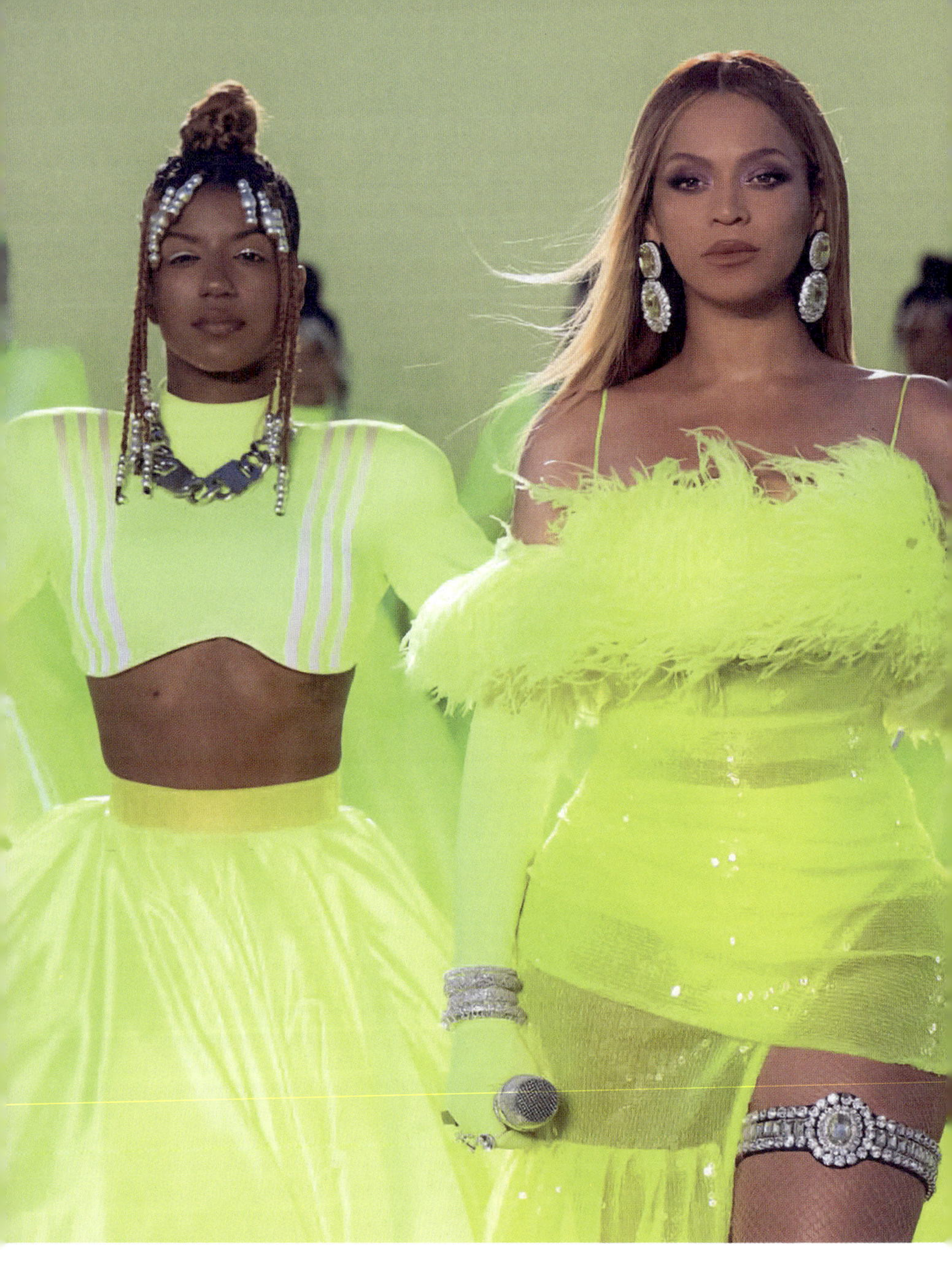

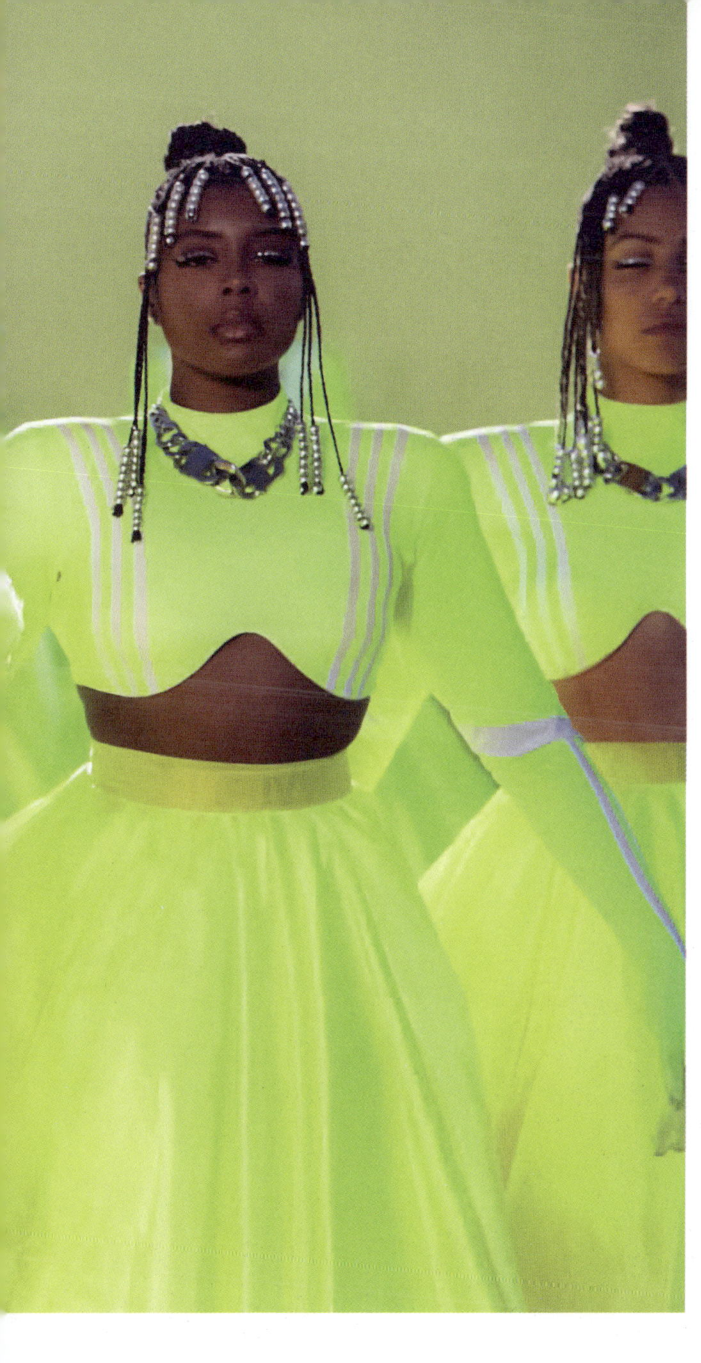

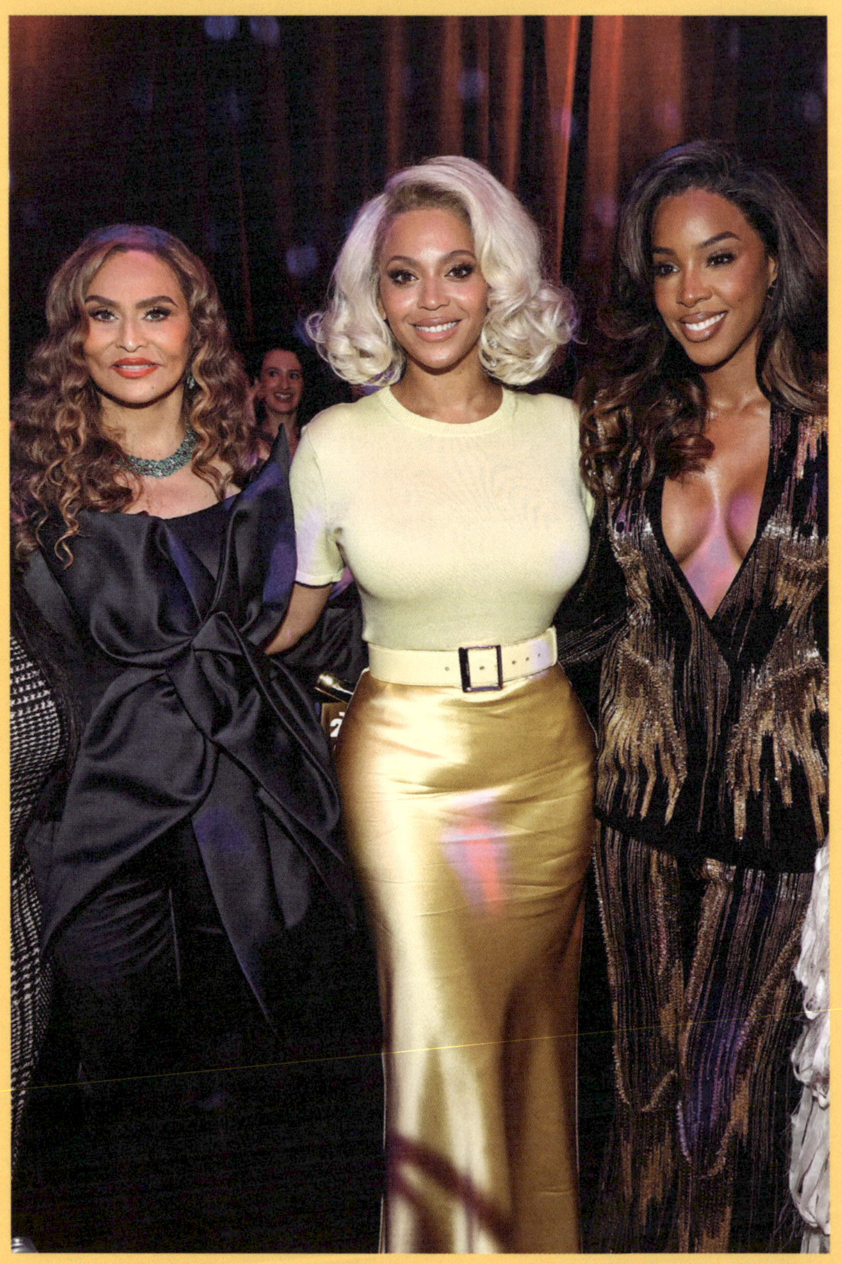

This is a woman who researches her references and her love for yellow almost certainly goes beyond merely a nod to the Beyhive. Speaking about the neon shade that was part of the Ivy Park collection, she said it was a direct response to the pandemic: "[it] brought me joy and made me smile in the midst of a tough time for all of us." Her instincts made sense – yellow has long been associated with happiness, thanks to it colouring elements of nature. The post-impressionist Vincent van Gogh said it "stands for the sun."

Sometimes Beyoncé's references are more specific. The Roberto Cavalli dress she wore in the video for 2016's 'Hold Up' was a beautiful shade of ochre meets canary yellow and chosen to send a specific message. With the Yoruba Orisha divine spirits thought to be a theme from 2016 album *Lemonade*, yellow represents Oshun, the deity symbolizing femininity and strength. Just the thing, then, to wear walking through a city smashing up cars...

While Beyoncé has not explicitly namechecked this reference, it's been a jump-off for scholars, both in academia and pop culture. Soon after the video's release, Yohana Desta, writing for *Mashable*, said 'Hold Up' was "Beyoncé channeling Oshun, the Yoruba goddess of water, fertility, love, sensuality. Powerful and beautiful and mythical."

So far, so Beyoncé. No wonder yellow is a colour to return to over and over again.

The golden child: Beyoncé in butter yellow – and Marilyn-style waves – to celebrate her mother Tina at the Glamour Women of the Year Awards in 2024.

> "*[Yellow] brought me joy and made me smile in the midst of a **tough time** for all of us.*"

BEYONCÉ

Always golden: a dress in deep ochre, by Vietnamese designer Nguyen Cong Tri, was the dream for the London premiere of *The Lion King* in 2019.

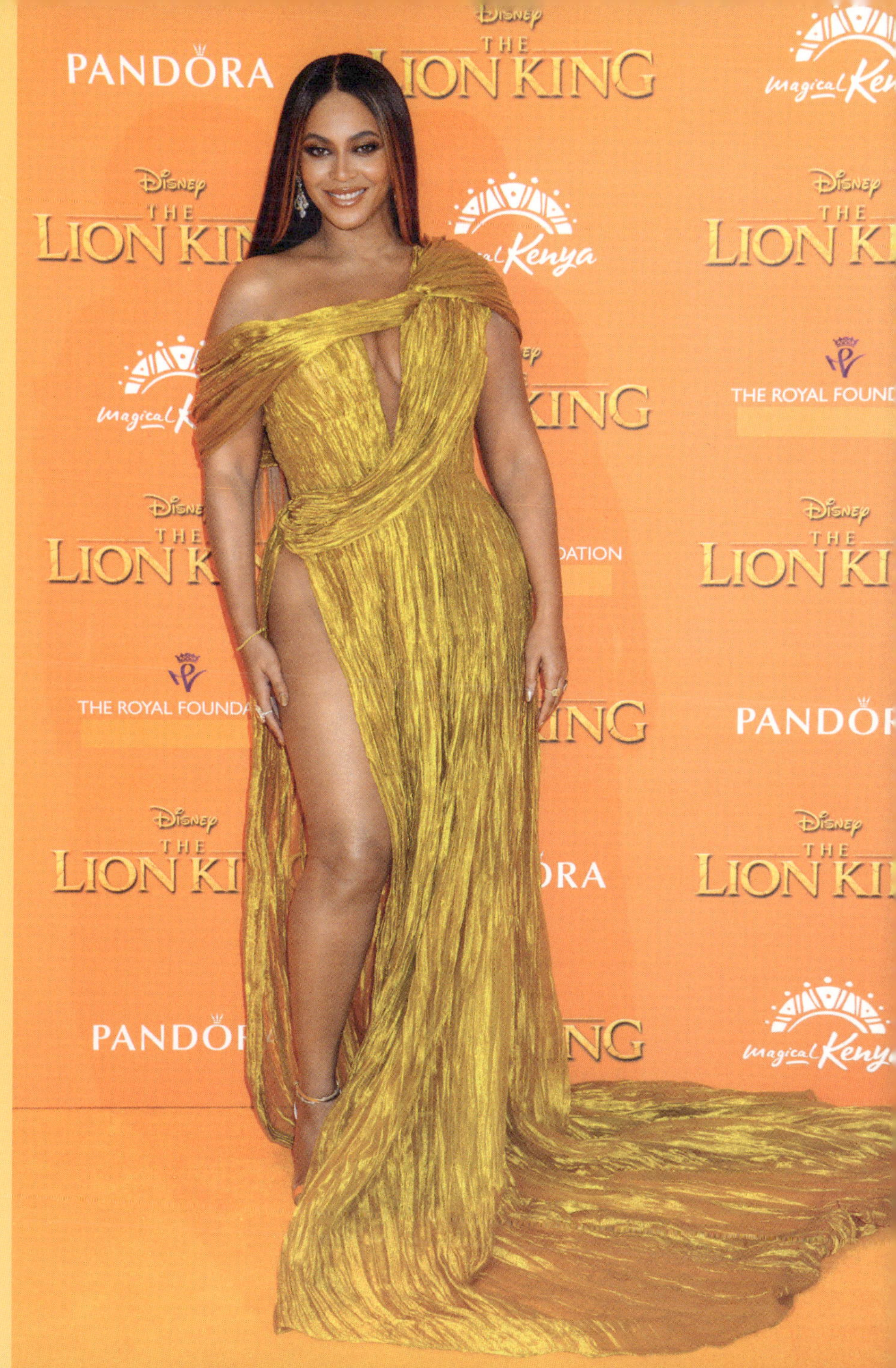

Disney
THE LION KING
PANDORA
magical Kenya
THE ROYAL FOUNDATION
Disney
THE LION KING
magical Kenya
THE ROYAL FOUNDATION
Disney
THE LION KI
PANDORA
Disney
THE LION KI
Disney
THE LION KING
PANDORA
Disney
THE LION KING
magical Kenya

Fashion with a capital F

As one of the most visible women of our time, fashion designers no doubt love seeing their work worn by Beyoncé. Data from the website Launchmetrics show just how much impact she has: Balmain gained $5.3m in Media Impact Value (the metric that measures the financial benefit from online buzz) by dressing her on the Renaissance tour.

A lyric, meanwhile, can swiftly put the spotlight on a label. This happened in 2023 with the song 'Summer Renaissance' where Beyonce praises Telfar bags over classic Birkins. Views of Telfar bags increased 85 per cent on The RealReal luxury resale site as a result.

OPPOSITE Like mother, like daughter: two generations of Knowleses showcase their style on the Council of Fashion Designers of America (CFDA) red carpet in 2004.

OVERLEAF Triple threat: Beyoncé, Giorgio Armani and Jay-Z at the celebrated designer's fashion show in 2006.

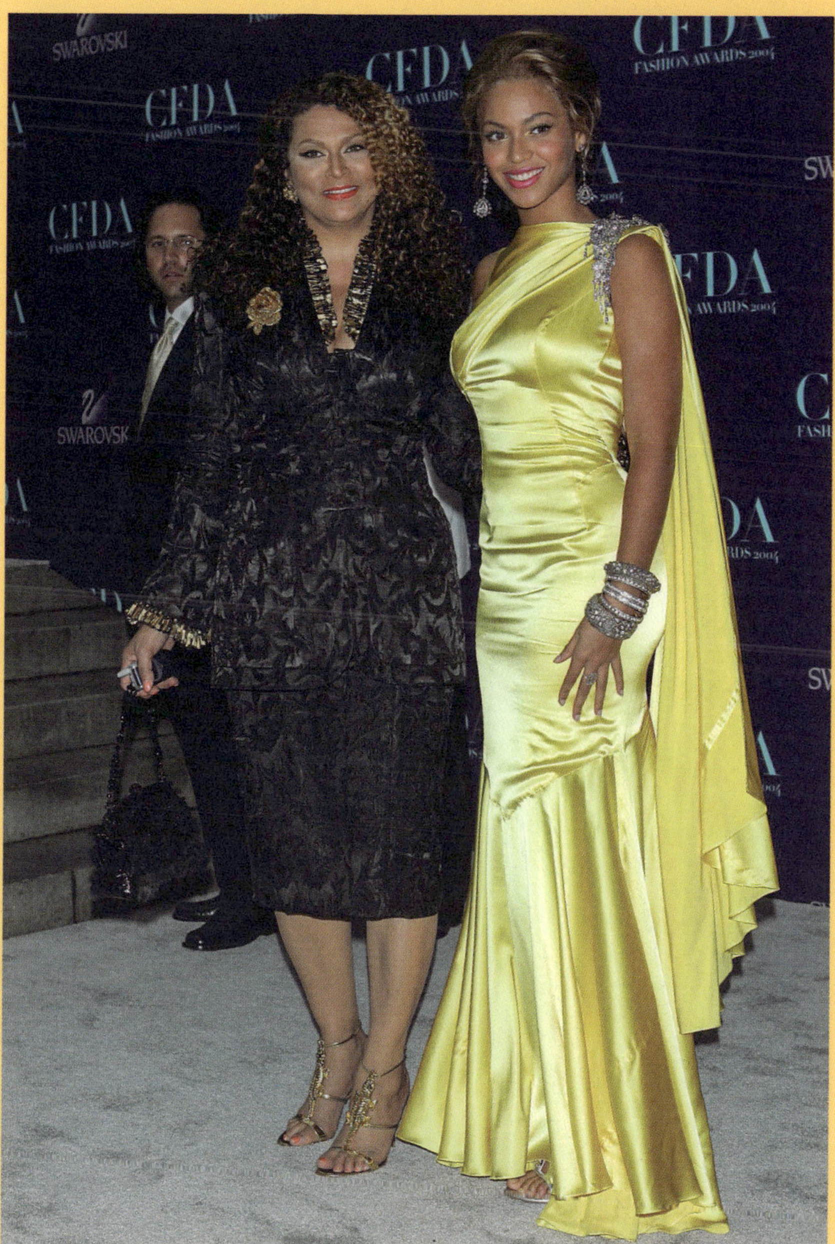

SWAROVSKI
CFDA
FASHION AWARDS 2004
CFDA
FASHION AWARDS 2004
CFDA
FASHION AWARDS 2004
SWAROVSKI
CFDA
AWARDS 2004
SW

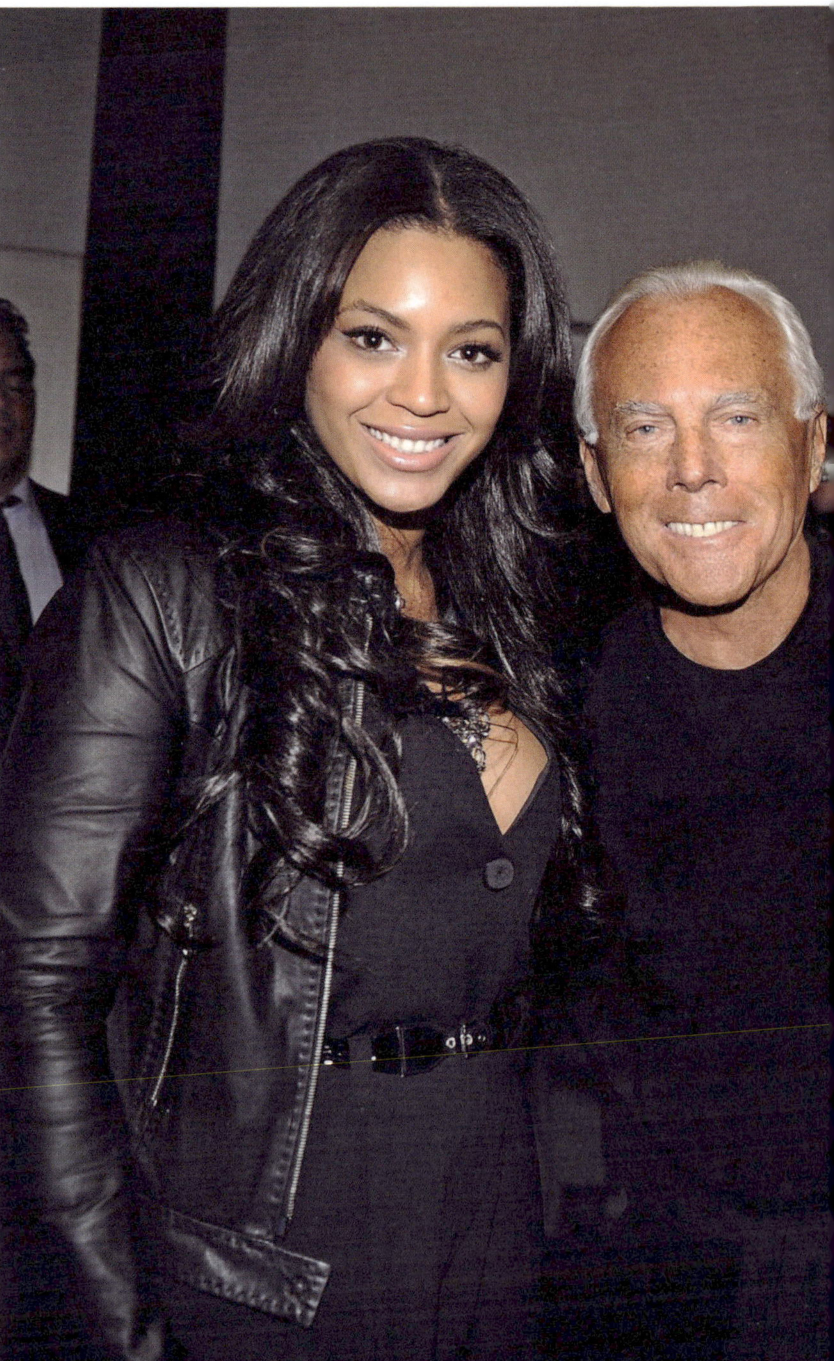

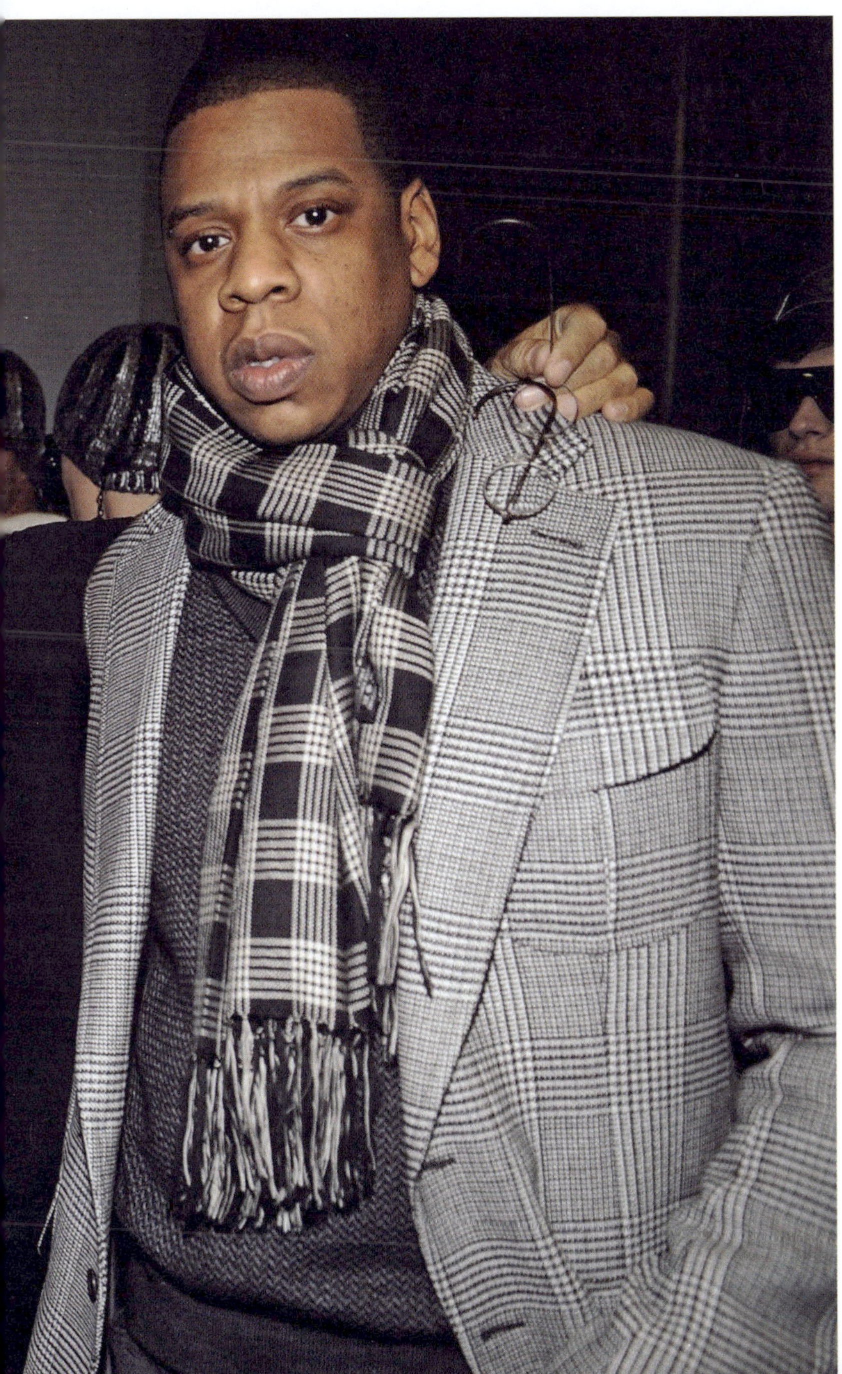

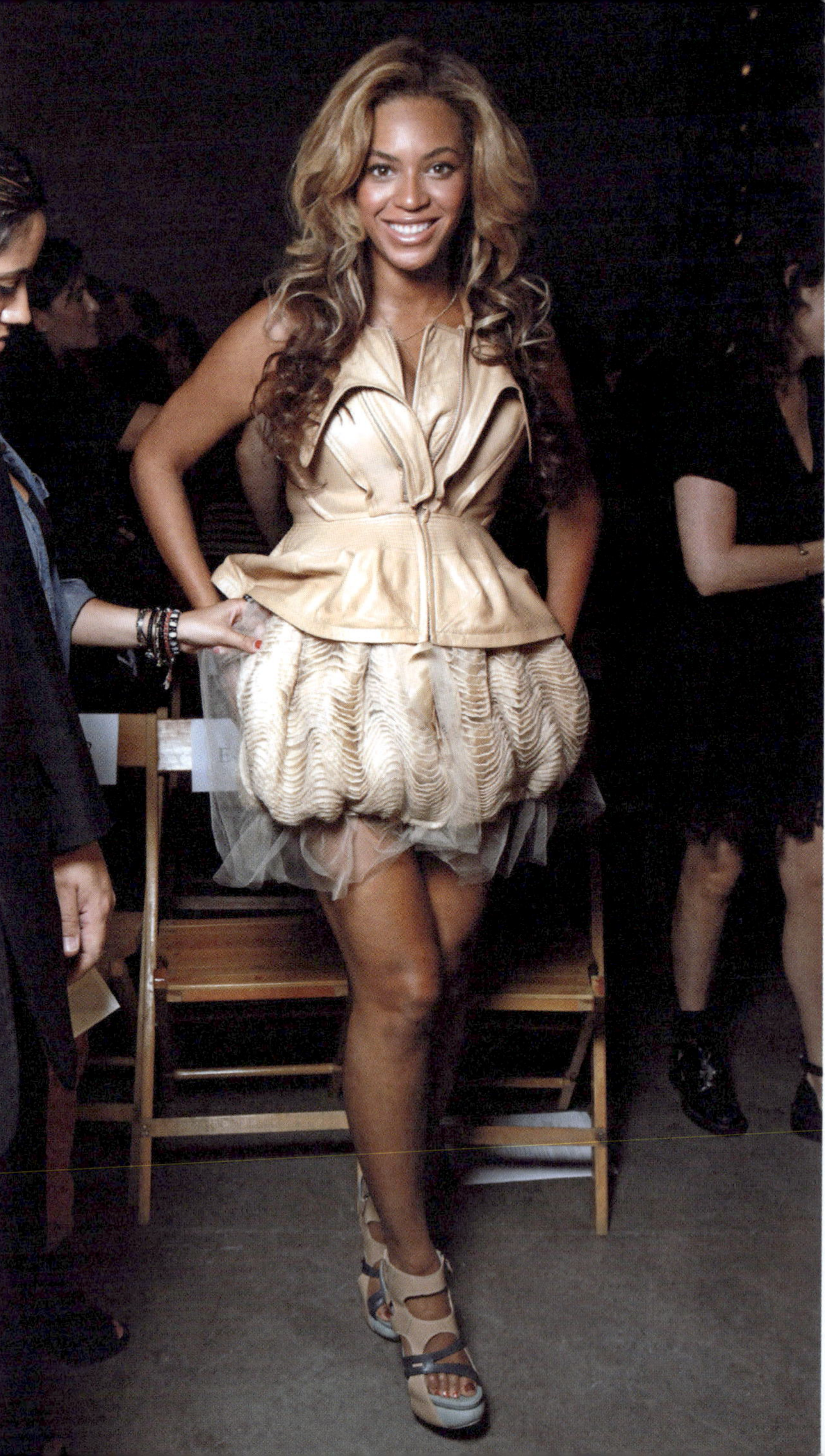

Beyond these co-signs, Beyoncé's mere presence at fashion shows has boosted luxury brands over the years. She has attended fashion shows for brands including Armani in 2006, Rodarte in 2011 and a Yeezy show in 2015 to support a pre-scandal Kanye West. As well as this, she's been a guest at the CFDA Awards, the event that honours fashion luminaries in America. Fittingly, she won Fashion Icon of the Year in 2016.

One of the most memorable of her fashion show appearances in recent years came in June 2023, when Beyoncé and Jay-Z joined an A-list audience including Rihanna and A$AP Rocky, Zendaya, Lewis Hamilton, Kelly Rowland and many more for the first Louis Vuitton show designed by long-time Beyoncé collaborator and producer, the alpha multi-hyphenate Pharrell. Wearing a pair of what looked like the world's most luxurious pyjamas and oversized sunglasses, she glowed with star power. In fact, Beyoncé's very presence, a gesture of support, may have backfired – with guests keeping eyes on her, rather than the catwalk, while the show took place.

Front row regular: Beyoncé shows her fashion credentials in a directional outfit for Rodarte's show in 2011.

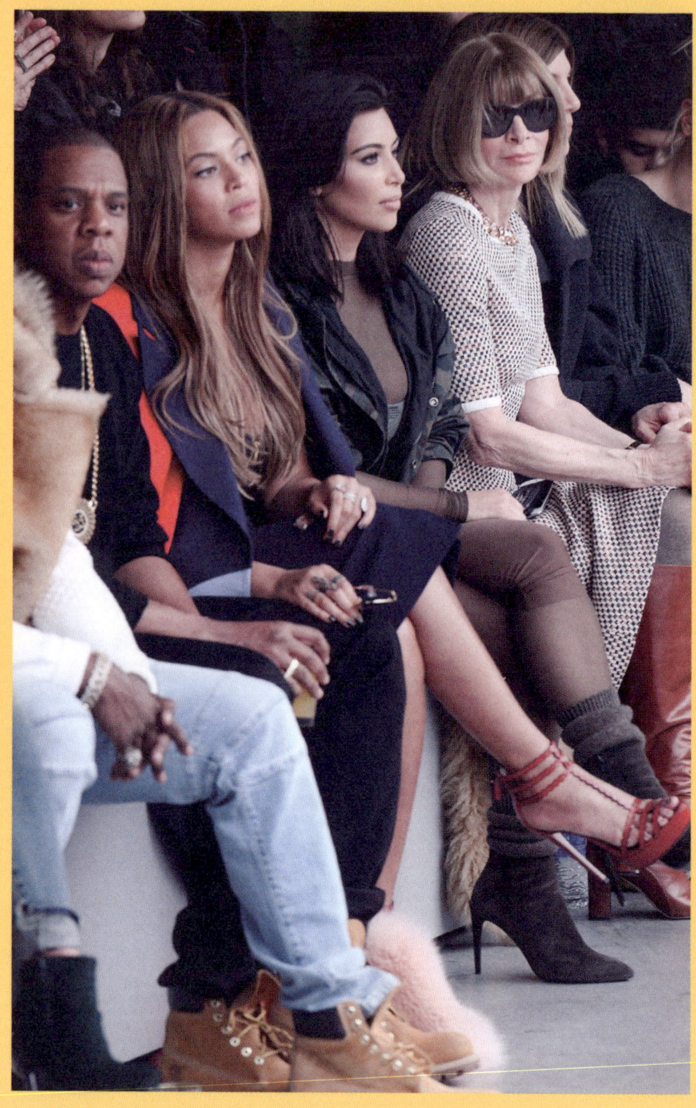

ABOVE Amongst the A-list: Jay-Z, Beyoncé, Kim Kardashian and *Vogue*'s Anna Wintour watch the Yeezy show in 2015.

OPPOSITE Shades and pyjamas: a low-key combination is taken to another level, when worn by Beyoncé to a Louis Vuitton show in 2023.

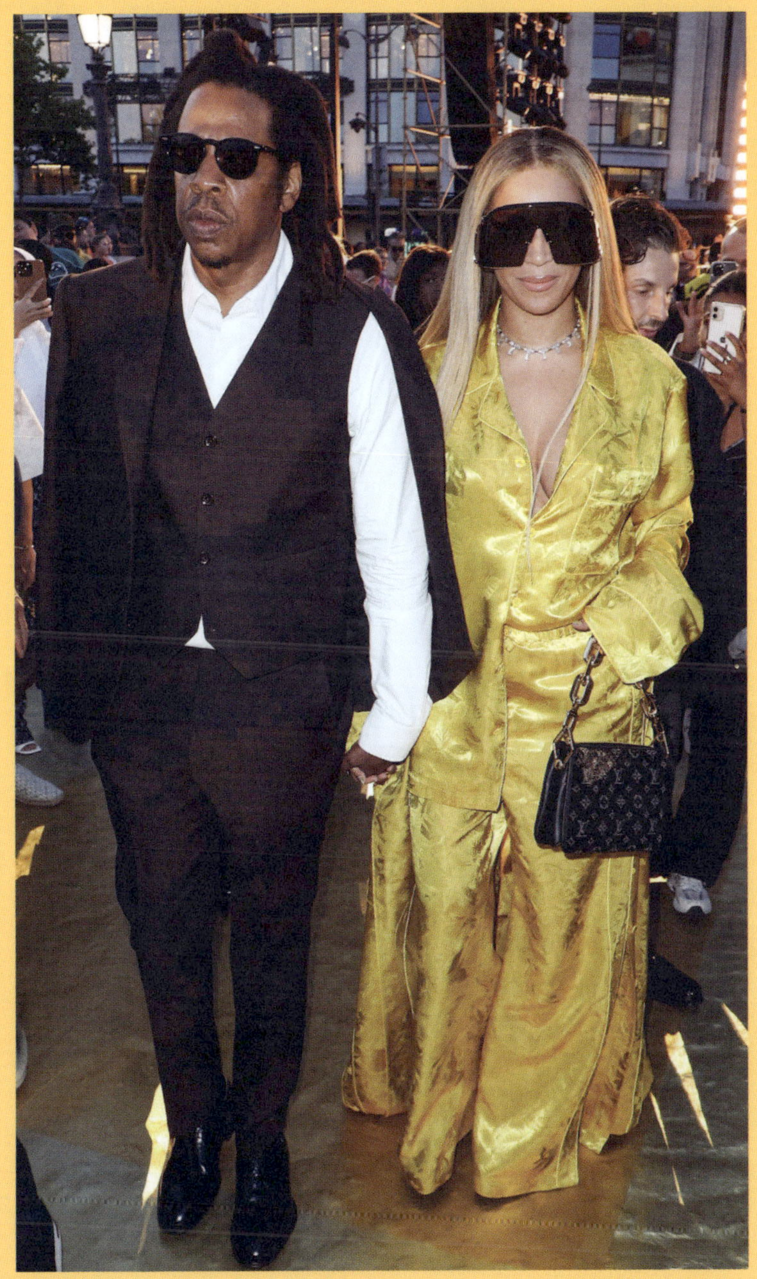

Beyoncé Inc.

With many of Destiny's Child's early outfits designed by Tina Knowles, it was perhaps only a matter of time before she brought her skills beyond the women in the band. The clothing line House of Deréon – a collaboration between mother and daughter, named after Beyoncé's grandmother and entrepreneur, Agnéz Deréon – was launched on *The Oprah Winfrey Show* in 2005, with a show at London Fashion Week following a few years later.

"After so many years my fans say 'we want to buy these clothes somewhere,'" Beyoncé told CNN, "so it was a natural thing for us to do this line."

If House of Deréon closed in the 2010s, those fans soon had other things to buy. Beyoncé has consistently followed in the footsteps of her grandmother and expanded her footprint beyond merely music and culture to fashion and style too.

A family business: Beyoncé and Tina Knowles launch House of Deréon at Selfridges in London in 2011.

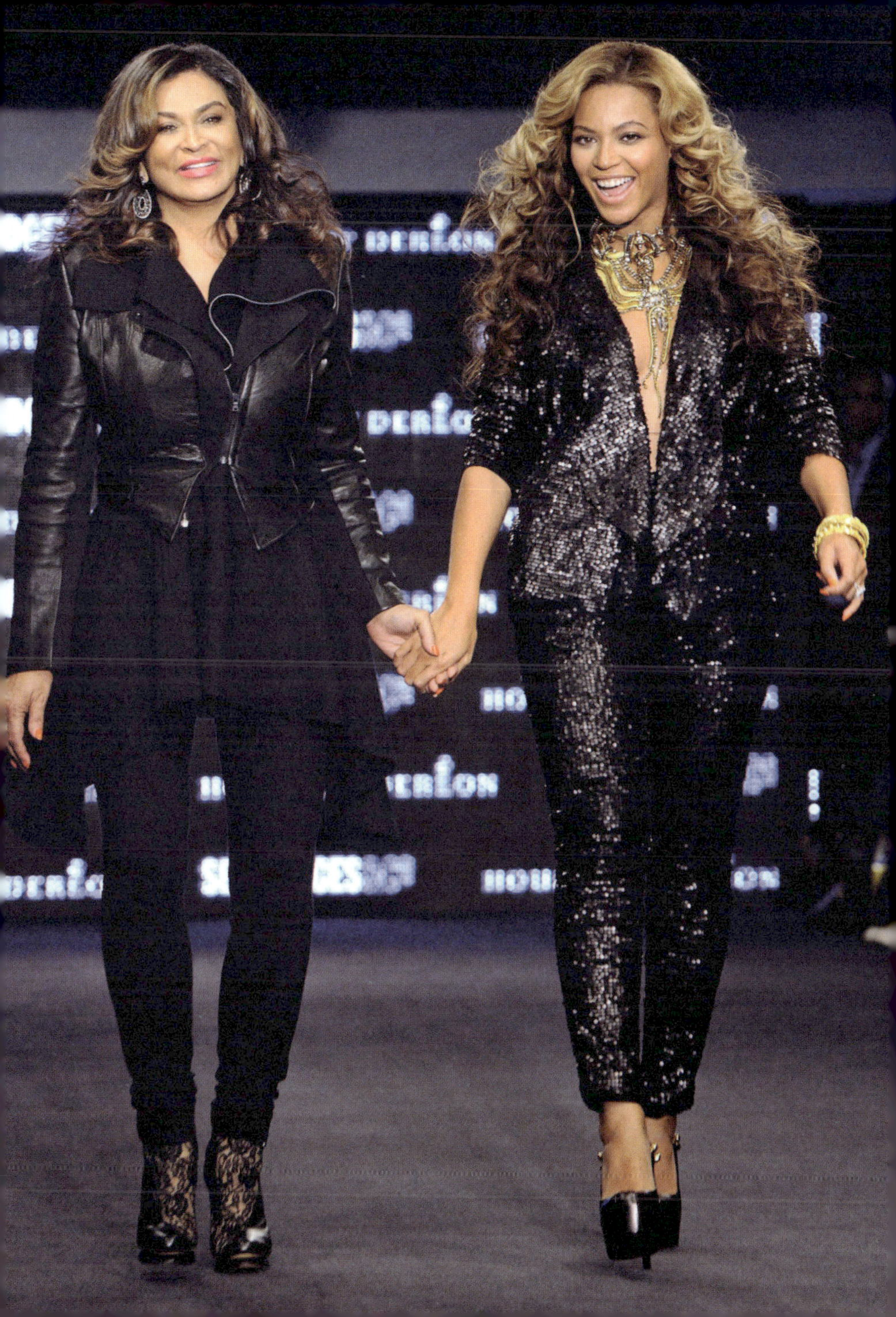

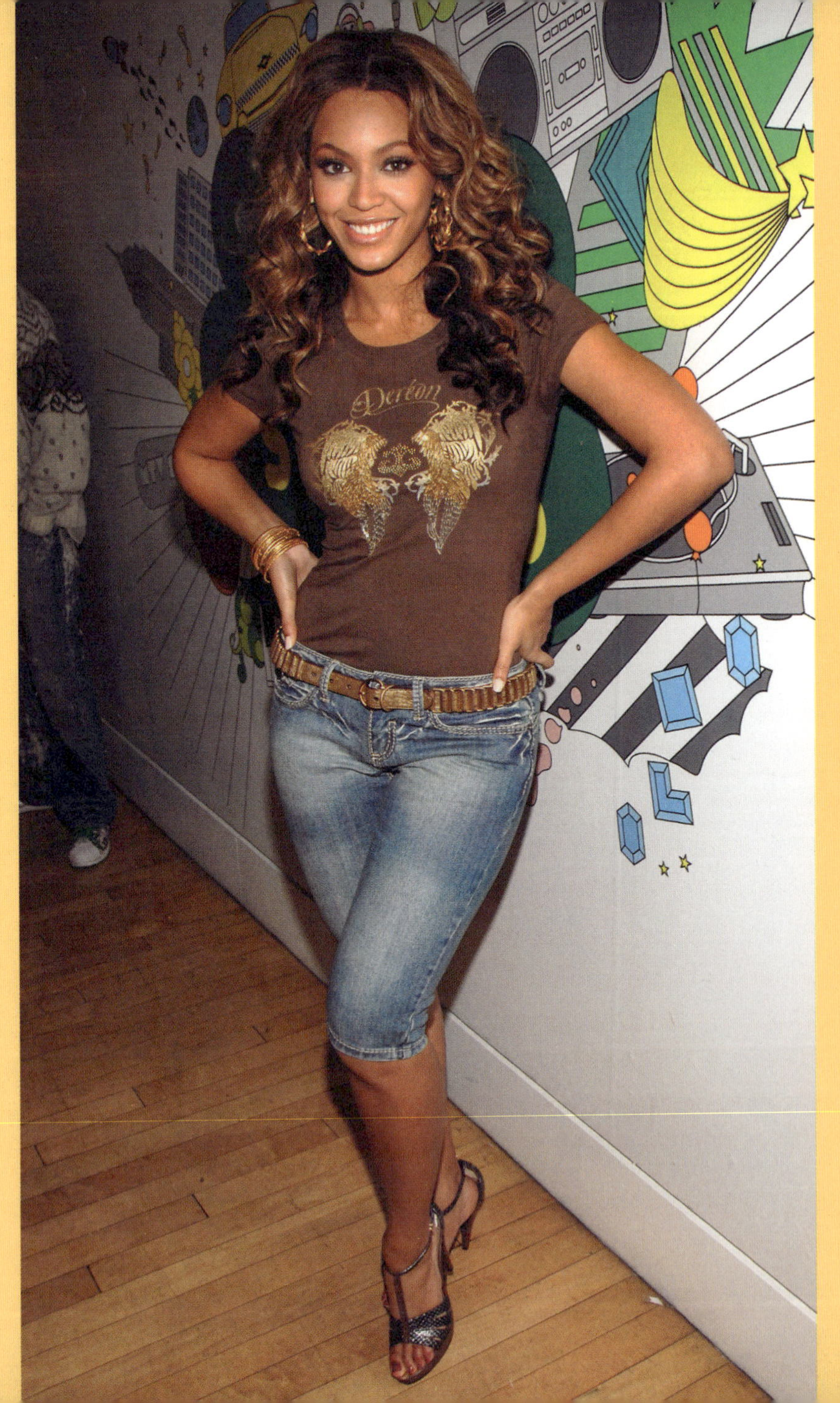

"After so many years my fans say 'we want to buy these clothes somewhere' so it was a natural thing for us to do this line."

BEYONCÉ ON HOUSE OF DERÉON

Face of the brand: Beyoncé wears House of Deréon to MTV TRL in 2006. It no doubt encouraged others to do the same.

In 2016, Beyoncé launched Ivy Park, an athleisure line. If
we now see this aesthetic as part of everyday style, the star
was a pioneer here, causing the *Guardian* to declare that the
label did something different – it "made sportswear sexy".
This sea change was no doubt boosted by the imagery, which
saw Beyoncé in an Ivy Park leotard on various types of gym
apparatus. Originally partnering with Topshop, collaboration
collections with Adidas produced in 2020 and 2021 swiftly
sold out.

Beyoncé turned to her family history in 2024 when she
launched Cécred (pronounced "sacred"), a haircare line. It
was once again in collaboration with her mother, a woman
who founded her own hair salon in Houston in the eighties.
Speaking to *Essence* about the product range, Beyoncé
described the thought process: "Cécred is a legacy project
for me, one that's probably the most rooted in my ancestry.
It's so far beyond business. Hair is our lineage; it's our family
story." Her family story was inspiration again later in the year,
when she launched SirDavis, a whisky named after her great
grandfather.

The Beyoncé empire continues to grow.

TOPSHOP
TOPMAN
5TH AVE & 49TH ST
5TH
AVE
TOPSHOP
TOPMAN
5TH AVE & 49TH ST

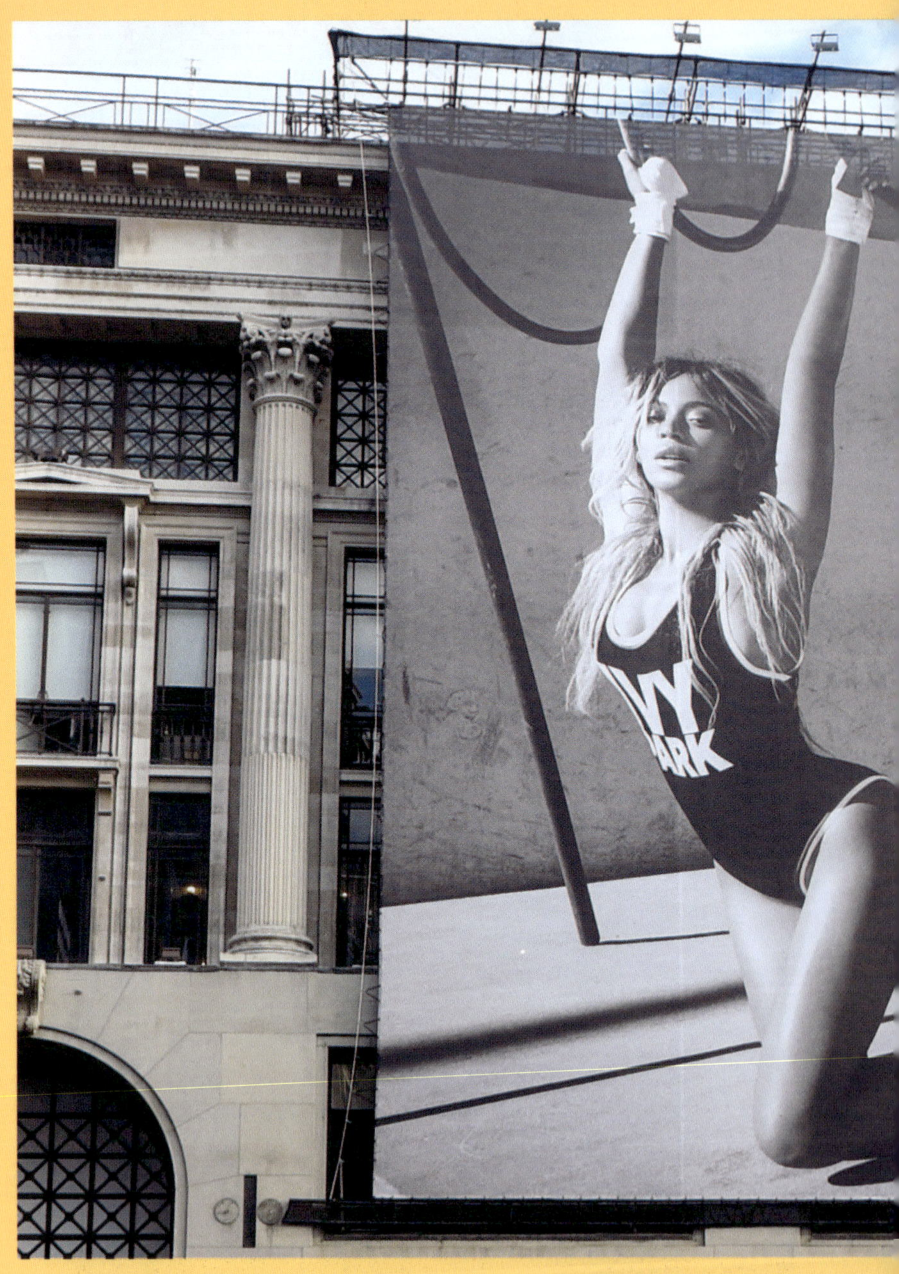
IVY
PARK

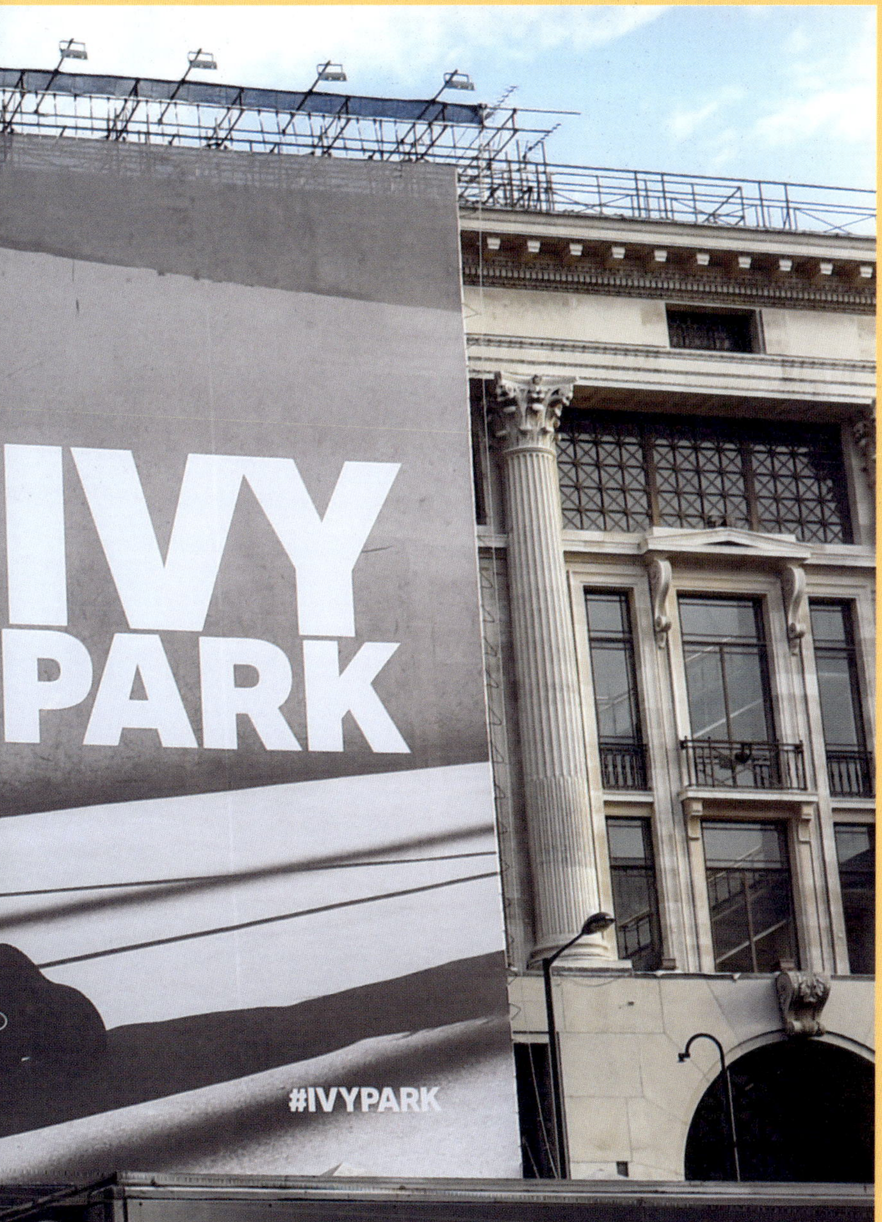
IVY
PARK
#IVYPARK

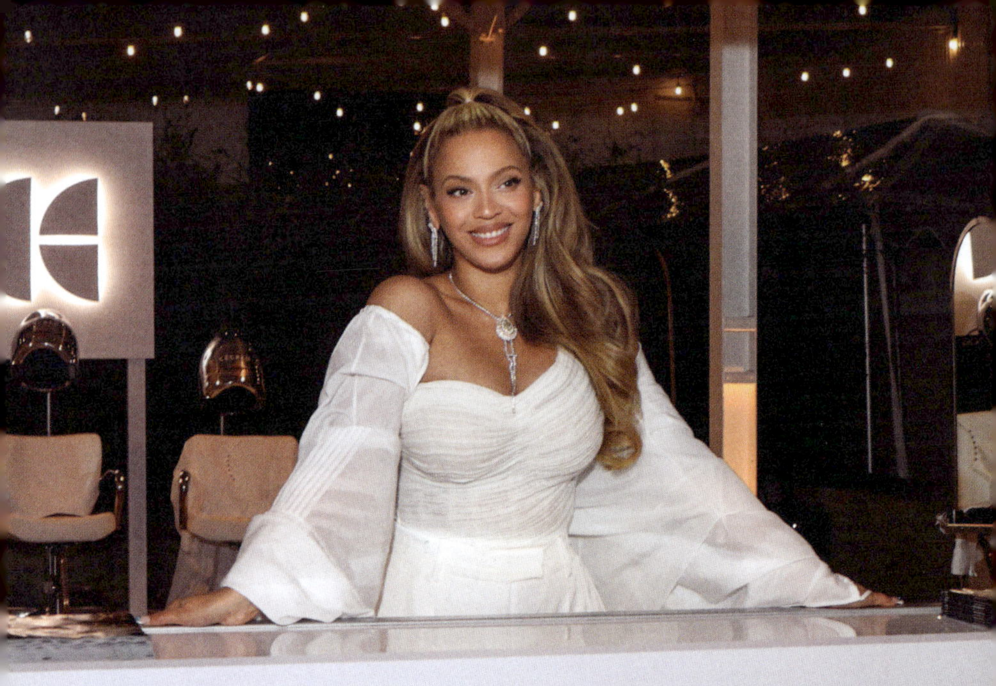
CÉCRED

> *"[Cécred is] so far beyond business. Hair is our lineage; it's our family story."*

BEYONCÉ

Hair do: the launch of haircare brand Cécred in 2024 – continuing the Knowles hair story, began in Tina's salon all those years ago.

Standing up, standing out

If pop stars and politics are not always the best of friends, Beyoncé has made her allegiances in American politics known in different ways throughout the years. Most recently, this was shown when she endorsed the Democratic nominee Kamala Harris on her presidential campaign in 2024, appearing at a Texas rally with Kelly Rowland in October. Harris was no doubt thrilled about this; a poll conducted by Newsweek in August 2024 found that 40 per cent of Gen Z would take notice of any Beyoncé-approved candidate. Sadly, however, even this megastar's magic wasn't enough for her to win the election.

In previous years, Beyoncé's involvement in politics has been explicitly signposted – often using fashion. She encouraged Texas voters to go to polling booths in 2020 – when Joe Biden was running for president – appearing on Instagram in a chic period-appropriate face mask.

OPPOSITE A model citizen: Beyoncé joins First Lady Michelle Obama's Let's Move! campaign in 2008, complete with slogan vest.

OVERLEAF Making the moment: Barack Obama's second inauguration in 2013 saw Beyoncé perform. She wore the sophisticated look – a Pucci dress and Dior coat – the occasion demanded.

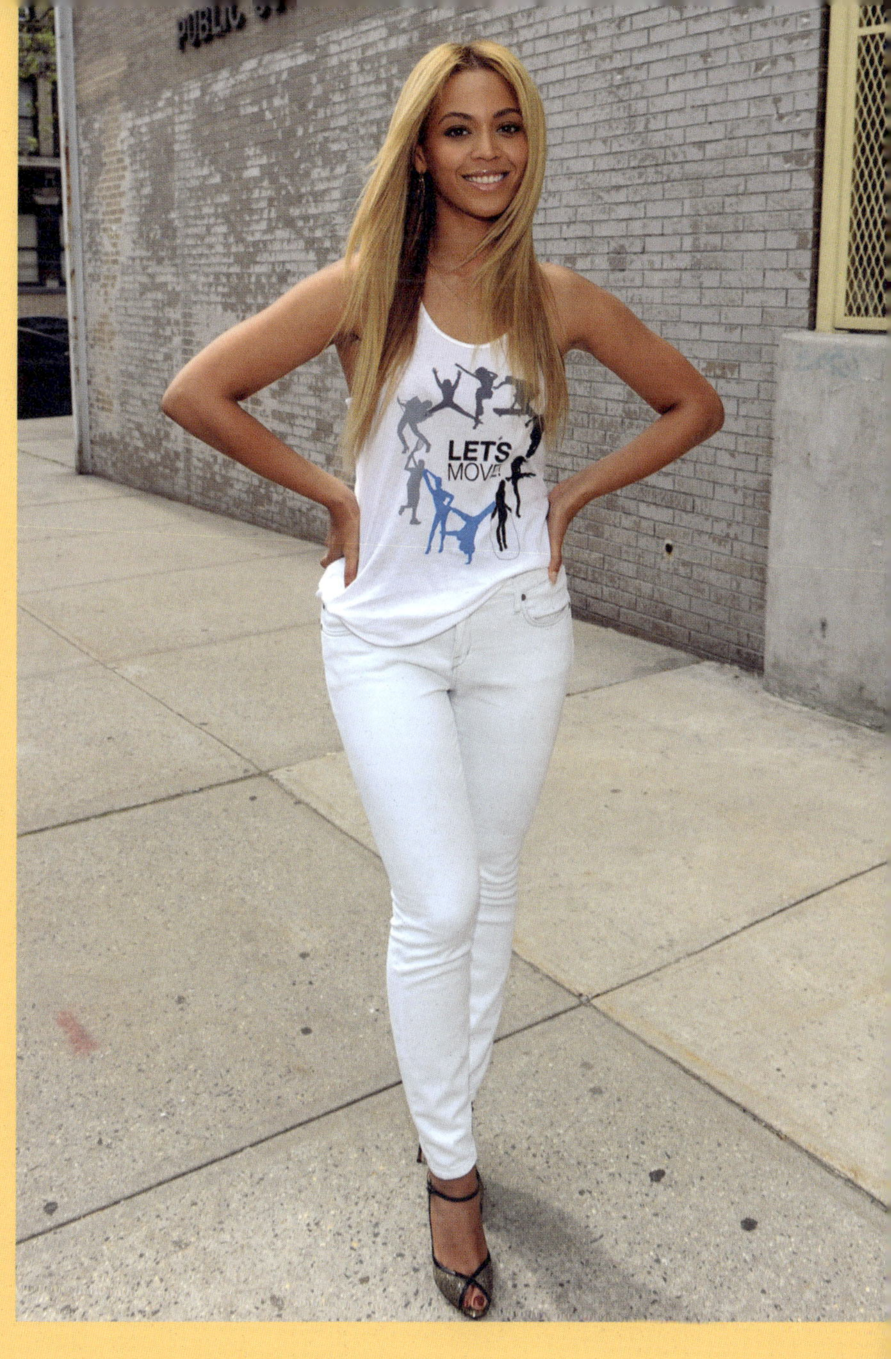
PUBLIC
LET'S
MOVE!

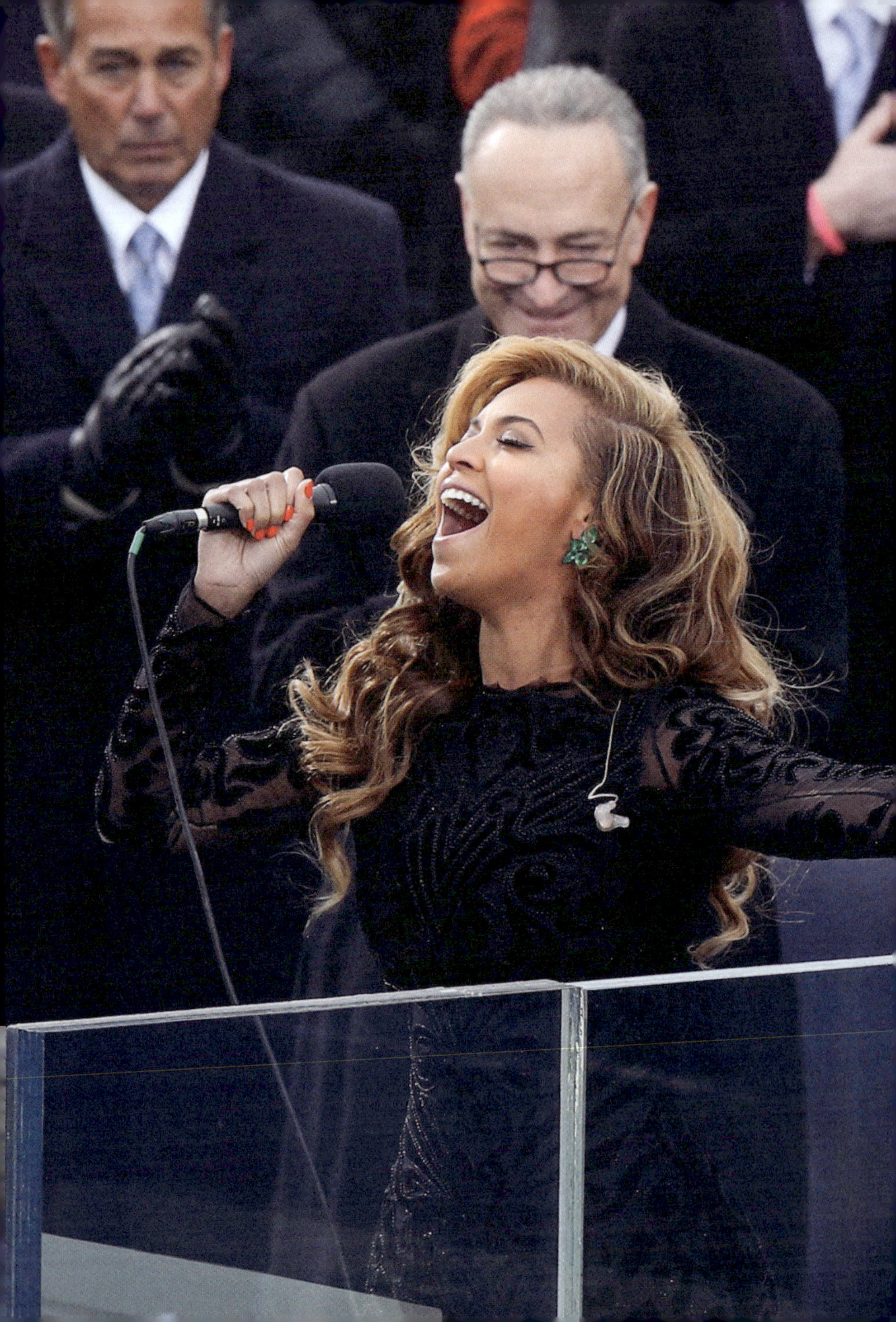

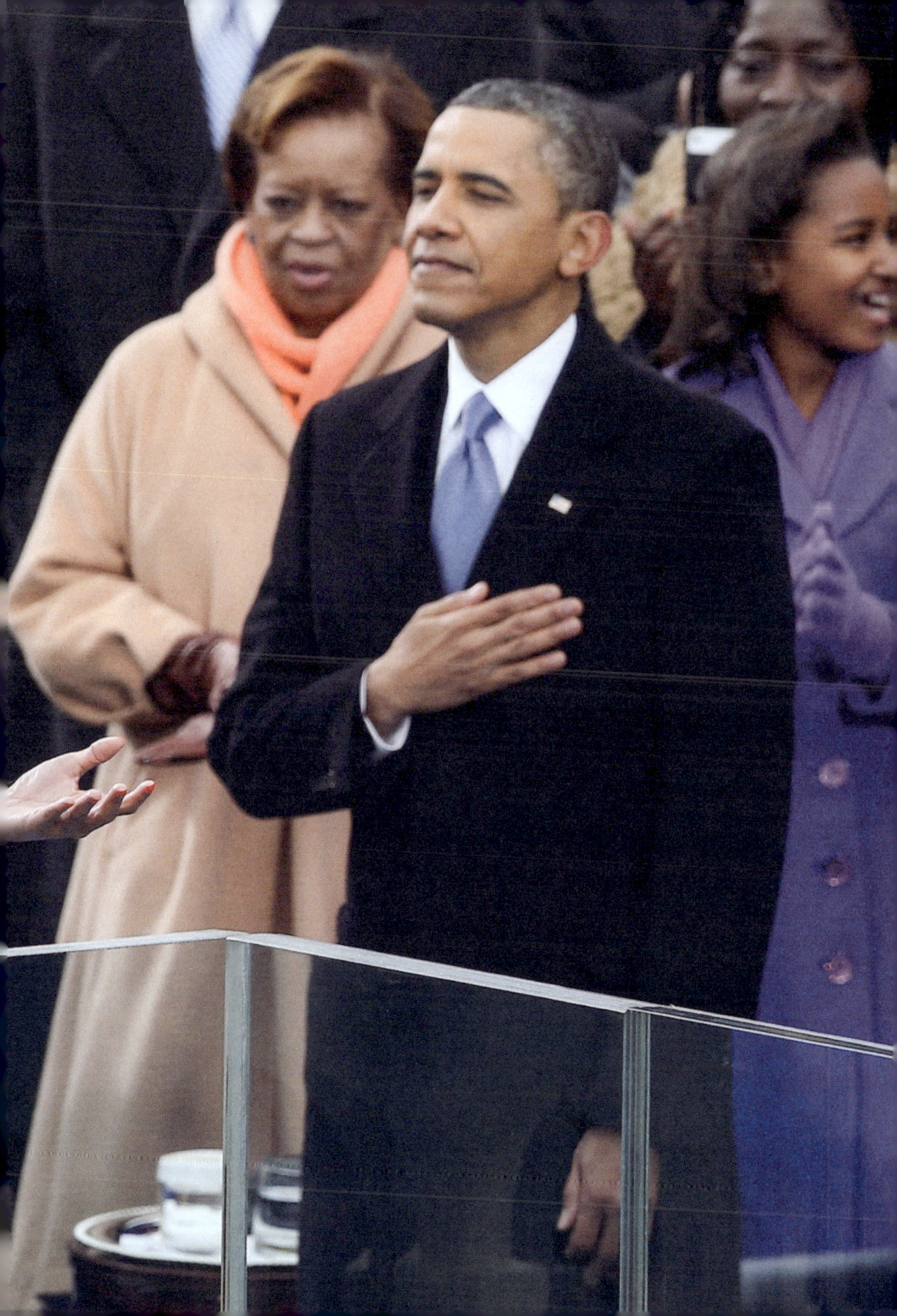

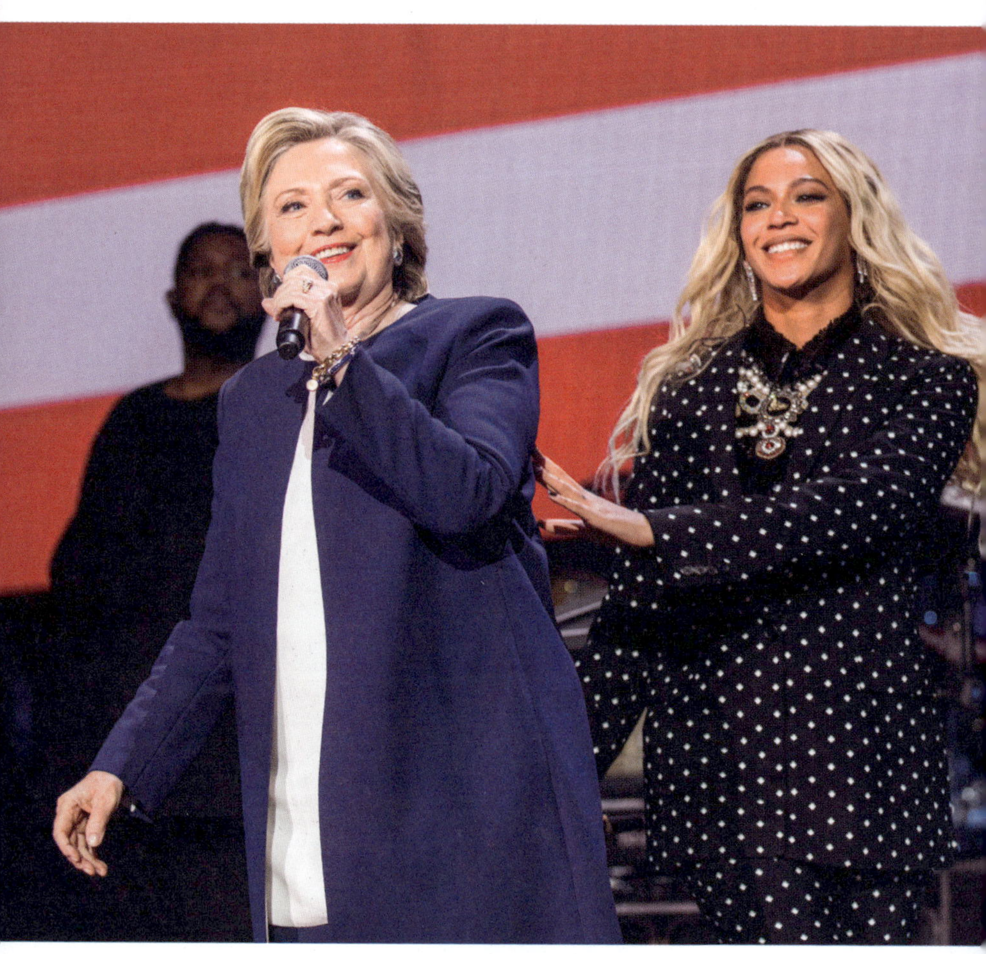

ABOVE Suits them: sartorial support for Hillary Clinton in 2016
came through suiting, the Democrat candidate's trademark look.

OVERLEAF An update on suiting for Harris in 2024: oversized
or trouserless, all interpretations are welcome.

Her support for the Obamas, in the White House from 2008 to 2016, has been the most tangible. She performed 'The Star-Spangled Banner' at the second inauguration in 2013, looking every inch the establishment star. While she later admitted to lip-synching, she told reporters including the BBC that she didn't want to take any risks: "It was […] a very, very important, emotional show for me and one of my proudest moments," she insisted.

Those proud moments continued. In 2016, Beyoncé performed at a rally endorsing Hillary Clinton for president. In a sweet nod to Clinton's own look, the singer and her dancers wore pant suits, the dancers pairing them with the "I'm With Her" T-shirts of Clinton's campaign. "I've gotta say, didn't you love the pantsuits?" commented the nominee. Love for the pantsuits continued for the Harris rally in 2024 - Rowland wore an oversized pinstripe suit while Beyonce went for the fashion choice: a smart blazer worn with tights only.

This doesn't just centre around America. In 2018, Beyoncé performed at the Global Citizen Festival in South Africa, an event paying tribute to Nelson Mandela's legacy. Across six different outfit changes, a bodysuit and cape designed by Mary Katrantzou stood out: it featured a map of the 54 countries of Africa, each with its unique style of embroidery represented. This was perhaps a precursor to what was to come: *Black Is King*, Beyoncé's take on *The Lion King* dedicated to African culture, arrived two years later.

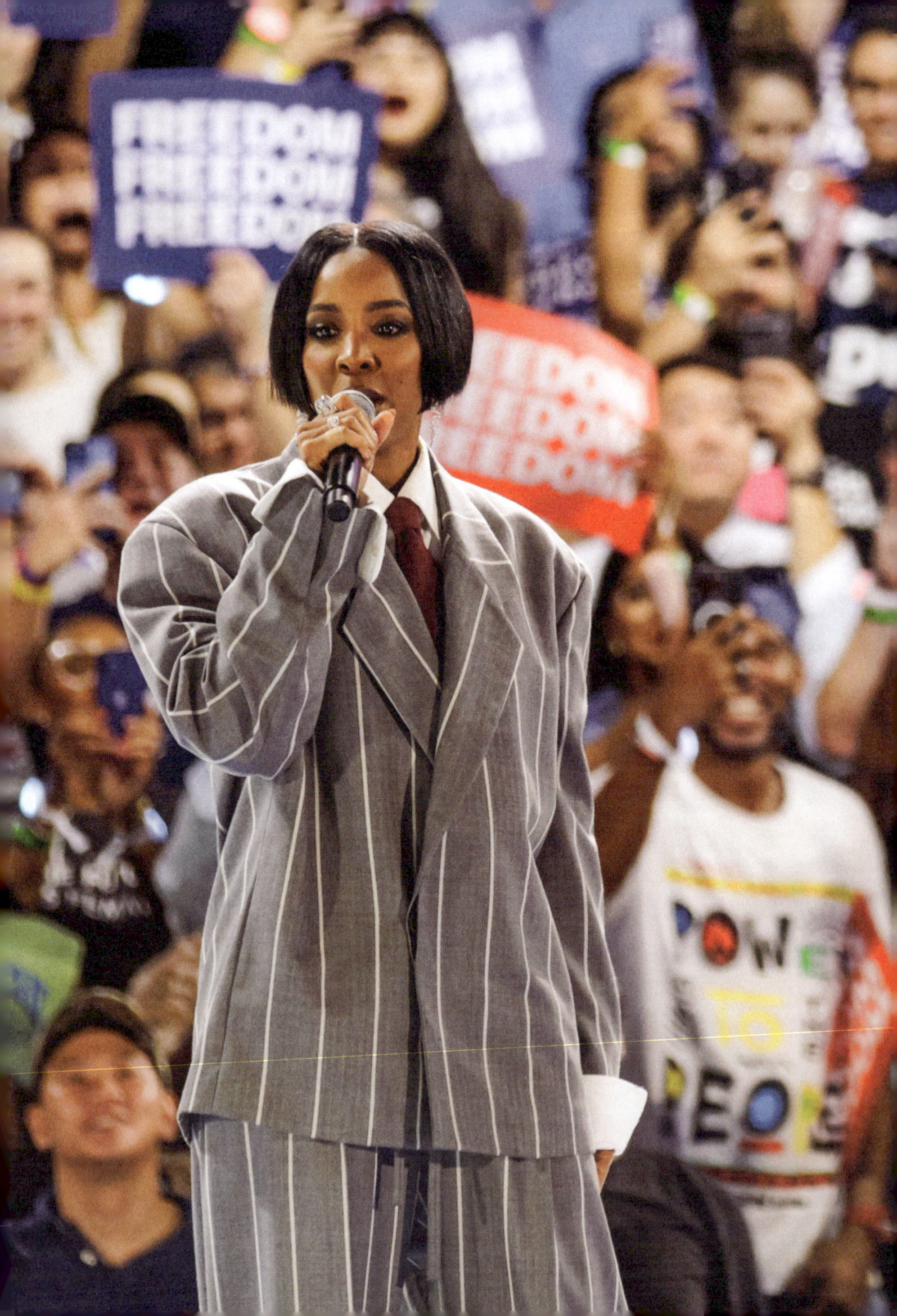
FREEDOM
FREEDOM
FREEDOM
POWER
TO THE
PEOPLE

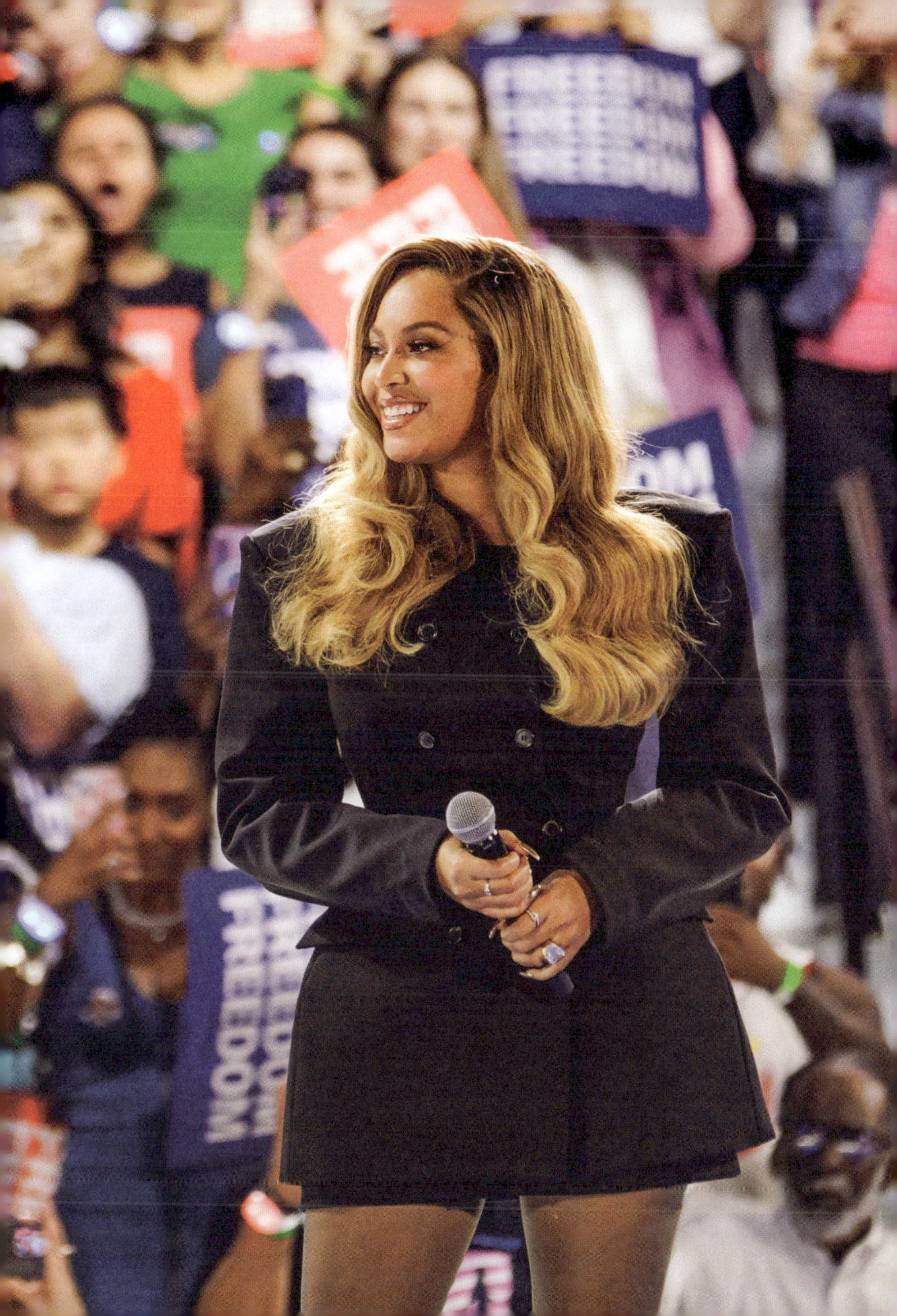

Completely unique

CHAPTER 3

Beyoncé's Looks

2006: A real dream girl

While on her Renaissance tour in 2023, Beyoncé celebrated her birthday in Los Angeles – with something of a surprise guest. Diana Ross, then 79, led the gig's audience in a rendition of 'Happy Birthday' for the 42-year-old. Beyoncé, ever the professional, was nevertheless somewhat emotional. "This is the legendary Diana Ross," she said. "Thank you so much for all of your sacrifice and your beauty and your grace, thank you for opening doors for me."

Ross, who first came to prominence in the sixties as part of one of the classic Motown groups, The Supremes, is indisputably a trailblazer when it comes to Black female megastardom. She was also, of course, an inspiration for a crucial moment in Beyoncé's career: playing the part of Deena Jones in the 2006 film, *Dreamgirls*. Telling the story of fictional girl group, The Dreams, it was partially based on the story of The Supremes and Ross's rise to fame in the sixties and seventies.

A star as a star: Beyoncé in full early sixties glam, playing Deena Jones in the 2006 film *Dreamgirls*.

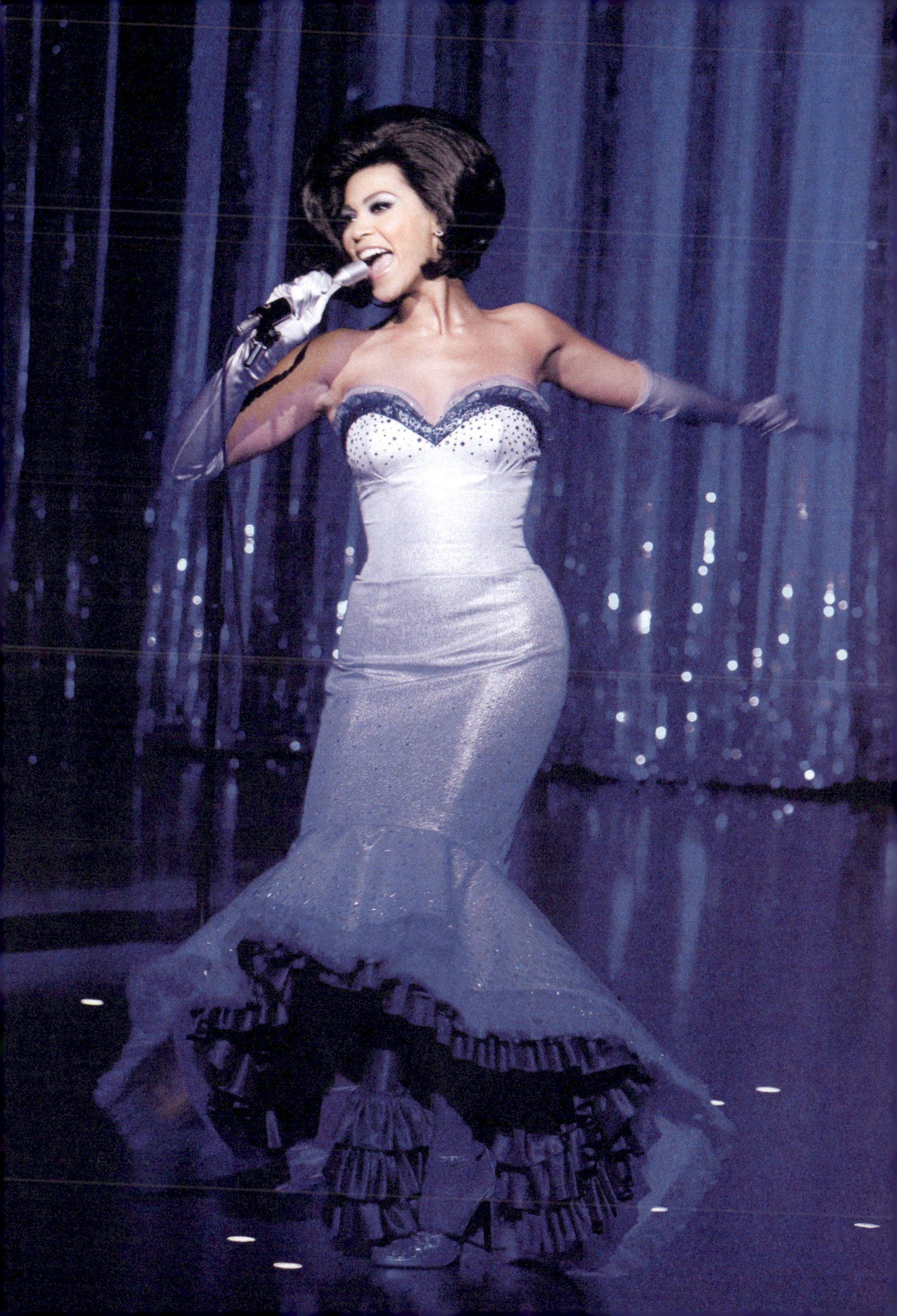

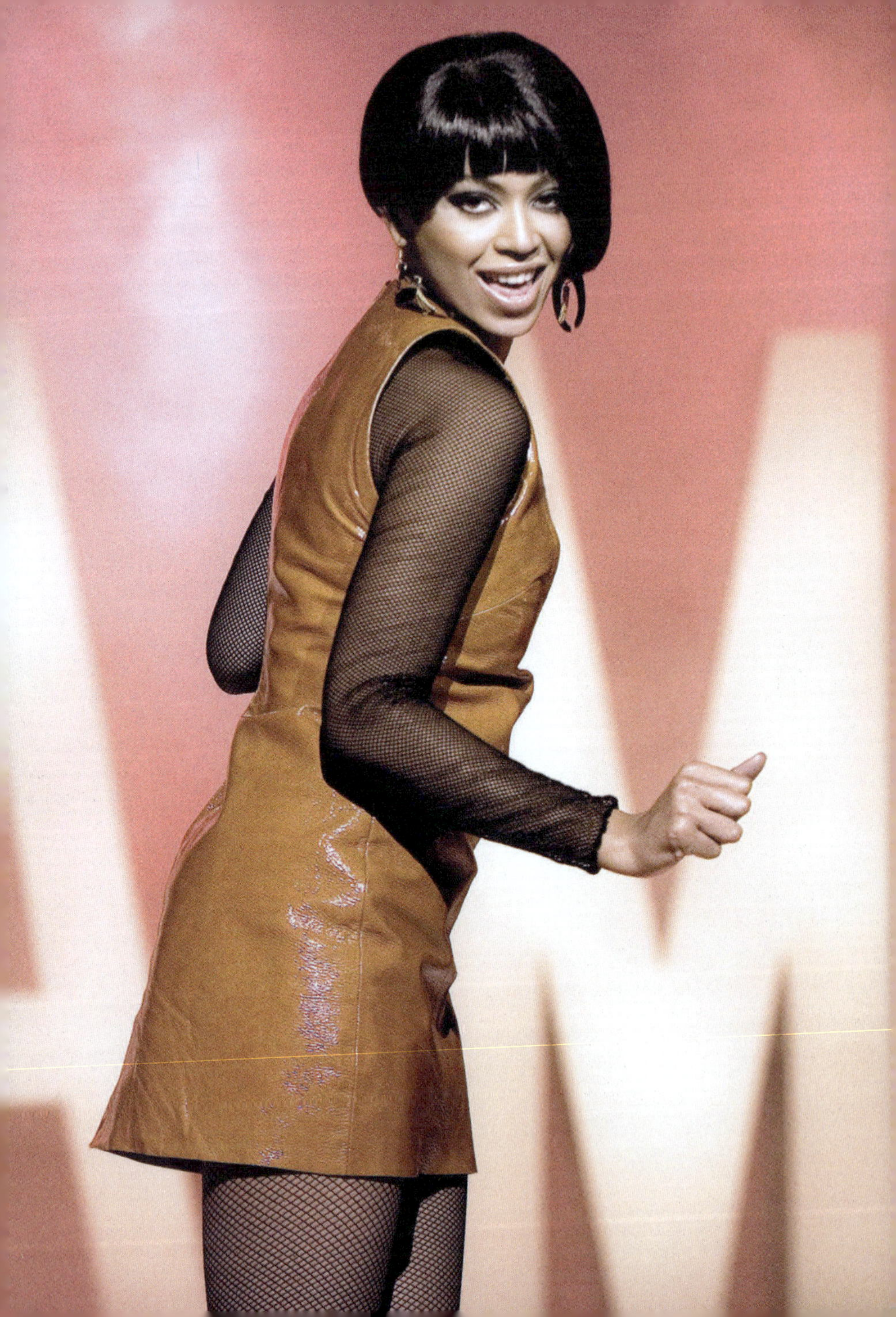

If *Goldmember* had shown that Beyoncé's star power could translate to the silver screen, *Dreamgirls* was a far more serious proposition, one that she was more than up to. As someone who shared the trajectory of moving from a much-loved group to solo star, Beyoncé no doubt brought some personal experience to the role. Interviewed on *Letterman*, she also said that she had a "shrine" to Diana Ross in her trailer.

With Destiny's Child's costumes inspired by groups like The Supremes, Beyoncé would have seen parallels in the costume changes here – from the coiffed and glamorous looks of the early sixties to the Mod-ish styles later in the decade, complete with eyelashes, miniskirt and Vidal Sassoon-worthy bob. Think of it as a sartorial tribute to a living legend.

A real pop look: a different perspective on the sixties for the same character – featuring a hairstyle that defines the era.

2008: The other Tina

When Tina Turner died in 2023, at the age of 83, Beyoncé paid tribute to her online, describing her as "the epitome of power and passion". These twin attributes inspired the star from early on.

Beyoncé has regularly performed Turner classics 'River Deep, Mountain High' and 'Proud Mary'. Before a performance of the latter in 2005, when Turner watched on, Beyoncé told her, "I'll never forget the first time I saw you perform. I never in my life saw a woman so powerful, so fearless, so fabulous… and those legs."

Turner's stage style was focused around minidresses to show off those legs. She wore them throughout her career, from working with then husband Ike in the sixties and seventies to the eighties, in her triumphant solo career. This look no doubt influenced Beyoncé as much as her music and energy. She regularly paired wild hair with short dresses and heels, much like Turner, throughout the noughties.

Mountain high: Tina Turner in full flow – complete with that hair and those legs – for a concert during the eighties.

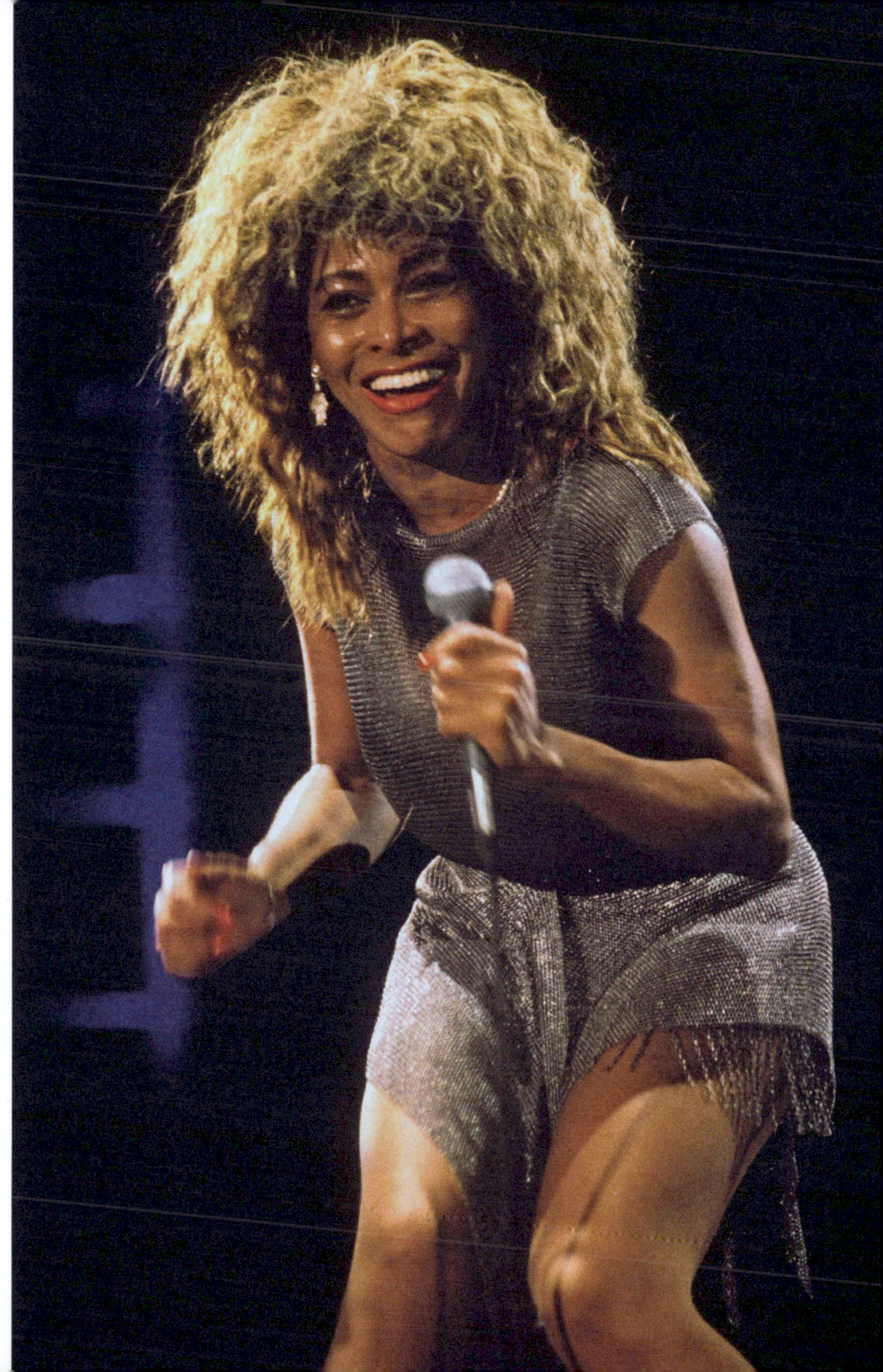

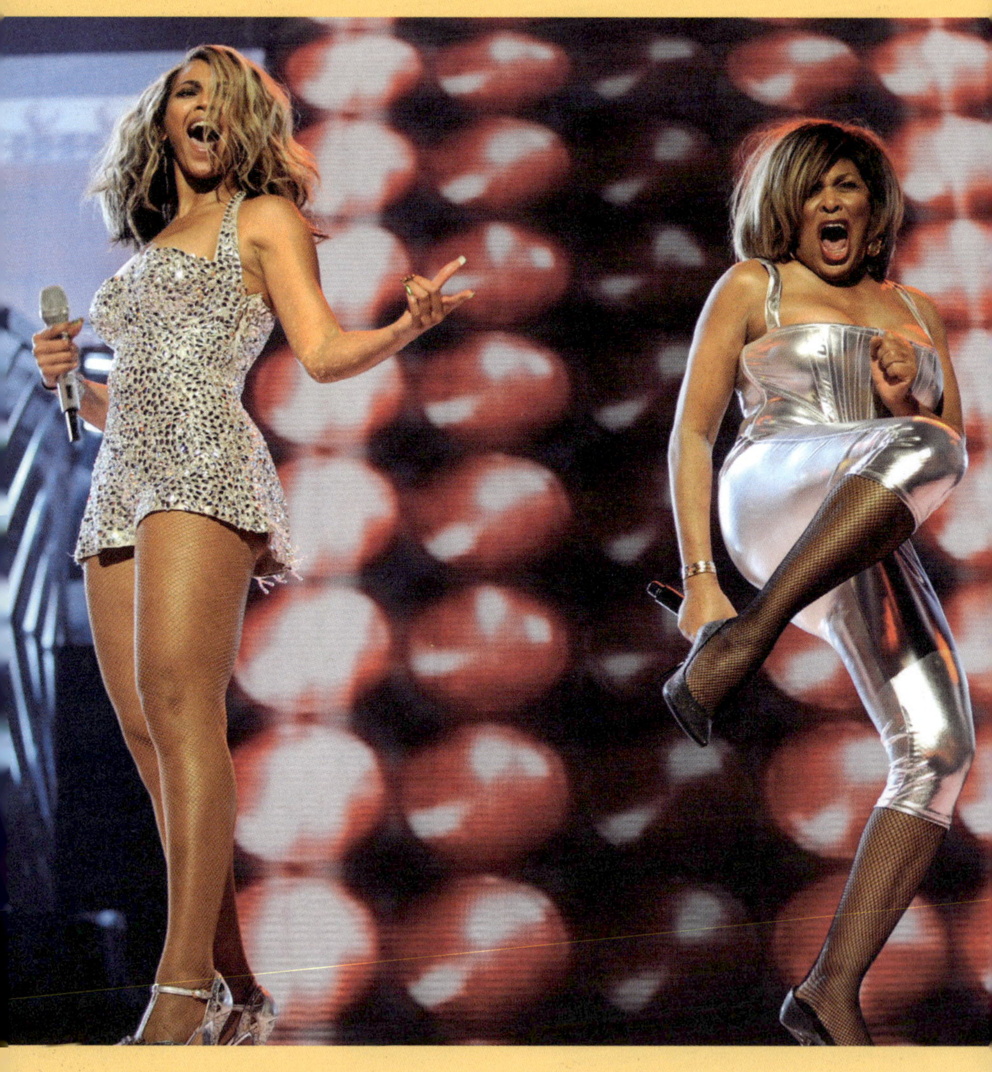

It was particularly touching when this combination was worn for a performance of 'Proud Mary' with Turner herself at the Grammys in 2008, with the two women wearing matching silver outfits. Beyoncé even had her hair waved in the way Turner wore hers in the eighties, and was able to bring a take on the singer's iconic dance moves.

A clip of backstage before this show circulated online after Turner's death, one which shows the excitement was palpable. Beyoncé skips over to meet Turner, elaborating, "When I was a kid and I saw her tapes, I wanted to be like her." As *Rolling Stone* reported in 2023, in their tribute to Turner, this showed the connection between the two stars: "In Beyoncé's pride and zeal, it was clear there *is* no Beyoncé without Tina Turner."

Hero worship: Beyoncé and Tina Turner sing classic 'Proud Mary' together, in matching silver, for the Grammys in 2008.

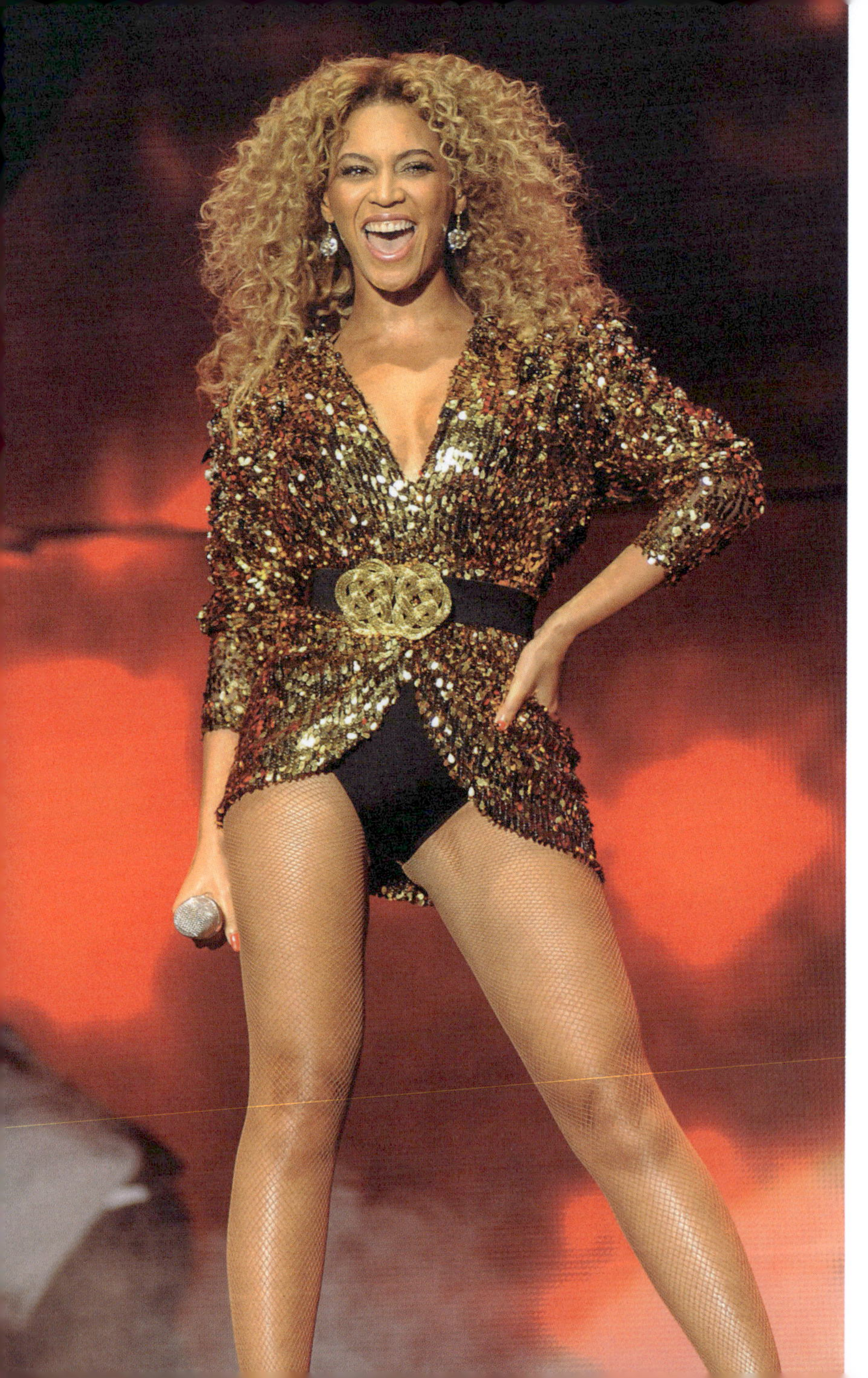

2011: Taking on Glastonbury

It's testament to the conservatism of rock music that when Jay-Z was announced as a headliner at Glastonbury in 2008, Noel Gallagher responded: "I'm not having hip hop at Glastonbury. It's wrong." Jay-Z famously responded by playing 'Wonderwall' by Oasis on stage.

Arguably, he also paved the way for his wife Beyoncé to take to the stage three years later in 2011, as the first solo Black woman to headline the Pyramid Stage. Despite more chatter on how she too didn't "belong" at the festival, she wowed in a set that began with 'Crazy in Love' and dropped hit after hit. In 2015, *Billboard* ranked it as one of the top-10 Glastonbury performances of all time.

Part of this was down to her look – a pair of tiny black shorts teamed with a gold sequin blazer from Alexandre Vauthier, airy blonde curls and an ear-to-ear smile. Unlike other shows, the star stuck to one look, perhaps partly because she was secretly pregnant with her first child, Blue Ivy.

Smile, you're headlining Glastonbury: Beyoncé making the much-loved Pyramid Stage her own, complete with iconic outfit, in 2011.

While the outfit is now categorically tied to the Glastonbury performance, it is a version of the bodysuit shape that Beyoncé has been wearing since the late noughties, with the advent of that famous alter ego: Sasha Fierce. Working with designer Thierry Mugler, who originally created bodysuits integral to his fashion shows in the nineties, Sasha wore his designs, sometimes covered in crystals, during the I Am... tour of 2009.

Only a year later, Ms Fierce was retired. "I don't need [her] anymore, because I've grown and now I'm able to merge the two," Beyoncé told *Allure* magazine. Glastonbury is perhaps hard evidence of this new Beyoncé era. This is a woman who performs at a jaw-dropping level, in an outfit of pure glamour, but realizes her own worth.

"I want to do something completely different," she explained to *Dazed*, ahead of the gig. "I feel like I've earned that right."

"I want to do something **completely** *different. I feel like I've* **earned** *that right."*

BEYONCÉ, ON HER
UPCOMING GLASTO
PERFORMANCE

2013: A superhero

From the moment Destiny's Child announced the breakup of the group in 2006, fans started to fantasize about a reunion. It finally came in 2013, with Beyoncé performing at the half-time show of the Super Bowl for the first time. Kelly Rowland and Michelle Williams arrived on stage with the star to run through a string of hits including 'Bootylicious' and 'Independent Women, Part 1'.

Part of the thrill was the outfits. In keeping with the established Destiny's Child approach to dressing, the reunited trio wore similar silhouettes – a series of short and black designs paired with over-the-knee black boots – that were just different enough. Beyoncé's was, of course, the most fabulous: a signature bodysuit with lace panels across the hips and a deep "V" running down to her navel. They weren't the only well-dressed women on stage: 120 backing dancers, dressed in a complementary way, featured for the 12 or so minutes that Beyoncé and her former bandmates performed.

Designed by lesser-known designer Rubin Singer, Beyoncé's
look – which began with a matching jacket with exaggerated
sleeves and peplum skirt, swiftly removed – was partially
inspired by Valkyries, female Norse warriors. This image of
female empowerment – always a theme for Beyoncé – was
fitting. It made sense that the set began with that now-classic
track, 'Run the World (Girls)'.

While there was some chatter before Beyoncé's performance
owing to the fact she had lip-synced for Barack Obama's
inauguration earlier in the year, this show silenced the
critics. It showed she was the complete package: a star who
looked great, sounded great, singing live and performing at
an interstellar level. The *New York Times* described her as "a
human pneumatic drill of intensity, constantly bouncing and
whirring" – in a really good way.

OVERLEAF Not all superheroes wear capes: Beyoncé in
a Rubin Singer bodysuit at the Super Bowl in 2013.

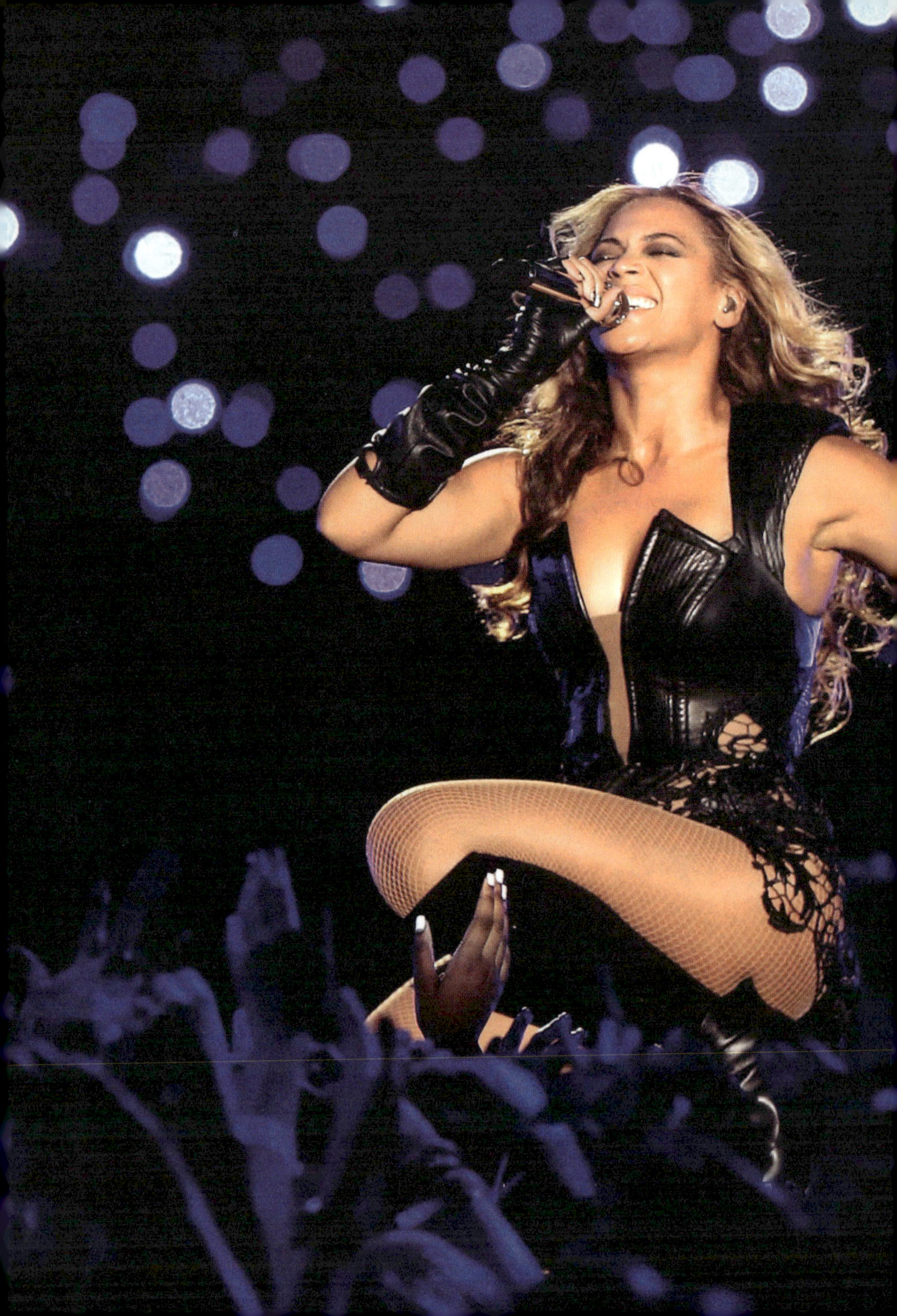

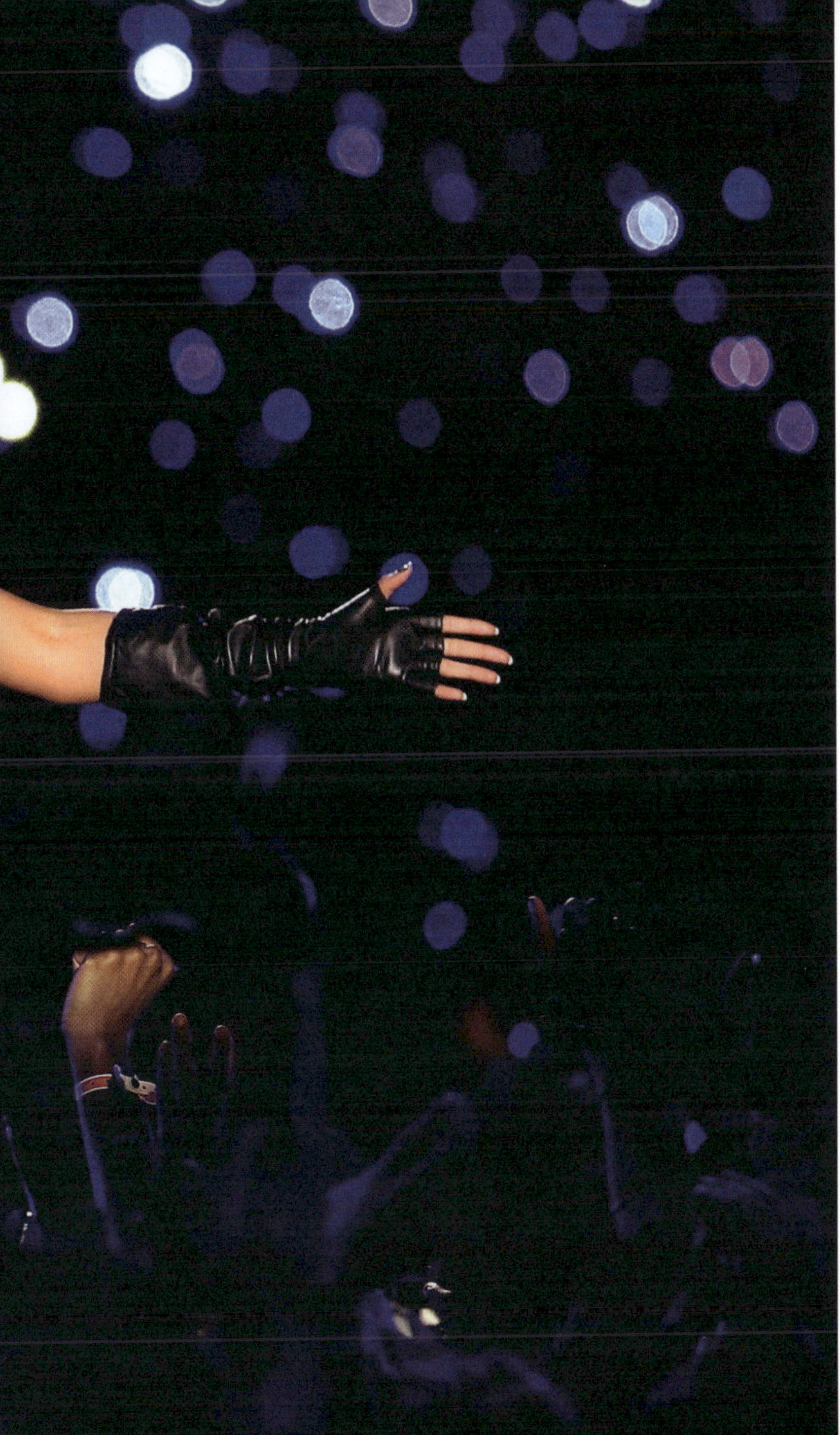

2014: A look with a story

By 2014, Beyoncé was a regular on the Met Gala red carpet and she wowed in Givenchy once again. Her stylist Ty Hunter described her outfit to *Billboard* as "[an] homage to Diana Ross, which is my favourite."

A few days after the event, said outfit became the centre of a different kind of news story when footage emerged of an argument between Jay-Z and Beyoncé's sister, Solange, in an elevator en route to an afterparty. Beyoncé is seen at the back, avoiding eye contact. Arguably the first proper scandal of Beyoncé's extremely well-executed career, the speculation online around the footage was at fever pitch. Beyoncé and Jay-Z even released a statement: "At the end of the day, families have problems, and we're no different," it read. "We love each other, and above all, we are family."

Beyoncé remained silent on the exact content of the argument but she may have used the interest in her personal life as inspiration for her seminal work. *Lemonade*, a visual album telling the story of a breakup and reconciliation as well as the Black female experience, arrived in 2016 and became the talking point of the year. Arguably, the move epitomized the much-quoted meaning of the title: Beyoncé was served lemons but she made *Lemonade*.

More than just a Met look: Beyoncé and Solange pictured on the night of the elevator incident.

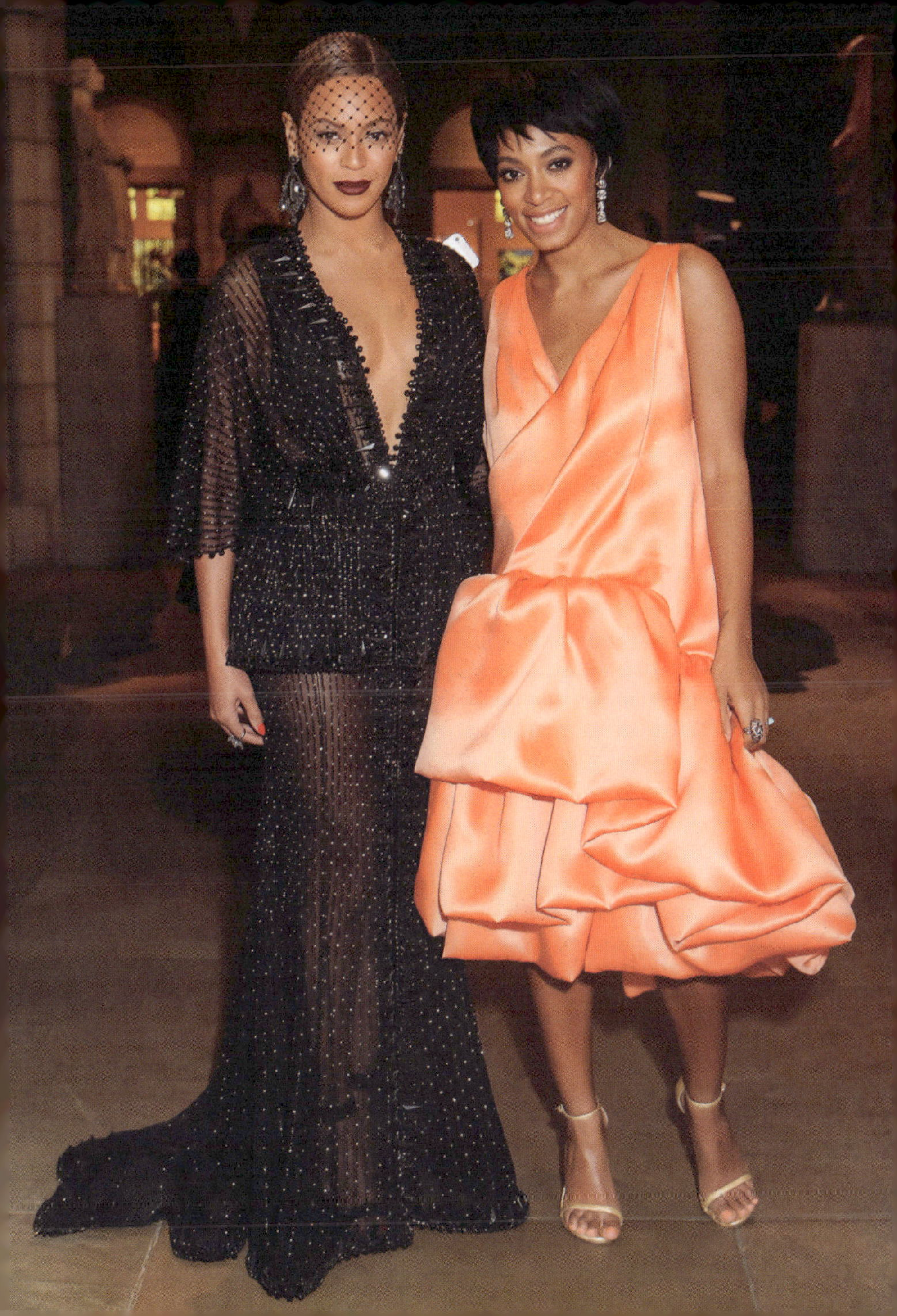

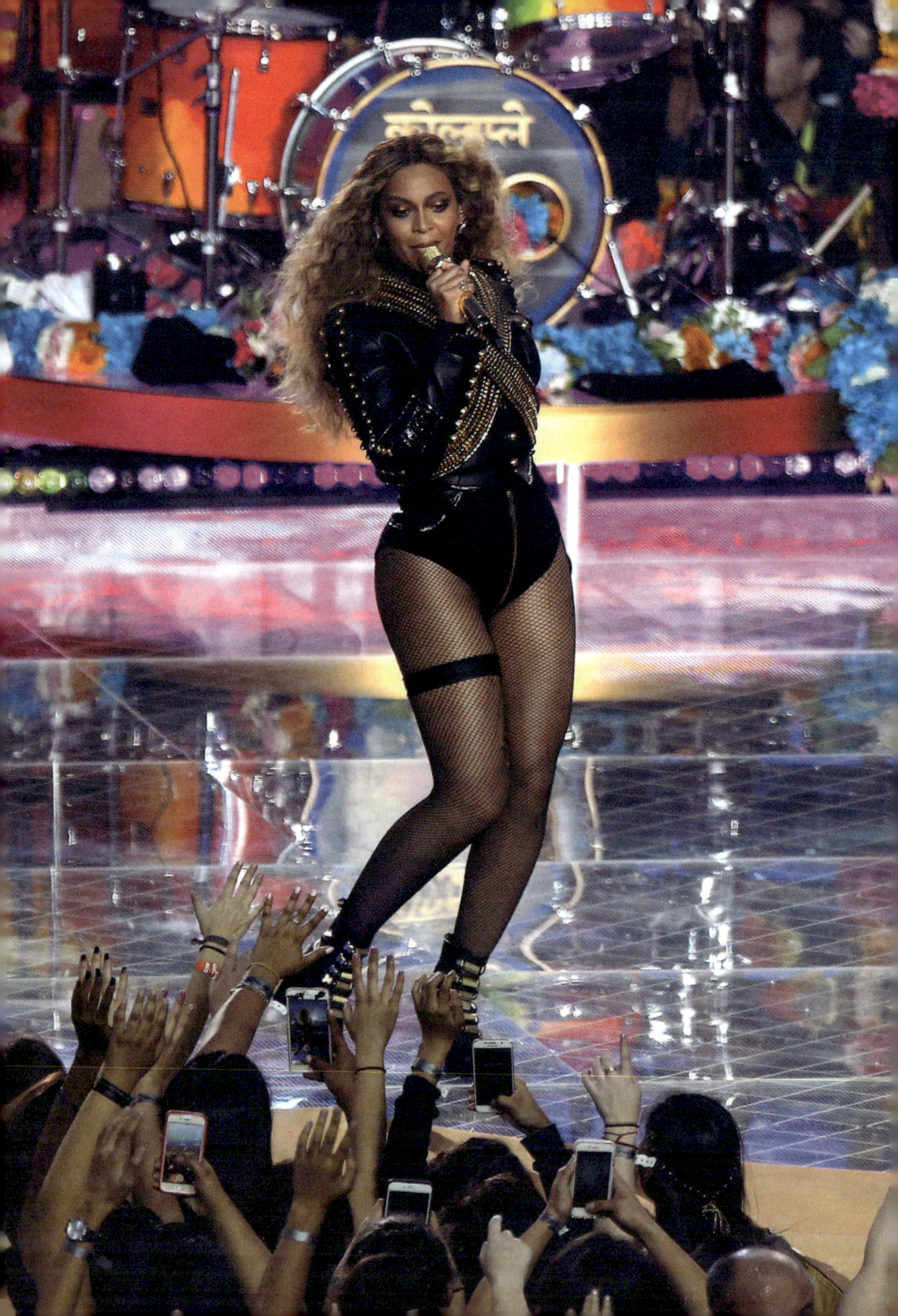

2016: A superhero sequel

The number of musicians who have performed at the Super Bowl is small, but the number who have done so more than once is even more select. Beyoncé is – of course – part of the latter group. Her second performance at the half-time show came in 2016.

If the first time out was about showing she was a performer up there with the best of them, this outing took things up a notch: it had a concept. In fact, this key performance could be seen as a clue to the content of *Lemonade*, which was released a few months later. An album that takes on racism and Black identity in the US as one of its themes, it is the most explicitly political work of Beyoncé's career. To breadcrumb that fact to her fans, she took to the stage in a military-style jacket. It paid tribute to one of her childhood heroes, Michael Jackson, and his half-time performance in 1992. This was when he was an undisputed icon of African-American excellence, one that a pre-teen Beyoncé no doubt watched with awe.

An outfit full of meaning: Beyoncé's second Super Bowl performance, in an outfit saluting Black history.

"It was important to [Beyoncé] to honour

the beauty of strong Black women."

STYLIST MARNI SENOFONTE, ON THE SUPER BOWL 2016 LOOK

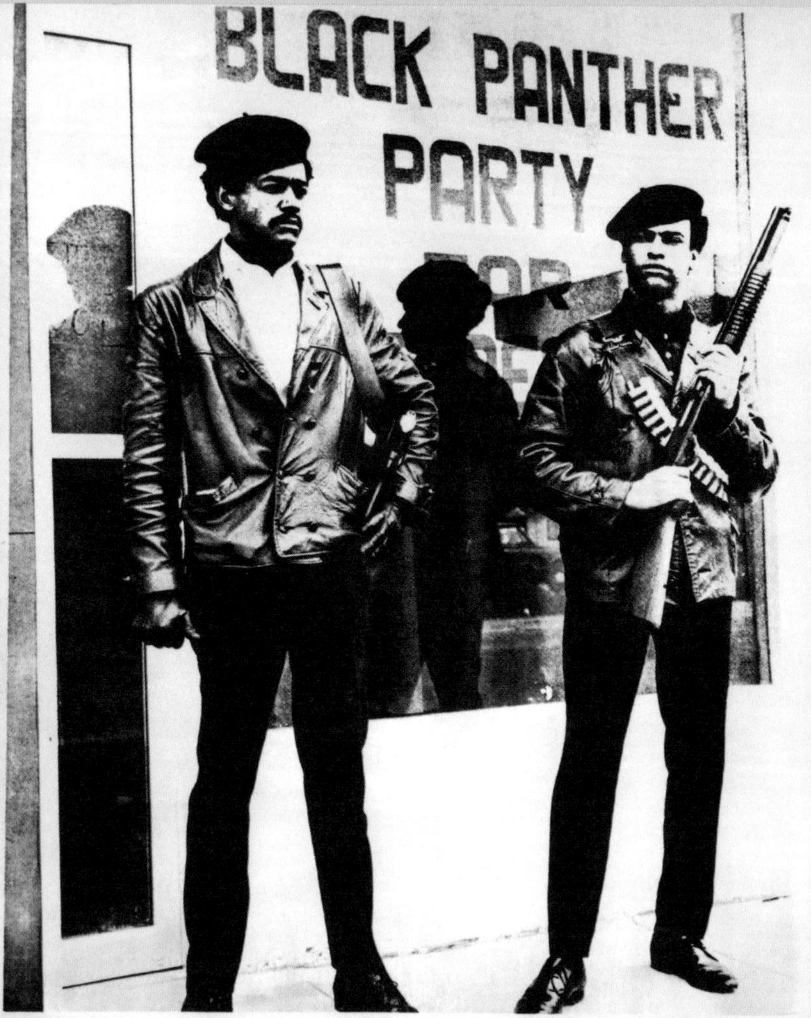

"THE RACIST DOG POLICEMEN MUST WITHDRAW IMMEDIATELY FROM OUR COMMUNITIES, CEASE THEIR WANTON MURDER AND BRUTALITY AND TORTURE OF BLACK PEOPLE, OR FACE THE WRATH OF THE ARMED PEOPLE."

HUEY P. NEWTON, Minister of Defense

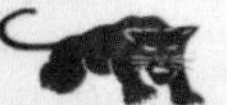

BLACK PANTHER PARTY
P.O. Box 8641, Emeryville, Calif.

Her dancers for the Super Bowl brought a different energy: they paid homage to the Black Panthers, the revolutionary anti-racist party from the sixties, who wore black berets and leather jackets. They looked great but this was not just a stylistic thing: Beyoncé was giving thanks to the women of the movement, including Angela Davis, Kathleen Cleaver and Afeni Shakur. Her stylist Marni Senofonte later explained what the symbolism meant to the star: "It was important to her to honour the beauty of strong Black women, and celebrate the unity that fuels their power. One of the best examples of that is the image of the female Black Panther."

If Beyoncé experienced some racist backlash for her direct referencing of the Black Power movement, the authenticity of the reference was praised by those within it. Activist William Johnson wrote: "As an original member of the Black Panther Party I thank Beyoncé for her courage to make a statement on national TV."

Black beret and leather jackets: the original Black Panther look, as seen on this poster from 1968.

2016: Brimming with style

In February 2016, Beyoncé released the video for 'Formation'. Covering everything from the aftermath of Hurricane Katrina to police violence against the Black community, it also features seven outfits in less than five minutes.

The hat that Beyoncé wore with the vintage black corseted gown became a signature – one that she wore beyond the video. Witness the moment when she accepted the CFDA Fashion Icon Award. Paired with a Givenchy suit featuring pinstripes of diamanté, she looked the worthy winner. She also wore it on the Formation tour, from July 2016. In fact, the announcement for the tour on Instagram featured the star walking into a stadium, sporting that unmistakable hat.

As with everything that Beyoncé wears, there's meaning behind it. The hat has been seen as a homage to Maman Brigitte, the death spirit found in Haitian Voodoo. It's also a nod to Mexican culture – stylist Marni Senofonte worked with a hat maker who created the designs from sombreros. Beyoncé donated her original hat to an auction raising money for lung transplants in 2017, where it sold for £27,000. The shape remains part of her style wheelhouse, however. For the Renaissance tour in 2023, it was there again, this time in silver.

The finishing touch: Beyoncé in her trademark wide-brimmed hat at the CFDA Awards in 2016.

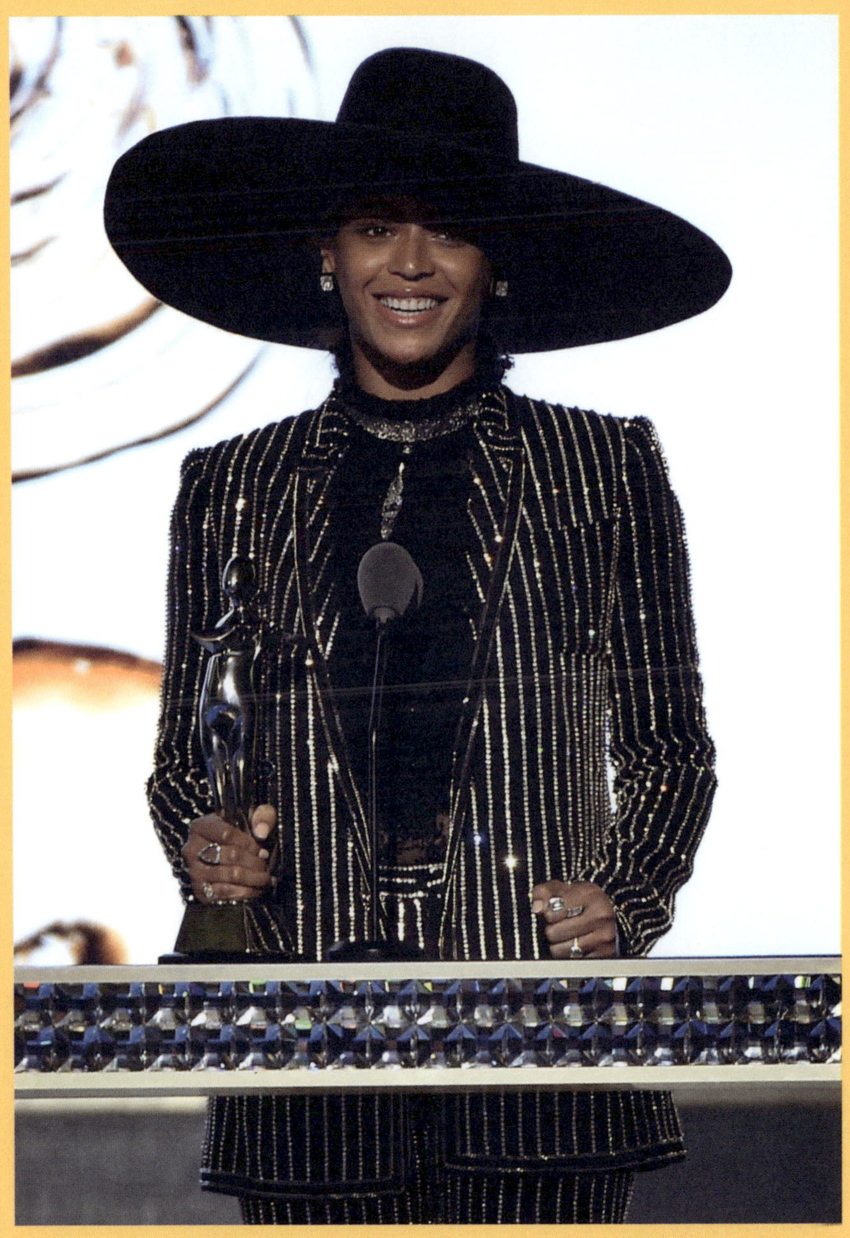

2017: An icon, in more ways than one

If, once upon a time, a pregnancy bump was something to conceal, it's now – rightly – a relatively normal sight. Beyoncé is part of that change. Her second pregnancy, with twins Rumi and Sir in 2017, coincided with a new era, post-*Lemonade*, where concepts fuelled her creative output.

See the outfit she wore to perform while several months pregnant at the Grammys. Created by former Pucci designer Peter Dundas, it turned Beyoncé into a modern-day fertility goddess – one that some critics say channelled the Christian Madonna, the Yoruba Oshun and the Hindu Durga all in one.

If that sounds like something of an ego trip from one of the biggest stars on the planet, it could also be interpreted as creating an image that celebrates motherhood and pregnancy for all women. Speaking to *Vogue*, she said that she changed after the birth of Blue Ivy in 2012: "From that point on, I truly understood my power, and motherhood has been my biggest inspiration." While most bumps are not decorated in hand-sewn sequins, women might now be more able to feel they can be celebrated nonetheless.

Stay golden: Beyoncé brings fertility goddess chic to the Grammys, in her Peter Dundas sequinned gown.

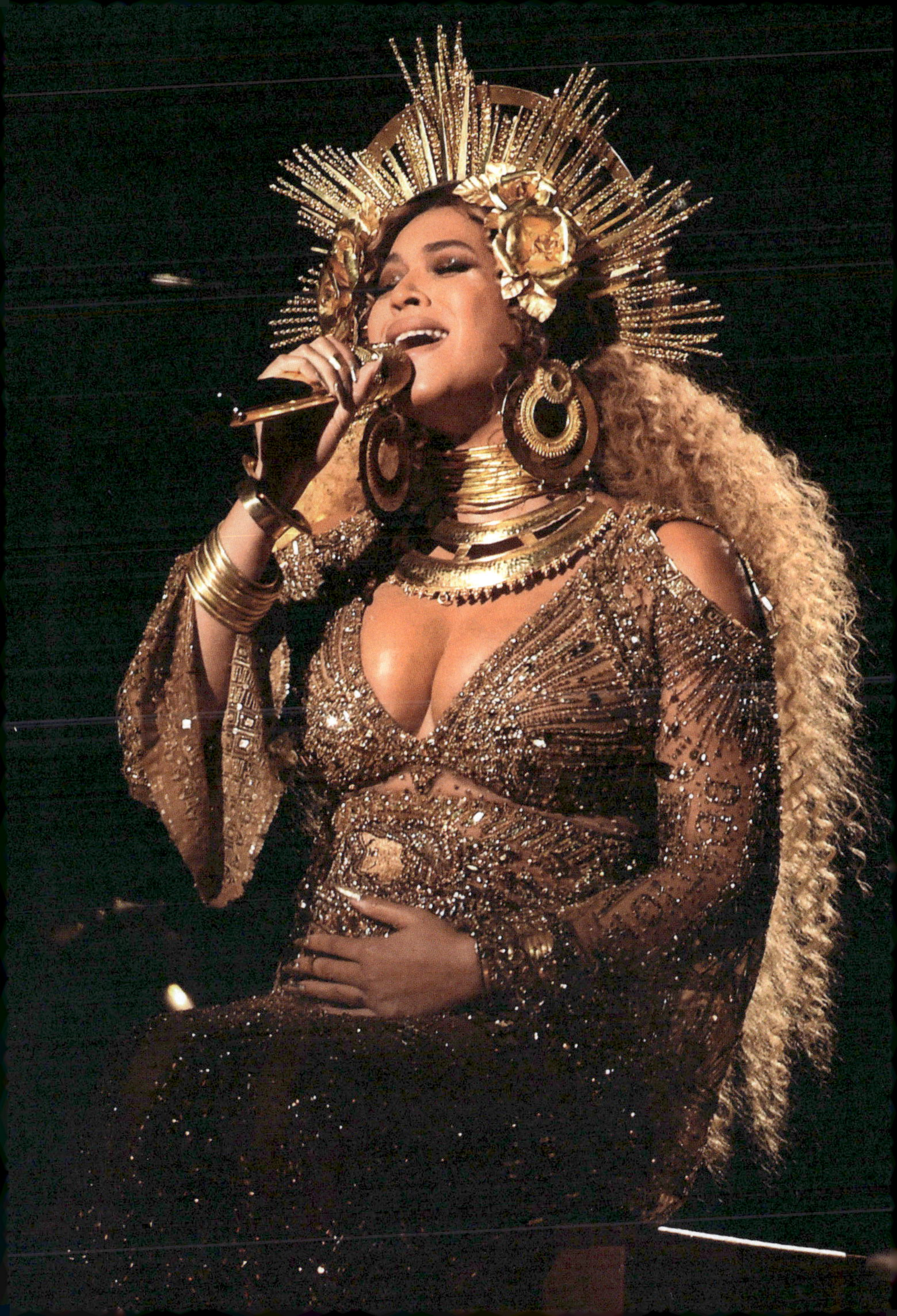

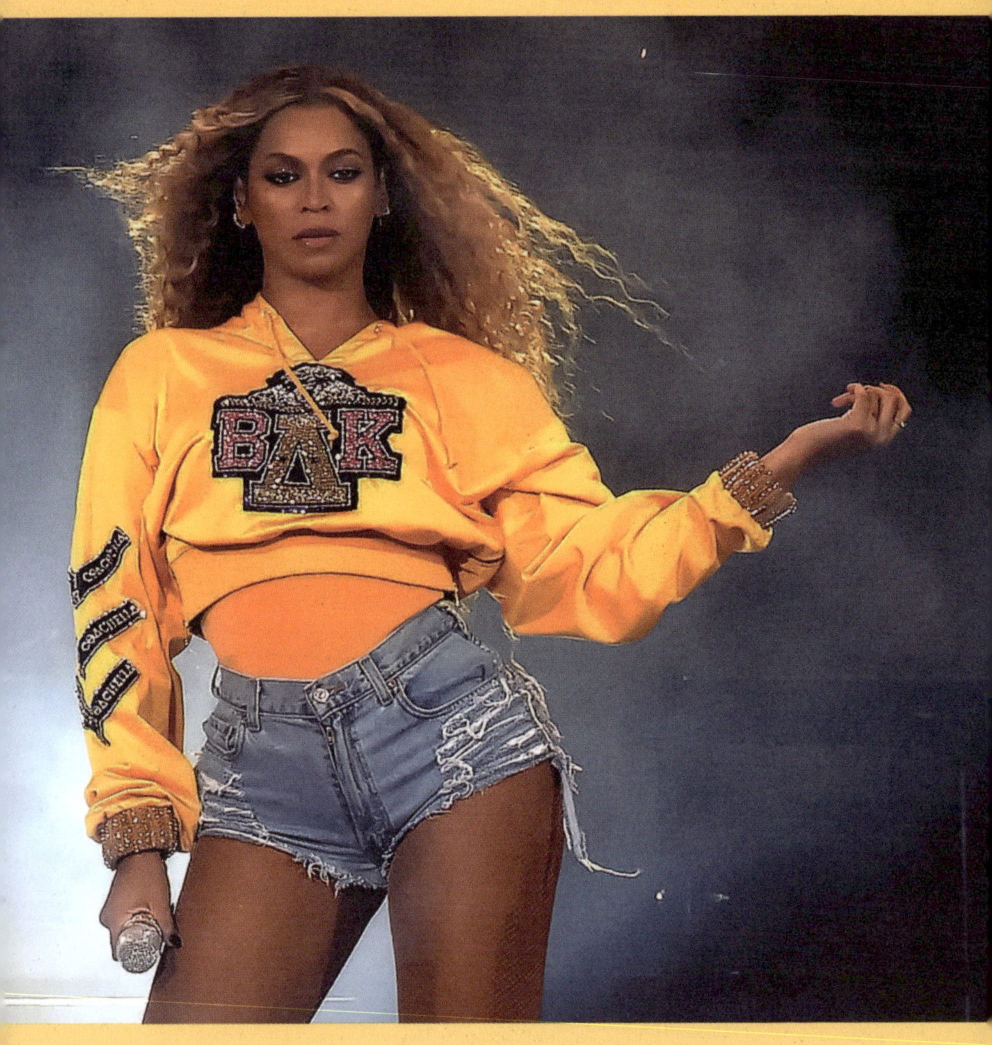
BAK
COACHELLA
COACHELLA
COACHELLA

2018: Coachella becomes Beychella

Fans had to wait a long time for Beyoncé to headline the Coachella music festival, and become the first African-American woman to do so. Originally scheduled to play in 2017, she fell pregnant with her twins. However, anyone who watched her – whether live, on TV or later in 2019's *Homecoming: A Film by Beyoncé*, the documentary that tells the story of the show – would testify that it was worth the year-long wait. So much so that the gig, taking place over two weekends in April 2018, was immediately rechristened "Beychella".

Beyoncé – as you might imagine – had made full use of her maternity leave to make a plan. "I had time to dream and dream and dream with two beautiful souls in my belly," she told the crowd at Beychella, "and I dreamed up this performance."

A hoodie and shorts as you have never seen them before: Beyoncé's now infamous ensemble helped make Beychella.

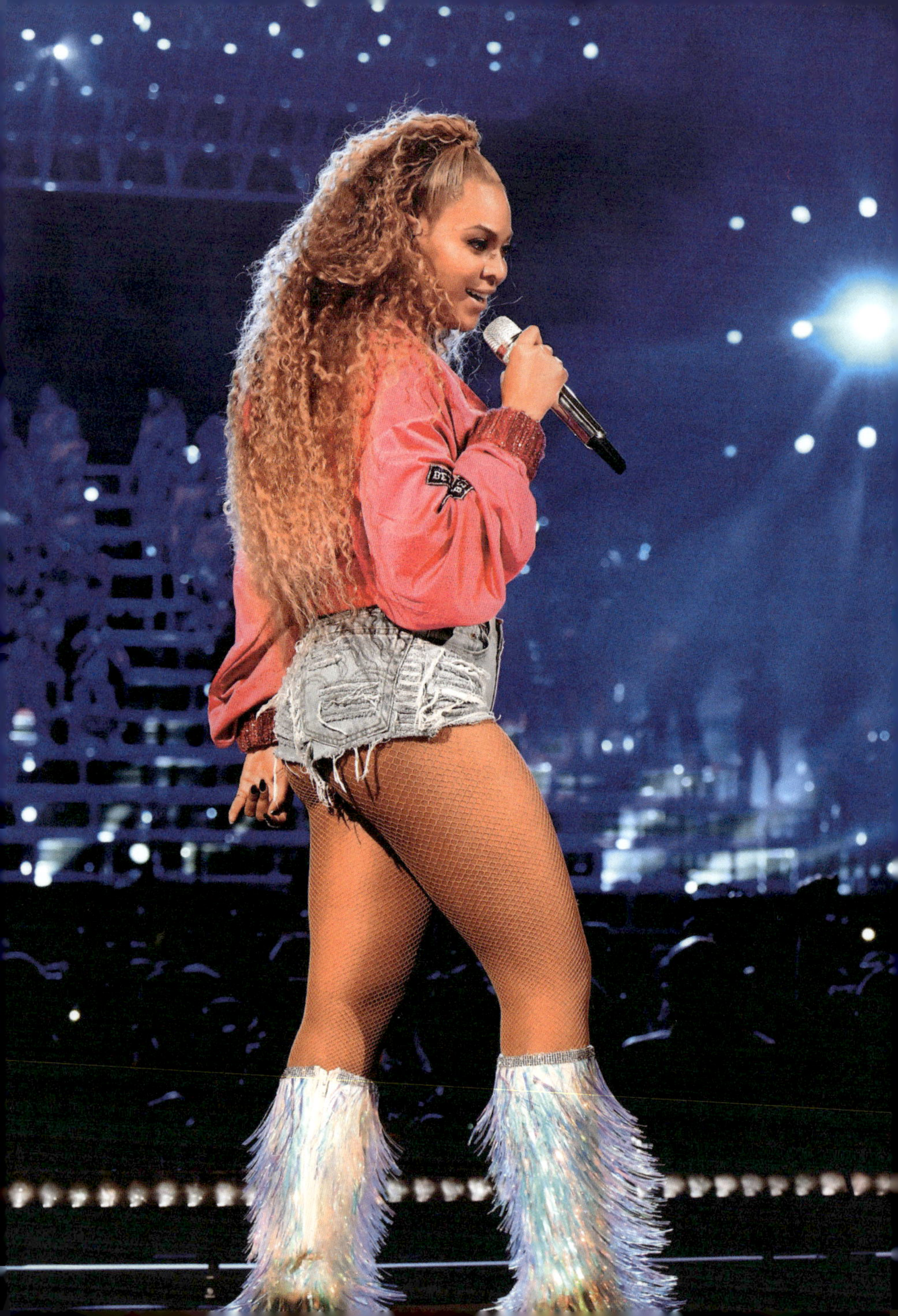

The dream centred, in large part, around going back to
school – to a HBCU, to be exact. Historically Black Colleges
and Universities have been seminal institutions for African-
American higher education since the nineteenth century.
Beyoncé paid tribute to their work by referencing elements
that were part of their college campus culture – see the
marching band and the majorette dancers.

Then there were the costumes. Created by Balmain's Olivier
Rousteing, they ranged from headdresses and capes to PVC
and mesh T-shirts. But it is the collegiate-like sweatshirts and
denim hotpants that have become iconic. Fans speculated
that Beyoncé was paying tribute to the first Black sorority,
Alpha Phi Alpha, with the yellow and black colour scheme.
But she also made her own: the sweatshirts read Beta Delta
Kappa – which one fan interpreted as "B for Beyoncé, Delta as
the 4th letter in the Greek alphabet [her favourite number],
K for Knowles." The marching band, meanwhile, wore
complementary sweatshirts with a collegiate-style crest. It
featured Beyoncé-ish symbols from across Black culture:
a Black Power fist, an image of Egyptian queen Nefertiti, a
(Black) panther and, of course, a bee.

Accessories are everything: changing her outfit from yellow to pink
over the two Beychella weekends, sparkly boots added pizzazz.

2021: Black joy

When Beyoncé accepted the award for Best R&B Performance at the Grammys in 2021, she made history, becoming the most decorated woman in the history of the awards show with her account – then – standing at 28.

The award was for 'Black Parade', the surprise song she released after George Floyd was murdered by a police officer in Minneapolis, an event that sparked Black Lives Matter protests across the world. Beyoncé, always intentional, released the song on Juneteeth, the holiday Black Americans celebrate to mark the end of slavery. The song shares its name with a directory she set up to platform Black-owned businesses. To launch it, Beyoncé wrote: "Being Black is your activism. Black excellence is a form of protest. Black joy is your right."

Beyoncé's triumph at the Grammys epitomized this spirit. With her hair frizzed out like a late seventies Donna Summer, she wore an outfit created by Daniel Roseberry, artistic director of Schiaparelli. The man to bring back surrealism back to fashion, Beyoncé's take was subtle: a classic ruched leather minidress with matching gloves, complete with gold "nails" over the top. As *Vogue* put it, this was "a look that was emblematic of her style: directional, powerful and uncompromising." Arguably, these are qualities that are unmistakably Beyoncé – whether applied to standing up for what she believes in or getting dressed for awards ceremonies.

The LBD reimagined: Beyoncé's appearance at the Grammys in 2021 was a moment to remember, with the dress to match.

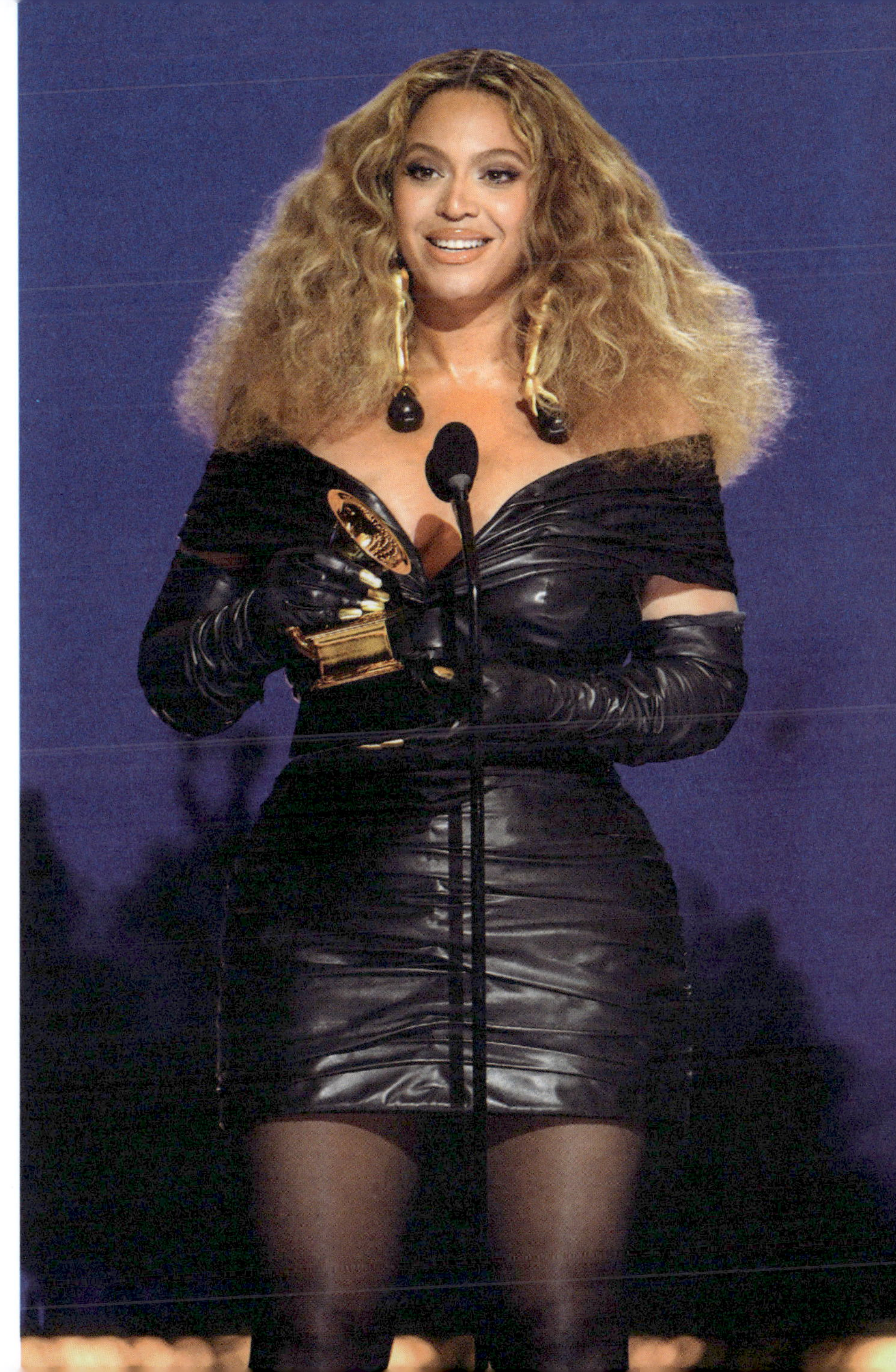

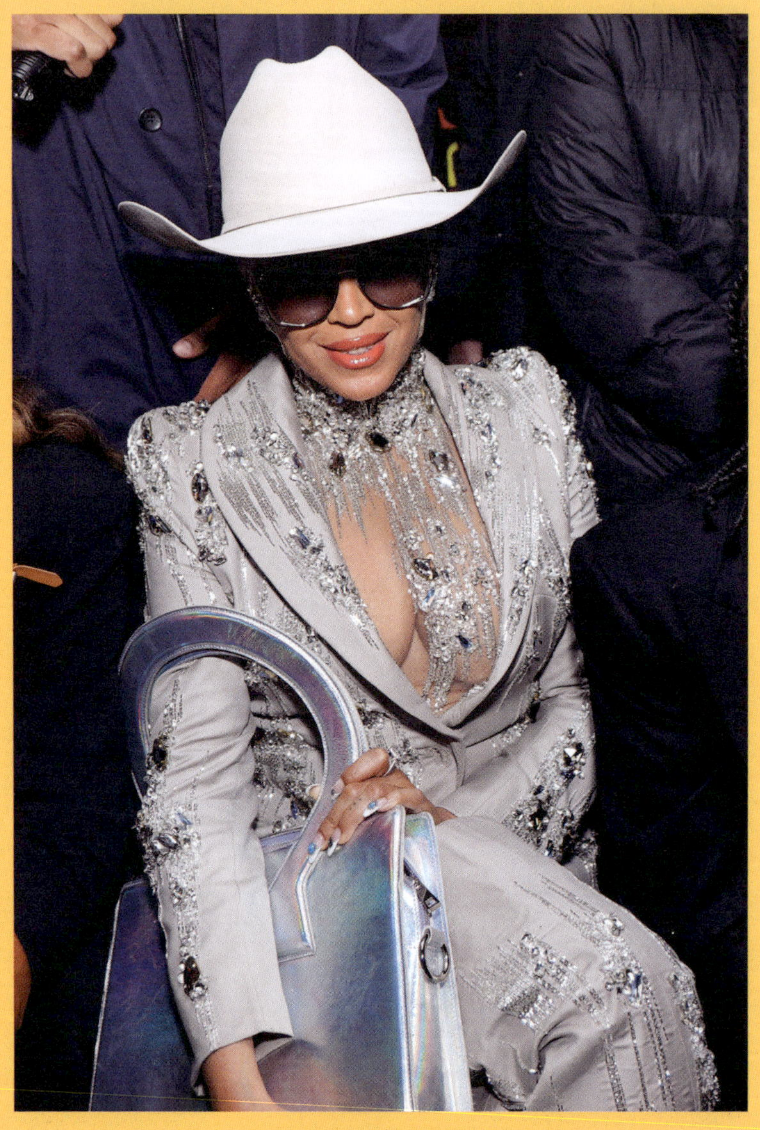

An unexpected joy: Beyoncé sitting in sequins and a cowboy
hat on the front row of the Luar show in 2024.

2024: A different kind of FROW

Luar, a New York fashion label designed by Raul Lopez, has been the recipient of a fair amount of hype recently. Known for his clothes but also his bags – particularly the Ana bag, worn by Dua Lipa and Patti LaBelle – Lopez won the prestigious American Accessory Designer of the Year Award for the first time at the 2022 CFDA Fashion Awards. His fashion shows, meanwhile, are always a hot ticket, often with crowds of tastemakers including playwright Jeremy O. Harris and model Paloma Elsesser forming outside.

Nothing compared to February 2024, when Beyoncé and her mother Tina Knowles attended the brand's show at New York Fashion Week. Influential *Washington Post* writer Rachel Tashjian dubbed Lopez: "The designer that brought Beyoncé to Bushwick". If a lot of celebrities are now paid to attend fashion shows, there's little chance that Lopez – an independent designer – would be able to afford the fee that a global megastar would command. Instead, as Tashjian wrote, this was "seemingly the rare moment of genuine fashion curiosity from a star whose co-sign can change a designer, dancer or musician's life."

Part of the appearance was down to Julez Smith, Solange's son. He walked in the show as his aunty and grandma looked on, while those in the audience gazed at them all. Dressed in a suit covered in sparkles and cowboy hat, Lopez would no doubt be thrilled by what Beyoncé carried on her arm: an Ana bag.

2024: A cowboy - or cowgirl? - comes to town

When Beyoncé released *Renaissance* in 2022, observant members of the Beyhive noticed that the title was preceded by "Act I". Accordingly, buzz (pun intended) began about a second act. Act II arrived and changed the game again in March 2024 (the final part of the trilogy remains outstanding at the time of writing).

If *Renaissance* came with style as bright and shiny as a disco ball, *Cowboy Carter* – as the name suggests – showed Beyoncé going country. Fittingly, her style changed again and saw her look to the culture around her childhood growing up in Texas, a state famous for cowboys. On the front cover of the album, she plays with this imagery. Sat astride a horse, carrying the American flag and wearing a cowboy hat, she could be the archetypal American Dream – except, perhaps, for the colour of her skin.

Country chic: for the Grammys in 2024, Beyoncé brought her take on country classics, including the cowboy hat.

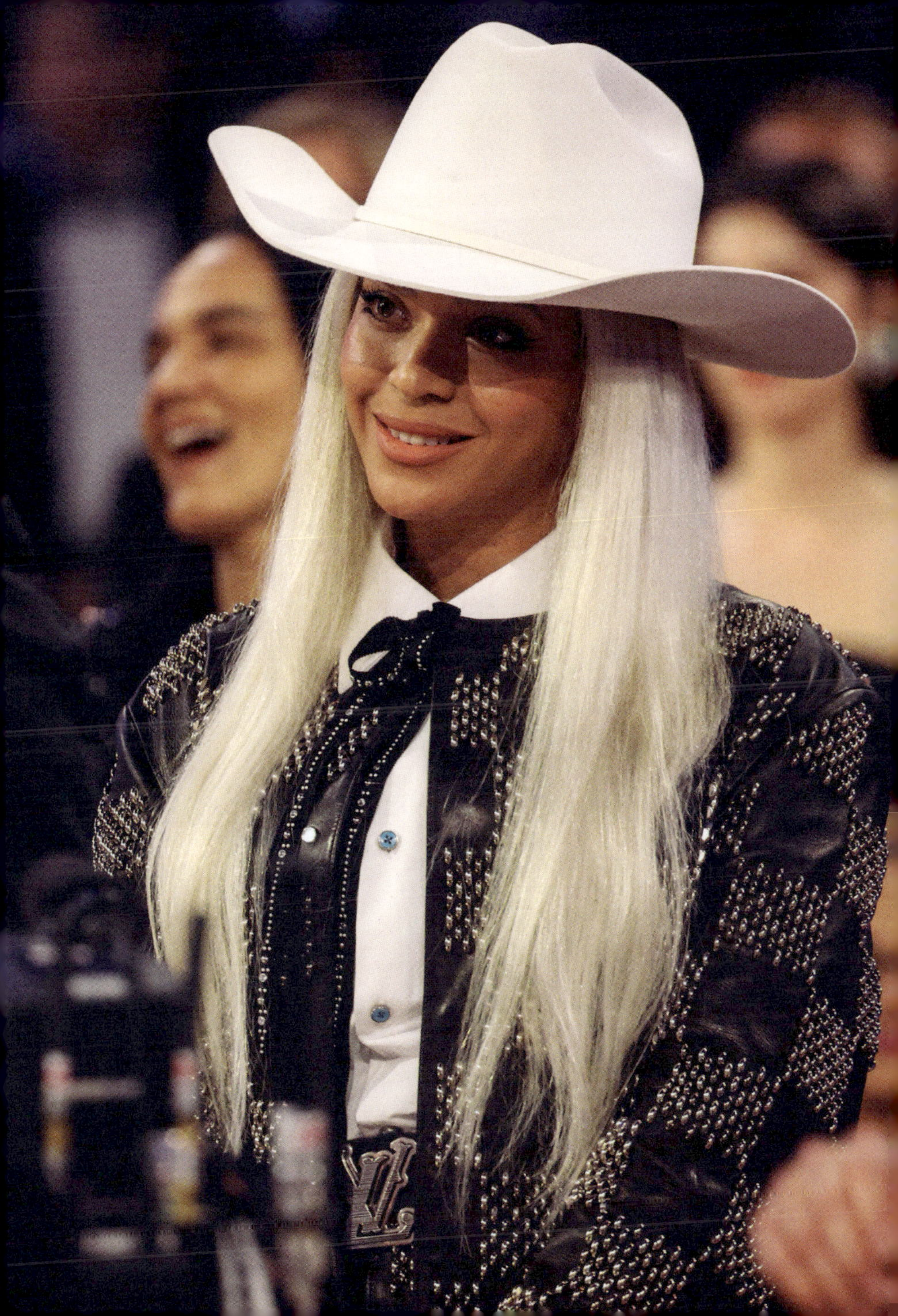

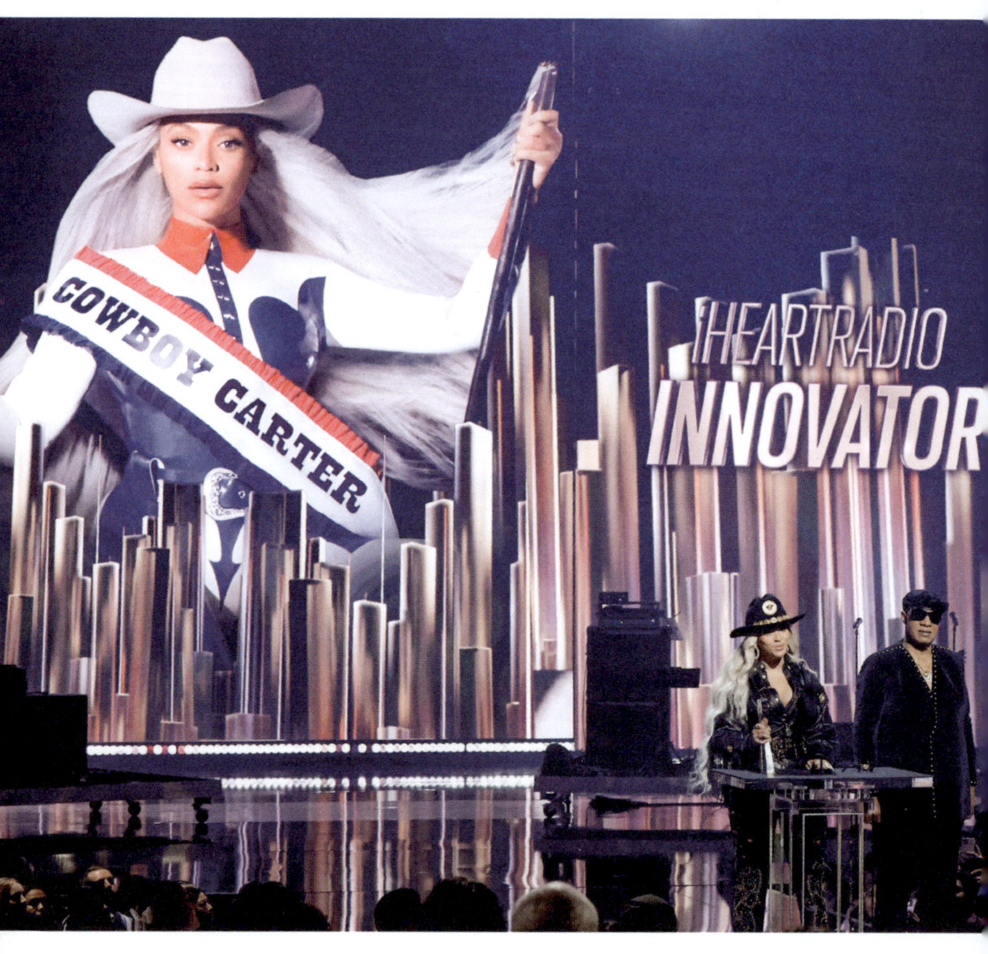

Cowgirls forever: Beyoncé wears vintage Versace Western wear, mirroring the outfit she wore on the front of her latest studio album, *Cowboy Carter*.

Writing about the development of *Cowboy Carter* on Instagram, Beyoncé explained that its genesis came about through her treatment following a performance of country-inflected 'Daddy Lessons' at the Country Music Association Awards in 2016: "It was born out of an experience that I had years ago where I did not feel welcomed and it was very clear that I wasn't," she said. Releasing an album of songs in the country tradition – and wearing the outfit that took its cue from that culture – is her way of resisting that racism. "These images are definitely a clapback to [that] experience," Francesca T. Royster, author of *Black Country Music: Listening for Revolutions*, told the *Guardian*.

When Beyoncé picks a theme, she runs with it. She has made the cowboy hat a signature item, one that actually runs from *Renaissance* in 2023 (she wore a sequin cowboy hat and not much else to announce the tour on social media). Cowboy moments in 2024 include a Louis Vuitton outfit for the Grammys and vintage Versace leather, with matching hat, to accept the I Heart Radio Innovator Award. In July when she showed her support of Team USA in the Olympics, wearing a swimsuit, cowboy boots and cowboy hat – all covered in the American flag.

Despite plaudits for the style and music, prejudice remains. When the CMA nominations were announced in September 2024, *Cowboy Carter* was roundly snubbed – it was up for zero awards. Consolation came in November with the Grammy 2025 nominations. Beyonce became the most nominated artist ever: *Cowboy Carter* was up for 11 awards, including Best Country Album.

Breaking our soul

Renaissance World Tour Style

Forget the wardrobe, this is the tourdrobe

For five glorious months of 2023, people around the world experienced extreme joy. This was thanks to the Renaissance tour, Beyoncé's first in seven years and one that took her everywhere from Stockholm, where it began, to Kansas City, where it ended. Audiences enjoyed a show spanning around two and half hours, double digits of hits, multiple dancers and – of course – outfits to bring most observers' jaws to the floor. It all confirmed what we already knew: no one does a show like Beyoncé.

Now touring for over 20 years, each of Beyoncé's outings has been more mind-blowing than the last. For Renaissance, she had a big moment to top. The Formation tour of 2016 saw her in multiple bodysuits, walking a treadmill runway and dancing in a pool of water for 'Freedom'.

Handsy: the much-loved – and much-imitated – Loewe number worn to perform on the Renaissance tour in 2023.

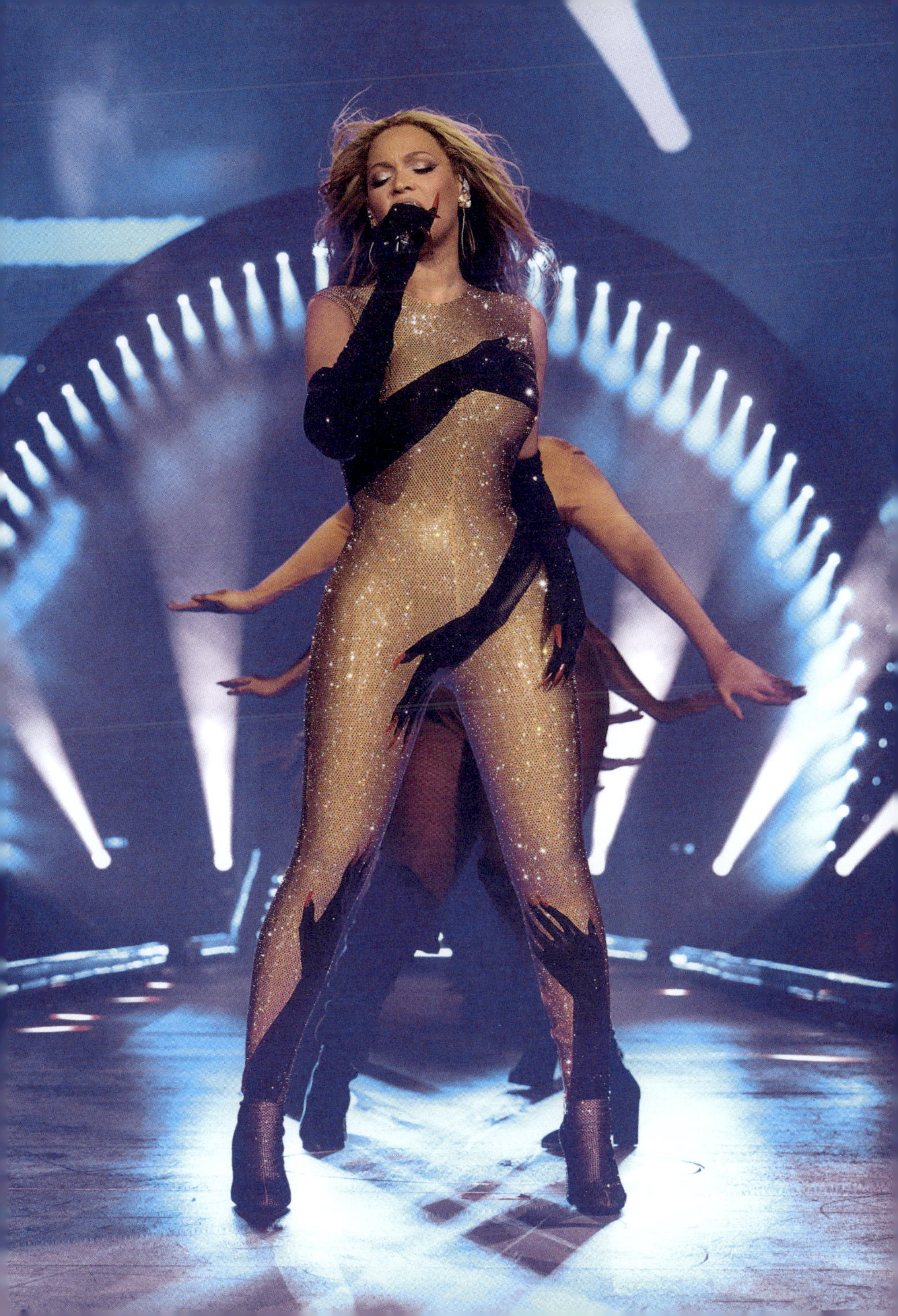

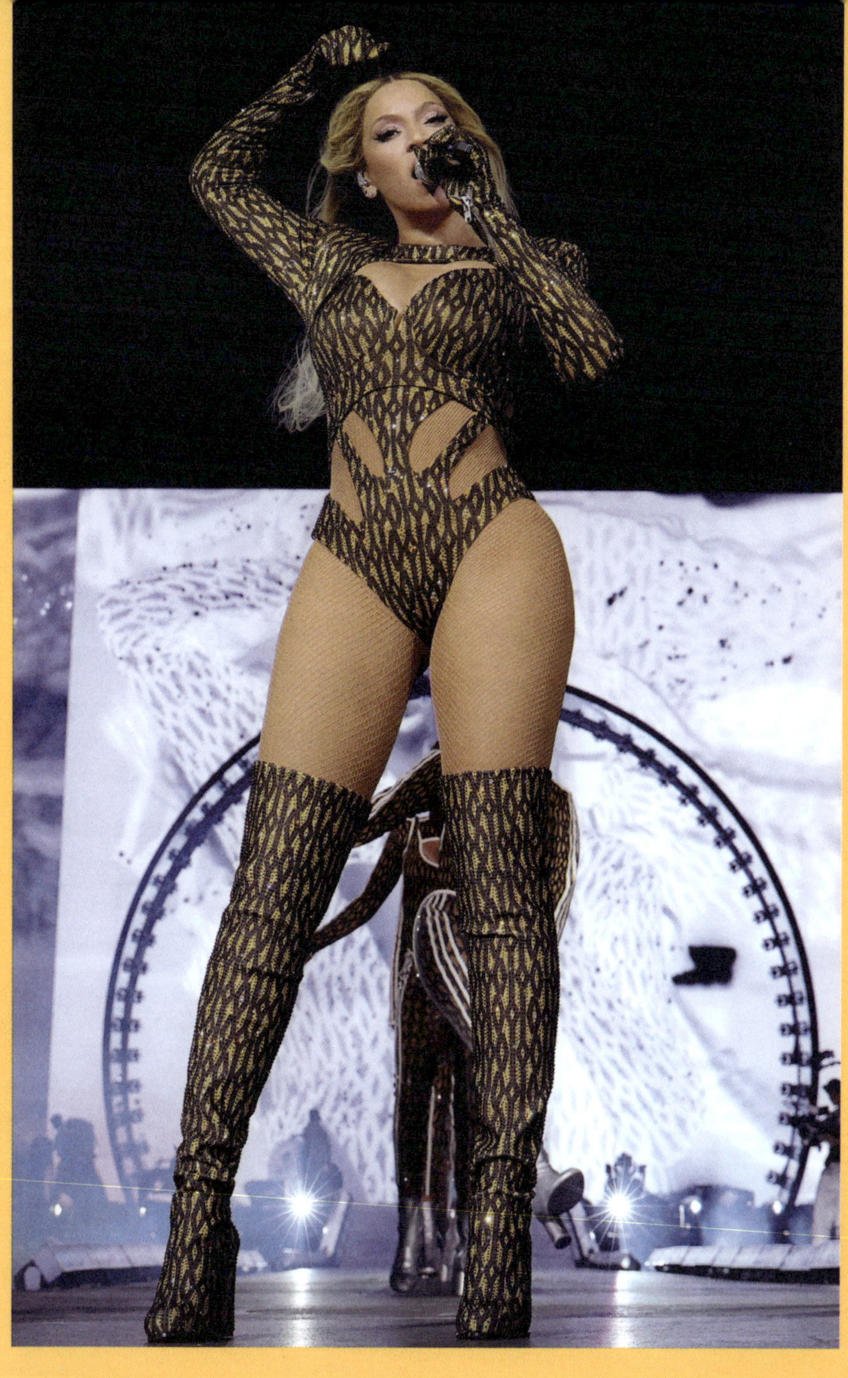

The outfits were one of the highlights of the Renaissance tour and ranged from holographic cowboy hats to sequinned camo. *Vibe* magazine named their favourite as the spangled catsuit with strategically placed hands made by Loewe. She wore it for one of *the* moments of the show: singing the low-key album track 'Plastic Off My Sofa' inside an oversized shell.

Put together, the 148 outfits worn were swiftly dubbed a "tourdrobe". The designers involved saw the Beyoncé effect on their profiles. In an interview with the *Guardian*, David Koma, who made two outfits for the tour, said, "The visibility is incredible. Social media mentions, digital and print articles, and word of mouth – there's an immediate rise in interest." While most of the people watching Beyoncé on the Renaissance tour would have splurged on their tickets – and are unlikely to have the budget for designer clothes – the cut-through no doubt impacts on name recognition. And that's not to mention the honour of dressing a woman who remains, more than 20 years after that first tour, right at the top of her game.

OPPOSITE Boots and a bodysuit: a classic Beyoncé outfit, one that dates back decades, updated for the Renaissance tour.

OVERLEAF Attention: Beyoncé and her army of dancers, all in the Renaissance tour's trademark silver, take to the stage.

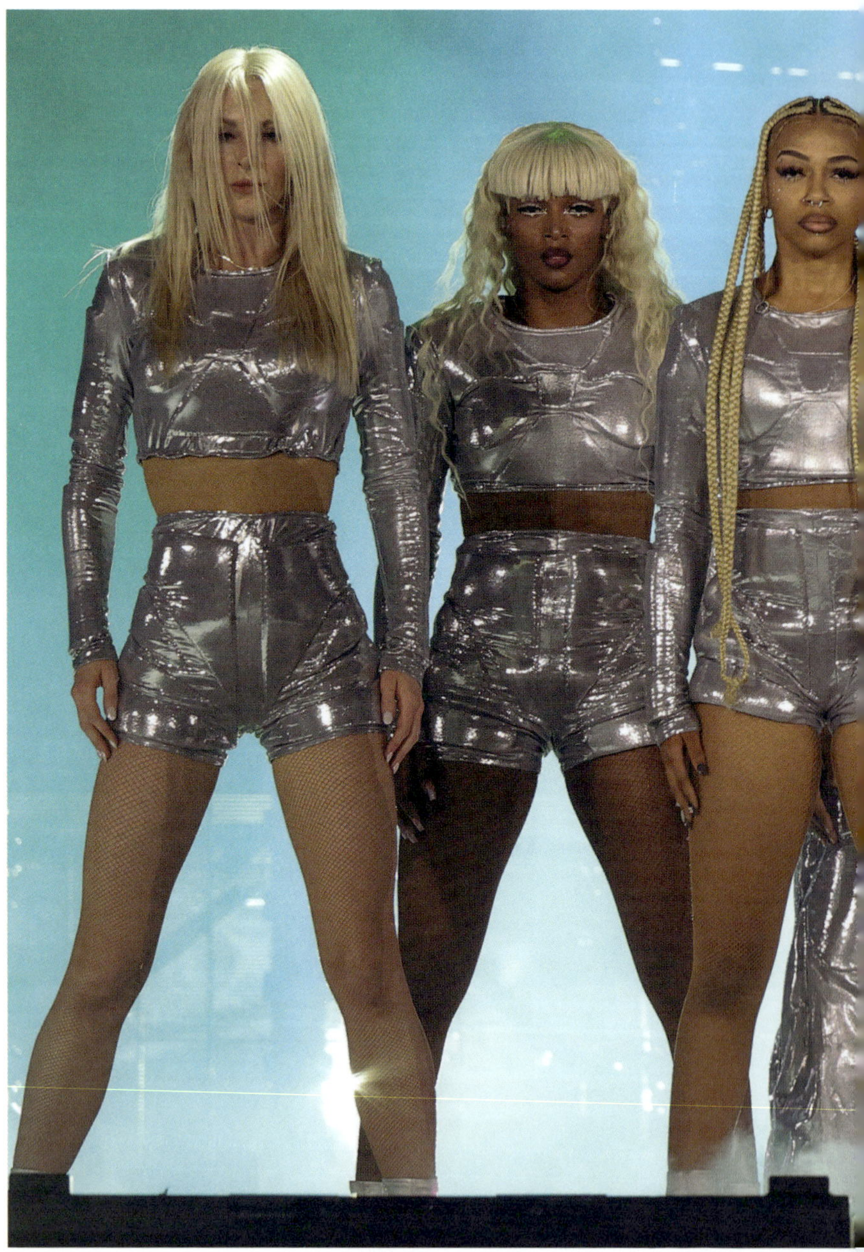

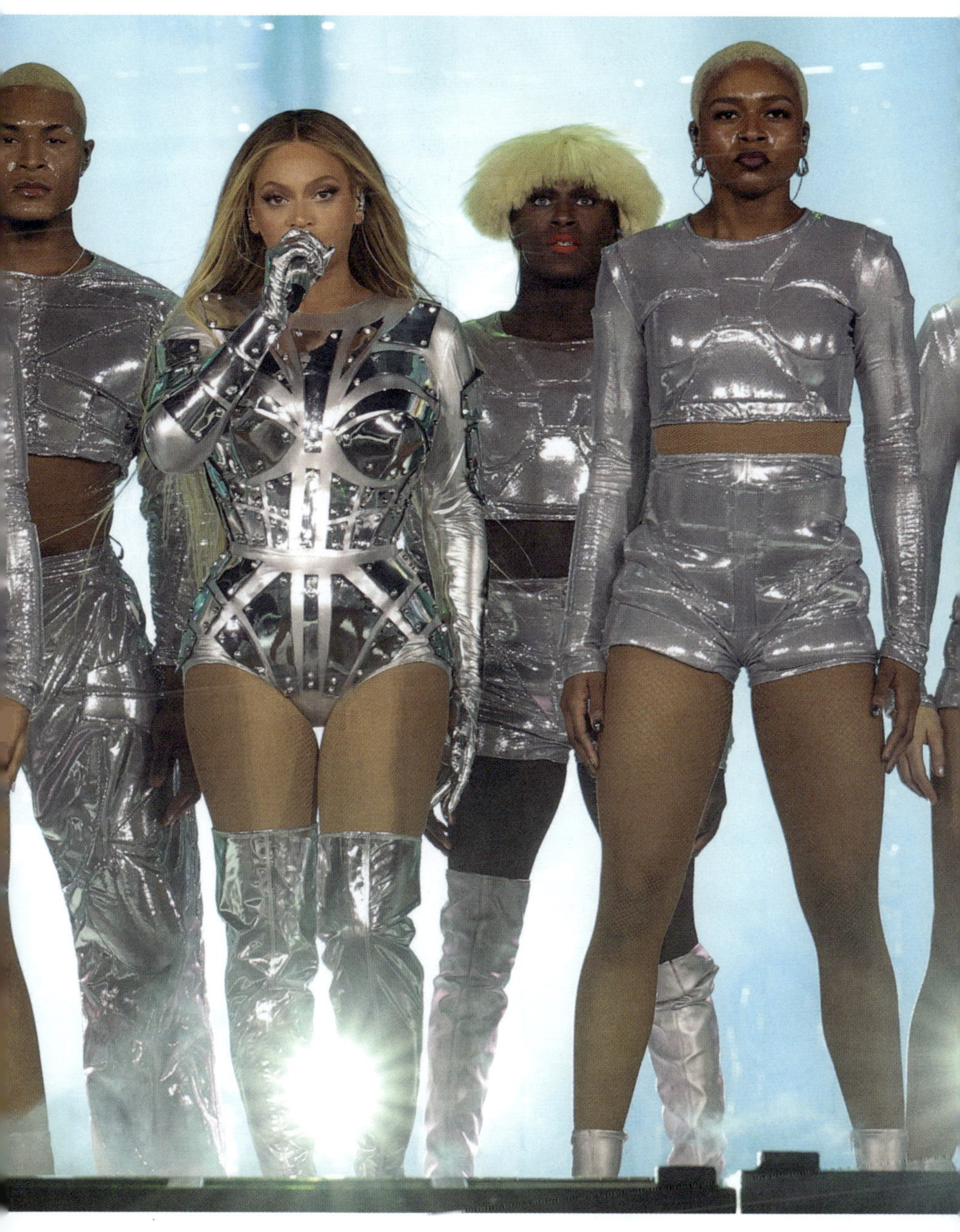

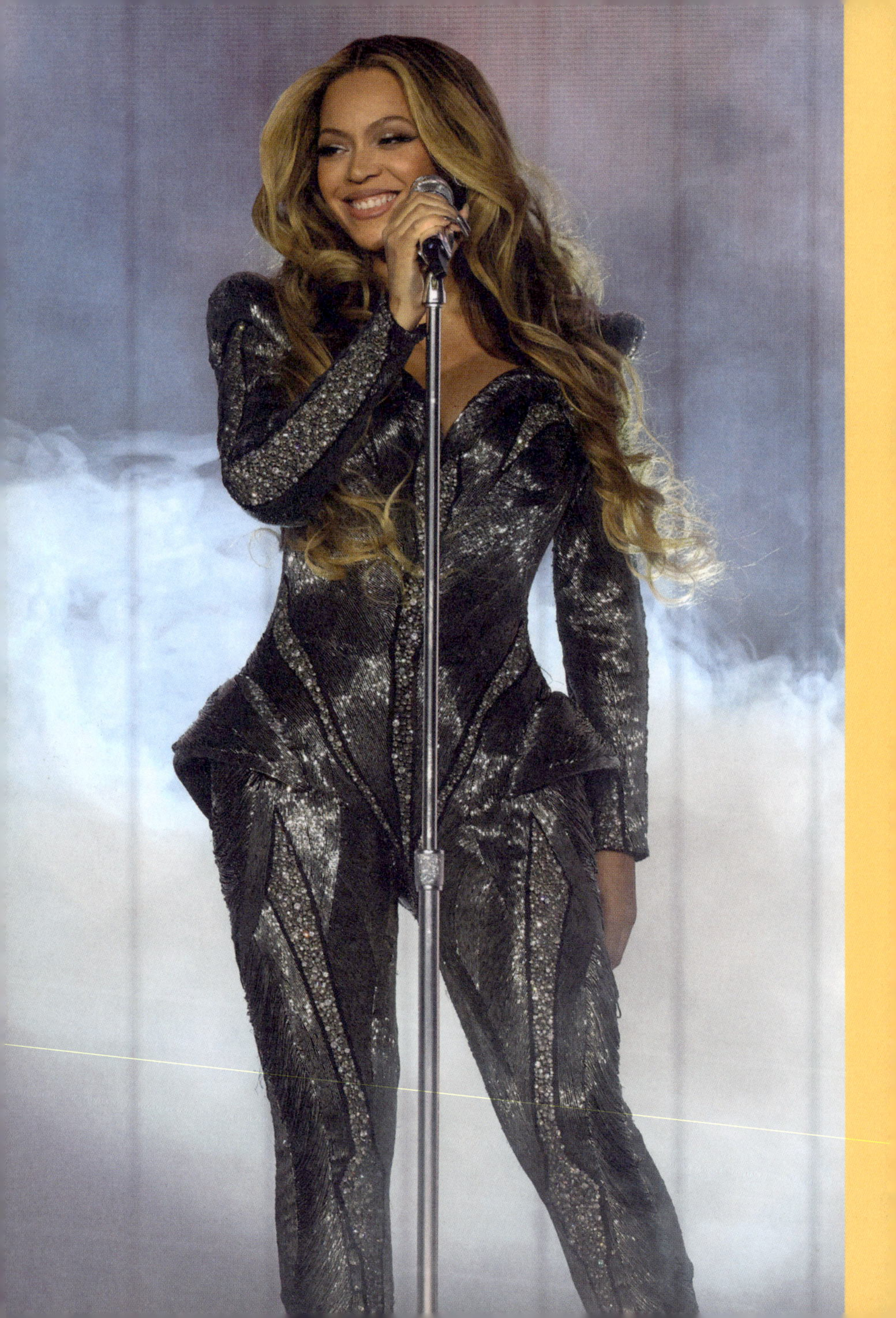

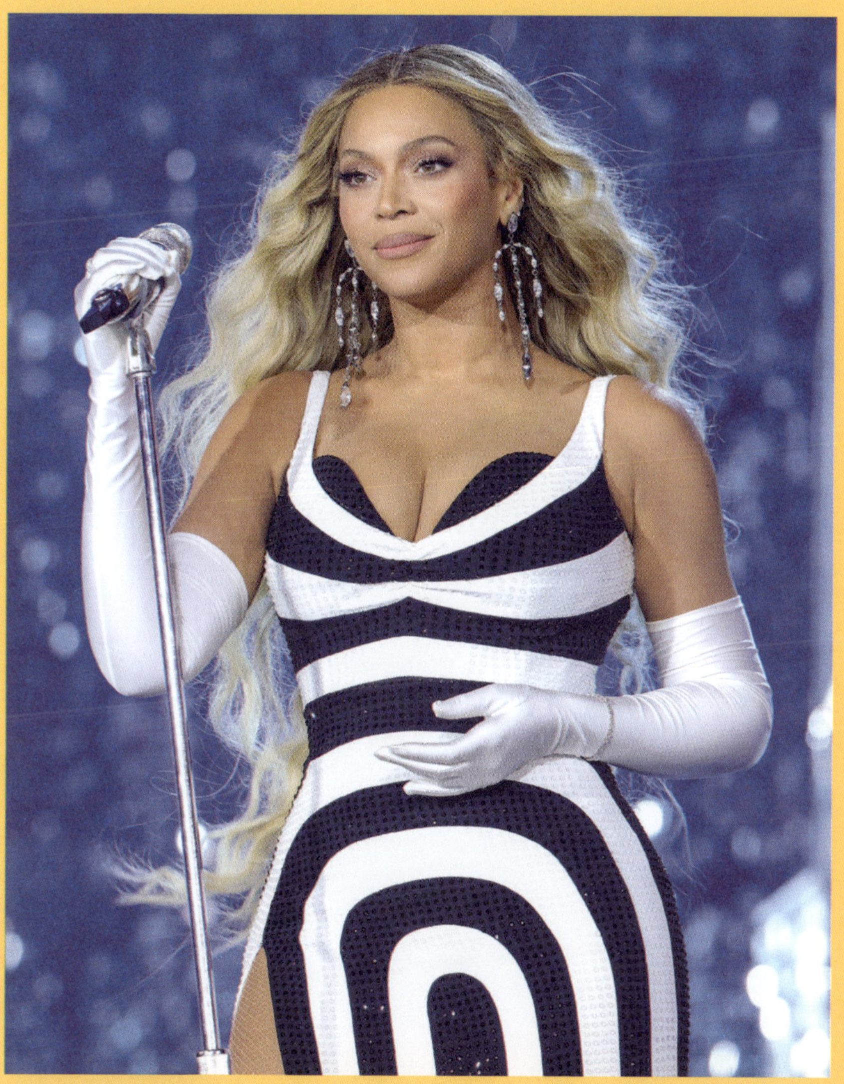

ABOVE Making it monochrome: a favourite colour combination,
mixed with Old Hollywood style, is a winning formula.

OPPOSITE More than a catsuit: the classic shape gets added glam with
hip and shoulder padding, not to mention sequins and sparkles.

Creating the buzz

Beyoncé fan Nerrisa Pratt kept it simple when talking about her outfit to attend the Renaissance tour: "I knew I had to come correct," she told *Vogue* in June 2023. She certainly did that. Pratt recreated Beyoncé's now-infamous Loewe hand catsuit, making it from scratch over five days. The video documenting her creation gained more than 700,000 views on TikTok.

If that sounds like the work of a particularly dedicated superfan, Pratt was actually only one of many devoted members of the Beyhive dressing up to see their queen and – crucially – each other. This is a community of like-minded individuals, after all.

Anthony Lee Pittman, who creates jackets with hand-painted images of Beyoncé on the back, wore one of his own creations to see the star in Paris. Other members of the crowd noticed it.

"I'm really shy and introverted so it was definitely outside my comfort zone," he told *Vogue*. "But just being able to be out there with the Hive ... t madeime feel a lot more comfortable."

A fan with a fan: a member of the Beyhive shows off their look at one of the Renaissance concerts, complete with statement hat.

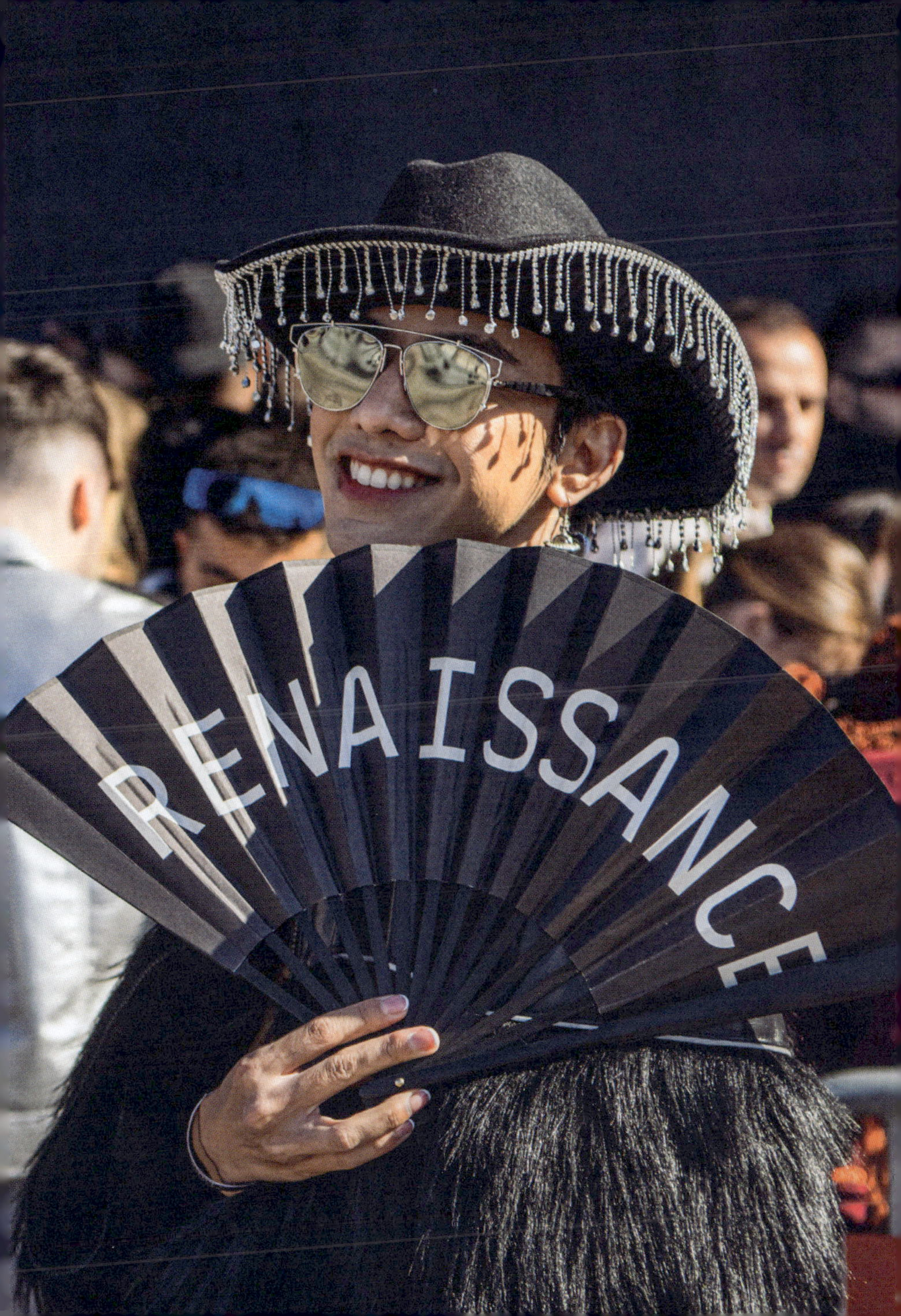

RENAISSANCE

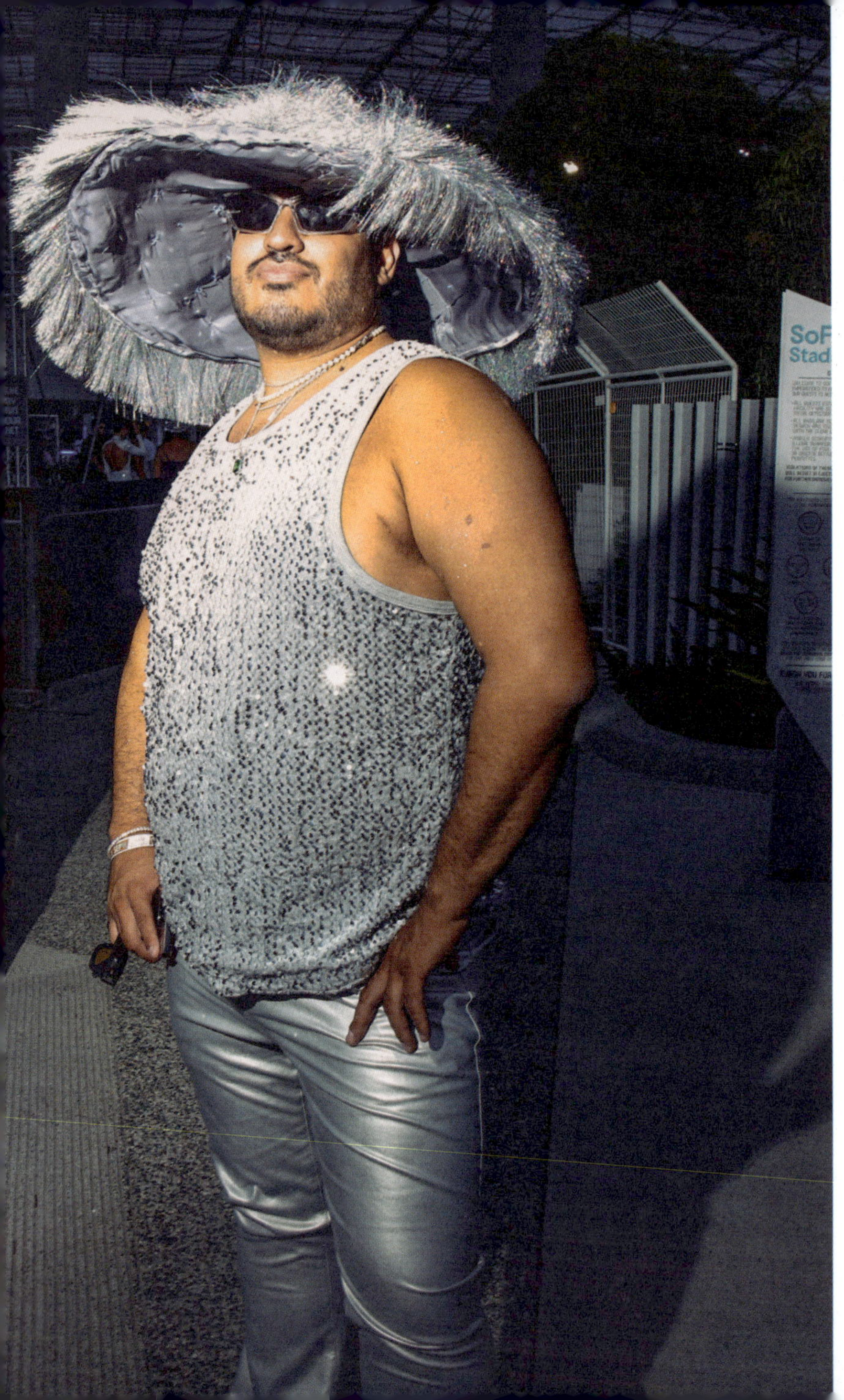
SoF
Stad

Of course, it wasn't necessary to go hard or go home. More
low-key fans were able to show their love through subtler
takes on the party atmosphere of the Renaissance shows. This
was thanks to two elements: silver and cowboy hats. Some
of this came as a directive from their leader – for the shows
in LA around her birthday in September, Beyoncé asked
concertgoers to "[wear] your most fabulous silver fashions".
The fanbase delivered both in the city and across the dates.
The cowboy hat, meanwhile, became a Beyhive signature
during the tour – months before *Cowboy Carter* dropped.
Bri Malandro, the founder of Black cowboy culture Instagram
account The Yeehaw Agenda, described it as "a very fun way
to show that you're down with the clique".

The dress-up went beyond the concert too. For the release
of the *Renaissance* film in December 2023, fans headed to
the cinema to relive their moments from the tour, with
outfits of upmost importance once again. Speaking to the
Guardian, one fan described the cinema trip as "the Met
Gala for the Beyhive".

Winning silver: a fan leans into the colour scheme of
the Renaissance tour at one of the concerts.

There's no "B" in team

As anyone who has seen the *Renaissance* film will attest, a tour of this scope requires a lot of people to work on it. This runs from the set builders to the caterers and – of course – the stylists. Speaking to *The Business of Fashion* in 2023 about working on outfits for the tour, designers gave more information. "There's so many people, it's not just one stylist…It's a big, big process," said Coperni co-founder Arnaud Vaillant, who created a silver cape and corset for Beyoncé to wear.

Vaillant was brought in by Julia Sarr-Jamois, fashion director for *British Vogue*, known for her quirky but exquisite taste. Sarr-Jamois worked on some outfits for the tour, sourced from Coperni but also Balmain and Courrèges: "Honoured to play a part in this historic moment," she wrote on Instagram.

Just the right amount of quirk: Beyoncé collaborator and stylist Julia Sarr-Jamois at an event in 2024.

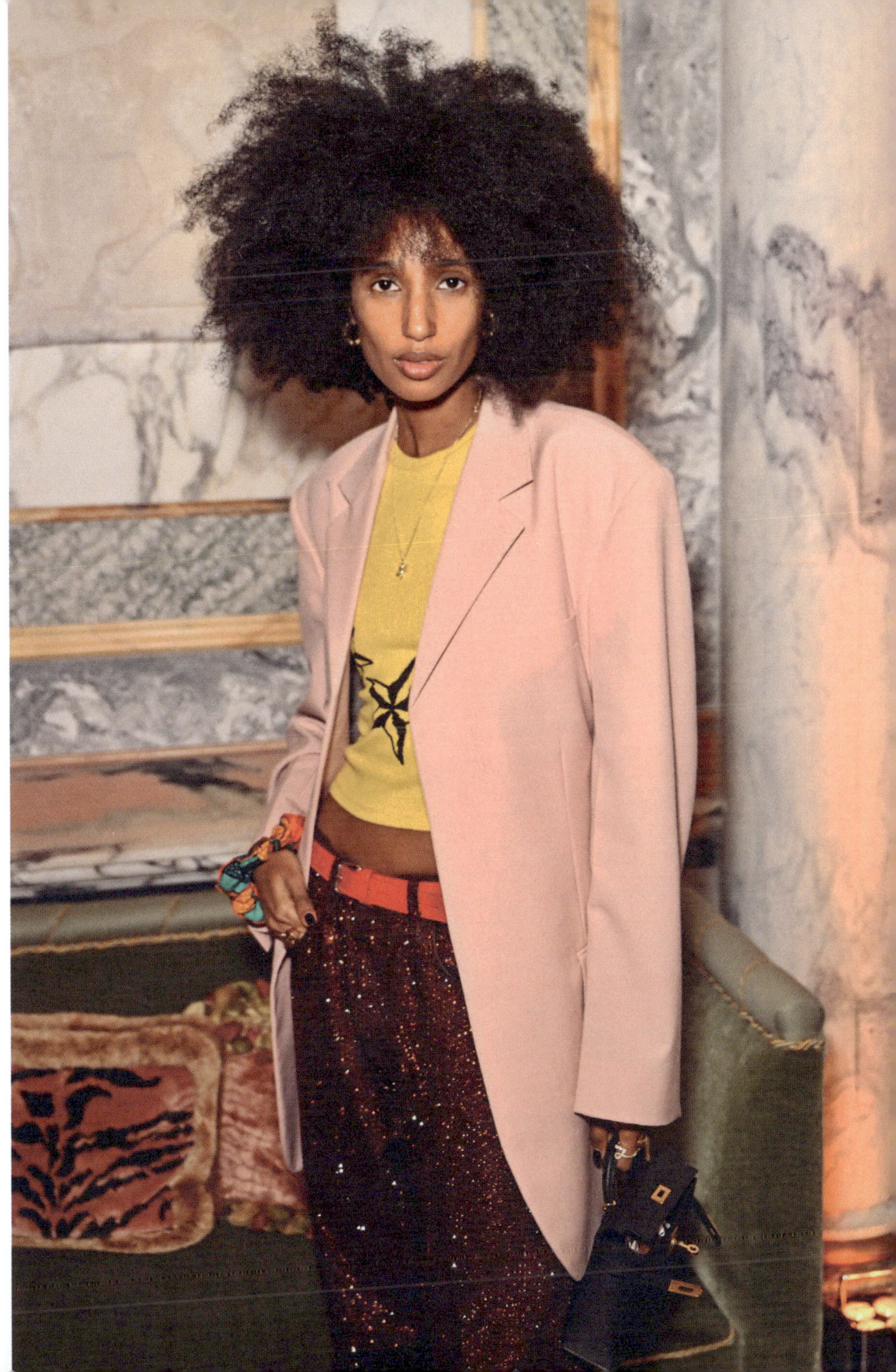

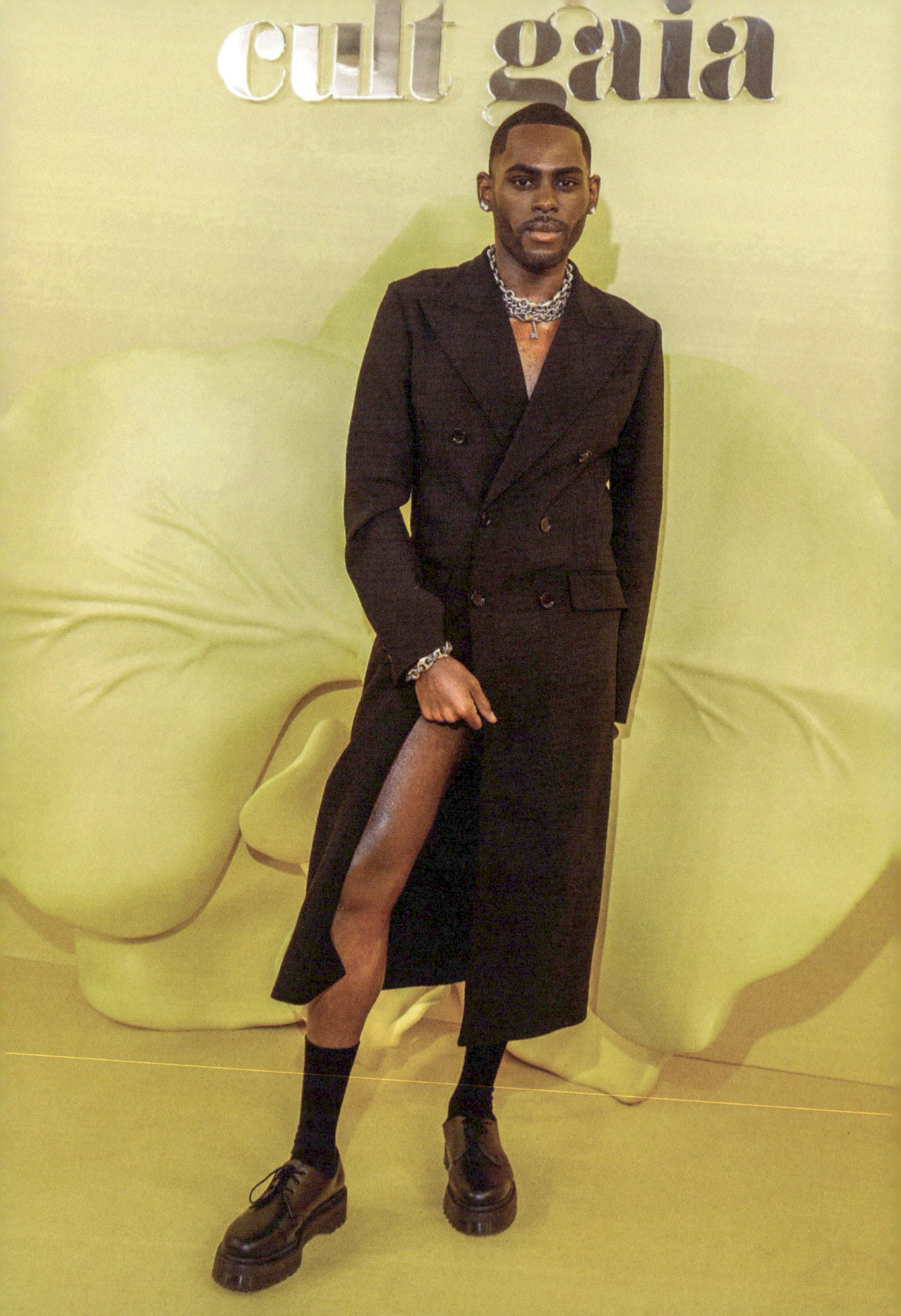
cult gaia

Also on board was Karen Langley, a fashion editor who cut her teeth on style magazines. Langley has long been part of Beyoncé's circle, styling Ivy Park campaigns and videos for *Lemonade*. She worked on outfits like a corset and sunglasses for the Renaissance tour. "[Beyoncé] comes to me when she wants to go beyond her comfort zone," Langley told *The Times* in 2016.

Elsewhere, other established collaborators dotted the roster. KJ Moody is perhaps the longest-serving – he is Beyoncé's cousin, after all. Previously working with Ivy Park, Renaissance was his first tour – one which saw him style looks from the opening night. It was, he told *ELLE*, a special experience – especially when he saw previous ideas reflected back at him among the fanbase. "I never imagined seeing everyone's interpretations on what this album means to them – until it hit the concert arena," Moody said. "Her fans really took it to the next level."

The Renaissance tour might have been focused around the brightest star but from the stylists to the fans, there is something to be said for the team effort.

Chic with a twist: stylist KJ Moody attends a fashion show in LA in 2024.

Index

Credits

The publishers would like to thank the following sources for their kind permission to reproduce the pictures in this book.

Alamy Stock Photo: Science History Images 184

Getty Images: Carlo Allegri 51; /Jason Armond/Los Angeles Times via Getty Images 214; /Al Bello 102-103; /Raymond Boyd 27, 40-41; /Vince Bucci 89; /Vince Bucci/Getty Images for AMA 75; /Larry Busacca 16, 96; /Fernanda Calfat/Getty Images for adidas 140; /Alo Ceballos/GC Images 66; /Jed Cullen/Dave Benett/Getty Images 217; /Julian Dakdouk/Parkwood Media/WireImage via Parkwood 150; /James Devaney/WireImage 101; /Steve Eichner 42; /Steve Granitz/WireImage 39; /Frazer Harrison 85; /Paul S. Howell/Houston Chronicle via Getty Images 14-15; /Mick Hutson/Redferns 44-45; /Peter Kramer 90; /Michael Loccisano 196, 199; /Stephen Lovekin 94; /Kevin Mazur/Getty Images for Anheuser-Busch 93; /Brooks Kraft 156; /Kevin Mazur/Getty Images for Parkwood 202, 203, 208-209, 210; /Kevin Mazur/Getty Images for Roc Nation 104; /Kevin Mazur/Getty Images for Sean Combs 105; /Kevin Mazur/Getty Images for Shawn Carter Foundation 86; /Kevin Mazur/Getty Images for TIDAL 71; /Kevin Mazur/WireImage 32-33, 57, 65, 144, 153, 168; /Kevin Mazur/WireImage for Parkwood 6-7, 9, 211; /Kevin Mazur/WireImage for Parkwood Entertainment 67; /Jamie McCarthy/Getty Images for Glamour 130; /Jason Merritt 78; /Metropolis/Bauer-Griffin/GC Images 77; /Jonathan Nackstrand/AFP via Getty Images 213; /Smiley N. Pool/Houston Chronicle via Getty Images 21; /Mason Poole/Parkwood Media/Getty Images for Atlantis The Royal 72-73; /Bob Riha, Jr. 68; /Tim Roney 53; /Ezra Shaw 176-177; /Karwai Tang/FilmMagic 97; /Theo Wargo 187; /Stuart C. Wilson 148-149; /Kevin Winter 81; /Kevin Winter/Getty Images for Coachella 190, 192; /Kevin Winter/Getty Images for iHeartRadio 200; /Kevin Winter/Getty Images for The Recording Academy 195; /Alex Wong 154-155; /Vinnie Zuffante 22, 24-25, 30, 37

Shutterstock: 35; /Eugene Adebari 166; /Ansa/EPA 136-137; /BEI 36; /Monica M Davey/EPA 180; /Dreamworks/Kobal 163 164; /Tabatha Fireman/Redferns 170; /David Fisher 28-29, 98; /Jonathan Hordle 143; /Domine Jerome/ABACA 141; /Frank Micelotta 189; /New Line/Kobal 61; /Gregory Pace/BEI 147; /Picturegroup 83, 91; /David X Prutting/BFA 179; /Sipa 138; /Startraks 54, 135; /Dan Steinberg/BEI 47; /Str/EPA 82; /Jason Sean Weiss/BFA.com 218; /Eric Workum/Starpix 74; /Richard Young 133; /Michael Gonzalez 158-159

Lauren Cochrane is Senior Fashion Writer of The *Guardian* and contributes to publications including *The Face, ELLE, Service95* and *Wallpaper**. Based in London, she writes about everything from catwalk shows to footballers' style and the return of the serif typeface. She is author of *The Ten: The Stories Behind the Fashion Classics*.